Arnhem:

Iain Ballantyne is the a[...] of military and naval history books, and [...]utor to television news and documentary programmes, and radio shows. In 2021 his *Bismarck: 24 Hours to Doom* was the subject of a major television documentary broadcast in the UK by Channel 4. Iain is a former newspaper reporter and currently Editor of a globally read defence magazine, occasionally writing for other publications. His other books include *The Deadly Trade* (Weidenfeld & Nicolson), a history of submarine warfare and *Hunter Killers* (Orion), covering the Cold War undersea confrontation. He is the host of Warships Pod.

Follow him on Twitter @IBallantyn

ARNHEM
TEN DAYS IN THE CAULDRON

IAIN BALLANTYNE

CANELOHISTORY

First published in the United Kingdom in 2019 by Agora Books

This edition published in the United Kingdom in 2023 by

Canelo
Unit 9, 5th Floor
Cargo Works, 1-2 Hatfields
London SE1 9PG
United Kingdom

Copyright © Iain Ballantyne 2019

The moral right of Iain Ballantyne to be identified as the creator of this work has been asserted in accordance with the Copyright, Designs and Patents Act, 1988.

All rights reserved. No part of this publication may be reproduced or transmitted in any form or by any means, electronic or mechanical, including photocopy, recording, or any information storage and retrieval system, without permission in writing from the publisher.

A CIP catalogue record for this book is available from the British Library.

Print ISBN 978 1 80436 367 6
Ebook ISBN 978 1 80436 368 3

Maps and Pegasus Emblem © Paul Slidel, 2019

Cover design by Philip Beresford

Cover images © Shutterstock

Main cover image © Imperial War Museum EA 44531. Used by permission.

Look for more great books at www.canelo.co

Printed and bound in Great Britain by Clays Ltd, Elcograf S.p.A.

For those who fought,

along with their families and loved ones

and for the civilians caught in the middle of it all

Concise Glossary of Terms and Abbreviations

British Ranks

General

Non-Commissioned Officer **NCO**

Commanding Officer **CO**

Royal Air Force

Flight Lieutenant **Flt Lt**

Army Ranks

Private / Trooper **Pte / Tpr**

Lance Corporal **L/Cpl**

Corporal **Cpl**

Lance Sergeant **L/Sgt**

Sergeant **Sgt**

Staff Sergeant	**SSgt**
Sergeant Major	**Sgt Maj**
Provost Sergeant	**Provo Sgt**
Regimental Sergeant Major	**RSM**

Army Officer Ranks

Lieutenant	**Lt**
Captain	**Capt**
Major	**Maj**
Lieutenant Colonel	**Lt Col**
Colonel	**Col**
Brigadier (US Brigadier General)	**Brig (US: Brig Gen)**
Major General	**Maj Gen**
Lieutenant General	**Lt Gen**
General	**Gen**
Field Marshall	**FM**

Navy

Lieutenant Commander — **Lt Cdr**

British Units

General Unit Abbreviations

Battalion — **Bn**

Brigade — **Bde**

Company — **Coy**

Division — **Div**

Regiment — **Regt**

Specific Unit Abbreviations

1st Border Regiment — **Border Regt / 'Borders'**

Air Landing Brigade — **Air Ldg Bde**

Airborne Division — **Airborne Div**

Airborne Reconnaissance Squadron — **Airborne Recce Sqn**

Army Air Corps — **AAC**

Dorsetshire Regiment — **'Dorsets'**

Duke of Cornwall's Light Infantry	DCLI
Independent Parachute Company	**Indep Para Coy**
King's Own Scottish Borderers	**KOSB**
Office of Strategic Services	**OSS**
Oxfordshire and Buckinghamshire Light Infantry	**'Ox and Bucks'**
Parachute Brigade	**Para Bde**
Parachute Field Ambulance	**PFA**
Parachute Squadron Royal Engineers	**Para Sqn RE**
Royal Air Force	**RAF**
Royal Army Medical Corps	**RAMC**
Royal Artillery	**RA**
Royal Engineers	**RE**
Special Air Service	**SAS**
Special Operations Executive	**SOE**
South Staffordshire Regiment	**'South Staffs' / 'Staffs'**
Tactical Air Force	**TAF**

United States Army Air Force   USAAF

German Ranks

* with British Rank Equivalent

Waffen SS Ranks

Rottenführer	L/Cpl
Scharführer	Sgt
Untersturmführer	Lt
Hauptsturmführer	Capt
Sturmbannführer	Maj
Obersturmbannführer	Lt Col
Standartenführer	Col
Obergruppenführer	Lt Gen

Wehrmacht Ranks

Obersdeutnant	Lt Col
Generaloberst	Gen
Generalfeldmarschall	FM

'And the Germans themselves had coined their own name for our tiny perimeter. They were calling it The Cauldron.'

—Major General Roy Urquhart,
Officer Commanding,
1st Airborne Division[1]

Operation Market Garden

The Arena of Struggle 17-26 Sept 1944

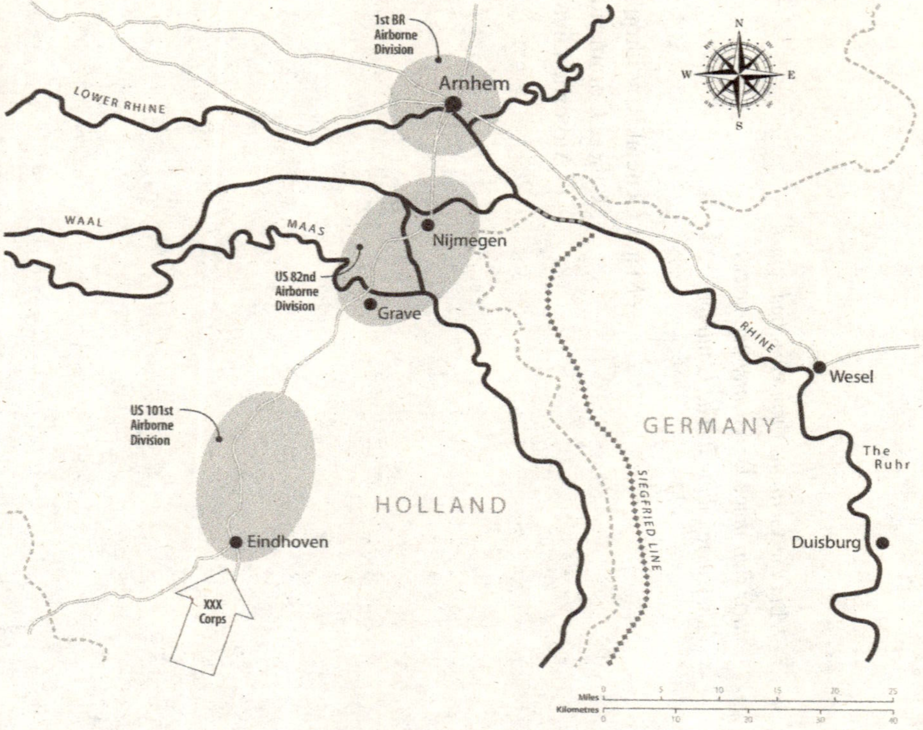

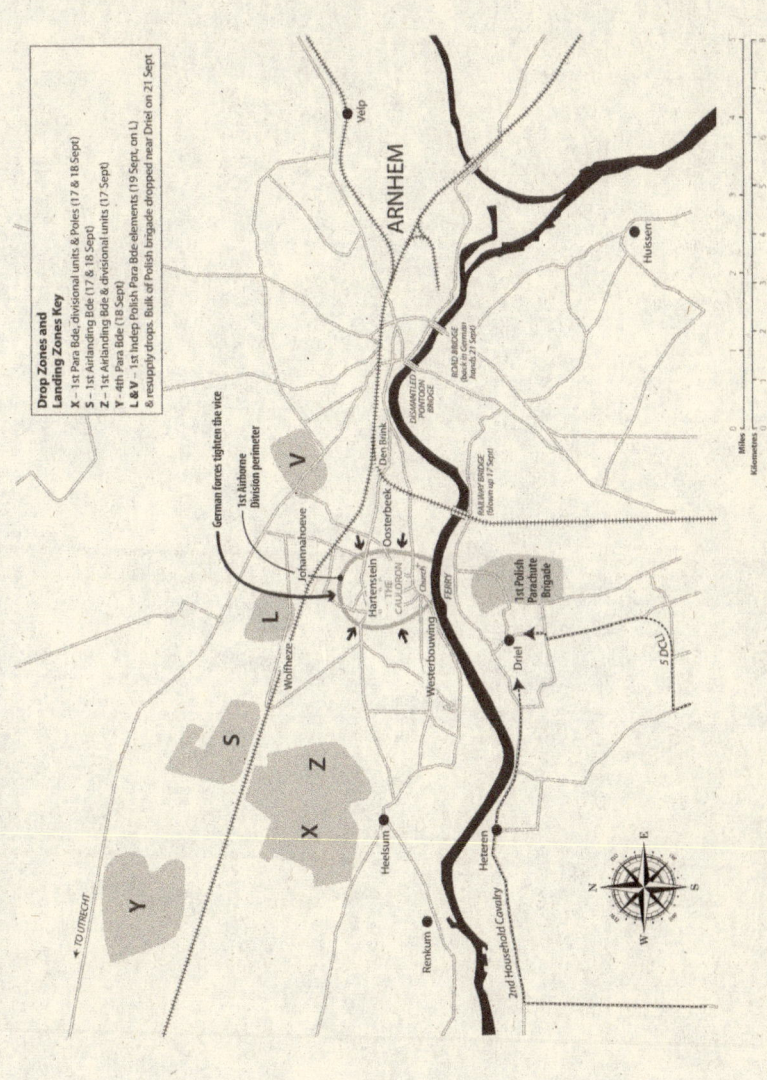

ARNHEM: The Battleground by Sept 22 1944

The symbol of all British Airborne Forces since 1942 is often referred to as the Pegasus emblem but in fact shows both the famous winged horse of Greek mythology and the warrior Bellerophon said to be swooping through the air to destroy a monster.

Prologue

*'...alone and unheralded,
like thieves in the night.'*

—By Air to Battle: The Official Account of the British
Airborne Divisions

The roaring four-engined Halifax bomber has towed the Horsa glider up into the sky from Tarrant Rushton airfield in Dorset, southern England. It is one of six such combinations taking off at around 10.30pm on 5 June 1944.

Thirty soldiers belonging to D Company (Coy) in the 2nd Battalion (Bn), The Oxfordshire and Buckinghamshire Light Infantry, are crammed into the lead glider along with their weaponry and equipment.

They sit down the sides of the Horsa, facing each other and enduring uncomfortable, hard wooden seats for their flight into history. Lieutenant (Lt) Den Brotheridge, 26-year-old commander of 25 Platoon, sits opposite 31-year-old Major (Maj) John Howard, the assault commander of Operation Deadstick. They, and 150 men carried in the other five gliders, will be among the first – if not *the* first – Allied troops to touch the soil of enemy occupied France on D-Day.

After many months of planning, training and gathering of military might across the British Isles, the Ox and Bucks are going in ahead of many tens of thousands of Allied soldiers, airmen, and sailors. They are all engaged in a massive, multi-dimensional military enterprise – filling the air, covering the sea (even lurking under it) and soon also to be projected ashore.

Most of the soldiers in the lead glider come from London and during the flight they sing cockney songs, puff on cigarettes, chatter, and joke. It does not entirely succeed in covering up the unnerving screaming wind forcing its way through the plywood covering of the timber-framed fuselage.

The troops watch Maj Howard closely to see if he will, as usual, succumb to airsickness and vomit. Tonight, he disappoints them, for he is so keyed up with adrenalin – his mind buzzing with thoughts about the mission to come – that he forgets to follow his usual custom.

Looking out a window as the glider is towed over the Channel, Lance Corporal (L/Cpl) Edward Tappenden, the company radio operator, sees invasion shipping below when the moon shines on the sea through a break in the cloud. He feels it looks 'as though you could step from ship to ship to France for certain…'[2]

To guarantee stealth, at nine minutes past midnight, as the French coast slides under them – and having exploited a gap in enemy Anti-Aircraft (AA) battery defences over Cabourg – the Halifax tugs let the gliders go, at between 5,000ft and 6,000ft. The enemy believes what approaches is just another bombing raid. As extra cover for their true intent, the Halifaxes will go on to bomb enemy targets along with other Royal Air Force (RAF) bombers flying across the Channel at the same time.

The divorce from the tug is signified by what one Airborne soldier on the mission describes as 'the familiar "twang" and jerk'[3] as the tow rope releases and falls away. With the rotary racket of the tug fading, Maj Howard shouts out to his men: 'Be quiet now!'[4] The soldiers fall silent, the lead Horsa diving steeply to get below the clouds, so the two pilots can navigate by studying the landscape laid out at their feet.

The glider creaks and groans, the scream of air replaced by a calmer 'sighing'[5] as the Horsa levels off at 1,000ft.

Lt Brotheridge undoes his safety belt and stands up. As he opens the door just behind the cockpit, Maj Howard and Tappenden hang onto him to make sure he doesn't accidentally exit the aircraft. A soldier at the back of the glider opens its other door.

Settling back down, Lt Brotheridge, Maj Howard and other soldiers near the doors watch as the Norman landscape flashes by below, inhaling the 'sweet, damp air'.[6] Howard finds it has 'an amazing tranquillising effect'. They spot horses and cattle grazing 'very, very quietly'[7] in fields laid out in a similar patchwork to those back home. The animals are unperturbed by the glider's passage close overhead.[8]

—

Six platoons of the Ox and Bucks – one to each of the Horsas – are tasked with taking two bridges a quarter of a mile apart in an audacious *coup de main* attack. They are accompanied in each Horsa by half a dozen Royal Engineer sappers whose job it will be to defuse and remove any demolition charges attached to the bridges. One of them spans the River Orne, near the village of Ranville, and the other the Caen Canal, close to the village of Benouville. Three gliders and 90 troops are assigned to assault and capture each bridge. It is archetypal use of Airborne forces – taking a gamble by coming down right on top of an objective to achieve total surprise. While it might cost a few casualties it should, with luck, swiftly deliver success. As one official history will later term it, the aim of the Ox and Bucks is to 'arrive at the bridges alone and unheralded, like thieves in the night.'[9]

The chosen troops and their glider pilots have for months trained intensively. The glider pilots scrutinised aerial reconnaissance photos of the actual bridges in Normandy and their surroundings, though they were not told where it was they were studying until just hours before take-off on the night of the attack itself. The glider pilots also repeatedly watched an astonishingly realistic film that presented a low-level fly-through, using a model of the target.[10] It had every detail realised in miniature, from German pillboxes to each bush and tree. The glider pilots memorised the landing spots and timings of their approach – the exact moment to follow a certain bearing for a certain duration after release from the tug, including when to take precise turns. They also rehearsed it for real, getting everything down to the split-second during simulated landings in the English countryside. These included a rehearsal of the raid itself, against bridges at Lechlade, a quiet and ancient little town on the southern edge of the Cotswolds.

The Ox and Bucks trained for their part in the mission at the Countess Wear bridges, near Exeter where, like the target in Normandy, there was a canal and river right next to each other. The troops used trucks in place of gliders, tumbling out of the back of them as if disembarking from Horsas. Had the troops and gliders trained with each other it would have risked death or injury, while making public the exact nature of the mission.

Training mishaps were still to be expected and thankfully there were not too many. One night in May 1944, during a night landing at Tarrant Rushton, a glider was released too far from the airfield, touched down safely but went through a hedge and slammed into a country lane with its nose wheel pushed up through the cockpit. Neither pilot was injured.[11]

During a landing rehearsal on Salisbury Plain there was a collision between gliders, with one spearing the other, while three others were involved in a landing pile up – again, miraculously, there were no deaths or injuries except for one pilot suffering a broken toe.[12] The fact that the fragile Horsas are largely made of wood and crumple on impact and that there is no fuel to catch fire helps avoid deaths in such situations.

One piece of new intelligence picked up via sources in France, and seemingly confirmed by an RAF photo-reconnaissance flight, is that poles appear to have been erected right where the gliders are to land alongside the canal bridge. Maj Howard worries about these a great deal and, just before the mission, asks the enthusiastic 24-year-old chief pilot of his glider, Staff Sergeant (SSgt) Jim Wallwork, if it is feasible to land safely in such a thicket. Wallwork replies that the distance between the poles is just right for clipping the wings of a glider and bringing it to a halt.

As the lead glider swoops low over Normandy, Howard resists the urge to stand up and place himself between the two pilots to watch their final approach to target – just to see if his fears about the poles are correct. He realises the pilots don't need him looking over their shoulders as they concentrate on the job at hand.

As they bring the glider in, Wallwork and co-pilot SSgt John Ainsworth find everything faithfully matches the photos and fly-through film. Wallwork sees the 'the river and the canal-like strips of silver in the moonlight.'[13] The burning city of Caen, around seven miles away, which has just been pounded by the Halifax bombers, acts as a useful navigation beacon. The glider flies inland towards Caen, takes a right turn, and then another to approach from the south for a landing by the canal bridge on its east side. The pilots work with intense focus, using a compass, and counting off the seconds to each turn on a stopwatch illuminated by a small lamp.

Wallwork yells out to the soldiers in the back:

'Hold tight!'

As trained, they link arms and raise their feet, the better to avoid broken bones and, hopefully, not go flying all over the place when the glider lands. Like a huge black bat, the Horsa swooshes out of the night, hitting the earth at 120mph and bouncing. Its undercarriage is torn off, the metal skid protecting the Horsa's belly striking sparks that are initially mistaken by those inside it for enemy fire. A parachute is released out the back of the glider to arrest its speed, which comes down to 60mph.

As the glider finally yields to the impact, there is a great splintering of wood, but there are no poles sticking out of the ground, merely holes where they are soon to be placed. Private (Pte) Denis Edwards recounts of the landing: 'There followed a sound like a giant canvas sheet being viciously ripped apart, then a mighty crash like a clap of thunder and my body seemed to be moving in several directions at once.'[14]

It is 12.16am.

The D-Day invasion has begun.

—

The Horsa smashes into a large cluster of barbed wire below an embankment that carries the road leading to the eastern end of the bridge. The pilots are injured as the cockpit collapses, with Maj Howard briefly rendered unconscious. On coming around, Howard fears he has been hit so hard on the head he has gone blind. In actual fact, his steel helmet has been pushed down rather violently over his eyes.

Shoving the helmet back up and doing a forward roll out of the broken wreckage, Howard is glad to see his troops pulling themselves together and shaking off the shock of the landing. Even the two glider pilots seem to be coming back to life. Howard cannot suppress a smile of gratitude for their reckless precision. Wallwork asked back in England where the major thought it best to end up and cheerfully agreed to put the Horsa's nose through the barbed wire, landing less than 50 yards from the bridge. In doing so, it removes another of Howard's nagging anxieties – how to get his troops through the wire while under enemy fire. Firstly, the way through is open, and, secondly, the enemy, incredibly, seems oblivious to what is happening. There are no bullets flying about – just an eerie silence, broken now by the second glider landing right behind the first and then, sixty seconds later, by the third carrying out its own controlled crash.

Pte Edwards is among those ready to charge across the bridge, having survived the landing unharmed, and despite sitting in the glider's 13th seat, right by the front door on the starboard side. The superstitious Army Air Corps (AAC) labelled his seat '12A', but he takes a perverse pride in thumbing his nose at such things. 'I always reckoned 13 was a lucky number, so I always used to sit in that seat,' he recalls. Even so, 'the whole [front of the] glider [was] stove right in, the woodwork completely blocked the doorway. We had to smash a hole through with our rifle butts to make a little hole to clamber out.'[15]

A few miles away, at around 12.18am, pathfinders of the 22nd Independent Parachute Company (Indep Para Coy) drop into Normandy. Their job is to mark the Landing Zones (LZ) and Drop Zones (DZ) for the rest of the 6th Airborne Division (Airborne Div), not least the 7th Bn, the Parachute Regiment (Regt).

It is due to arrive with the rest of the 5th Parachute Brigade (Para Bde) at 12.50am, with orders to link up with the Ox and Bucks at the two bridges. Once combined, they must hold off enemy attacks until Army commandos and assault troops of the 3rd Infantry Division (Div) – landing six miles away, on Sword Beach to breach Hitlers much-vaunted Atlantic Wall – can come to the rescue. The Airborne troops have to deny the use of the bridges to the enemy, for the Germans are expected to throw panzers and their own troops' reinforcements into the fight on the beaches, in a bid to push the British back into the sea.

The Allies will need the same bridges to launch their own assault by armour and infantry against the city of Caen, which it is hoped will be taken by the end of D-Day.

—

The German sentries on the canal bridge are confused about what has made all the noise, thinking something has fallen off an Allied aircraft shot down on its way to bomb Caen. Eighteen-year-old Helmut Romer[16], is still pondering what made 'a swishing noise, followed by a bang'[17] when a large dark shadow sweeps across the bridge, probably the third glider coming in to land.

On seeing soldiers clambering up the embankment and onto the road off the eastern end of the bridge, Romer is momentarily paralysed by fear. Armed to the teeth and with their faces blackened by camouflage paint, the intruders look terrifying. It is Lt Brotheridge who leads a charge of around two dozen screaming men across the canal bridge. Guns blazing, they are also hurling grenades with a lethal proficiency quite extraordinary for troops whose baptism of fire this is. Romer snaps out of it, fires a warning flare from a signal pistol into the air and yells: 'Alarm!'

He and a Polish conscript along with a fellow German named Sauer, run as fast as they can in the opposite direction, back across the bridge, towards a café, throwing themselves into an elderberry bush.

Their confused Non-Commissioned Officer (NCO) emerges from the pillbox where he has been slumbering, asking sleepily: 'What's wrong?'[18]

A burst of fire from Brotheridge's Sten gun sends the German NCO to eternity. Other defenders are more alert and begin to fire on the attackers. Bren gunner Pte Bill Gray has already claimed one German soldier, firing the machine gun from the hip as he runs.

Ahead of him, L/Cpl Tom Packwood – the soldier assigned as his number two, meant to hand him ammo magazines – steps aside and shouts:

'Come on Bill, you are supposed to be in front of me!'[19]

Gray keeps running and firing, felling another German on the other side of the bridge. Busting for a pee – though it is obviously unwise to pause for a toilet break right now – he smashes in the door of a barn he has been assigned to clear. Gray hurls in a grenade, fires a burst from the Bren, just to make sure of eliminating any enemy in there. It turns out to be devoid of enemy troops.

Lt Brotheridge has been hit in the neck by a bullet, tumbling to the ground by the café – a look of total surprise on his face.[20] Within two hours he will die of his wounds, a grievous loss to the Ox and Bucks. He was a very popular officer and they had lived with him and trained for war together for years. Now he has been cut down within minutes of going into action, possibly the first Allied soldier to die in combat on D-Day.

The only other death in the early moments of the action has been a private in the third glider, which veered into a pond to avoid crashing into the other Horsas and broke apart. The unfortunate soldier was trapped in wreckage and drowned.

The remaining Germans on the canal bridge do not put up much of a fight and either flee or die. Romer, Sauer, and the Pole stay undercover in their elderberry bush for the next 26 hours before being compelled by thirst and hunger to emerge with their hands up.

Sheltering in their cellar are Georges and Therese Gondree, who run the café. They have been the source of much intelligence on the local situation, which has been sent back to England via the Resistance. It is amazing what can be gleaned from the overheard conversations of German soldiers drunk on the café's unsophisticated Calvados brandy.

On this night the Gondrees and their two young daughters ignore the tremendous crashes on the other side of the bridge, also thinking it is associated with the bombing raid. They finally realise something unusual is going on when gunfire and explosions erupt on their side of the bridge.

Georges crawls on his hands and knees up to the first floor of the café building and peeps out a window. He can hear talking but cannot tell who might be responsible. His eyes grow more accustomed to the dark and he picks out a couple of soldiers sitting near the café's petrol pump. Beside them is a corpse.

Going outside to investigate, M Gondree is asked in French by one of the mystery soldiers: 'Are you a civilian?'[21]

Unable to tell if the inquisitor is German or British, Georges confirms in French that he is. The exchange appears to have exhausted the soldier's French vocabulary, so M Gondree returns to his cellar and decides to wait until after dawn to investigate further who is doing what to whom.

Not far away to the east, the Orne River bridge is taken without a fight, which is just as well, for the third glider assigned to the task has mistakenly landed by another bridge, over the Dives River, some eight miles away.

Its troops seize it anyway but then retreat under fire on realising their error, losing a few men while disengaging. At the Caen Canal and Orne River bridges, the sappers of the Royal Engineers (RE) discover the explosives have not even been placed to blow them up.

It is 12.31am.

Maj Howard goes to see how the glider pilots are getting on with off-loading equipment from the wreckage of their aircraft, finding SSgt Wallwork on his feet again and hard at work. Howard thinks the pilot has unusual war paint on his face – everybody else's is matte black, but Wallwork's has a sticky gleam to it, a different shade altogether. He realises the glider pilot's face is covered in blood from where he has been cut by Perspex shards and wood splinters.

—

Another air armada of transport aircraft sweeps over the Channel – the seas below by now crowded with thousands of invasion vessels carrying tens of thousands of troops.

Soldiers on the upper decks and sailors on watch aboard the ships gaze in awe at hundreds of twinkling navigation lights on the wingtips of the aircraft, their fleeting silhouettes revealed against a half moon sky. It is a staggering display of aerial supremacy. Along with the massive invasion fleet, the Allies hope it heralds the beginning of the end for the Nazi cause.

Maj Howard is mightily relieved at 12.50am to hear the roar of aircraft dropping the 3rd and 5th Parachute brigades. Thousands of parachutes blossom in the sky above over Normandy. However, it is all somewhat chaotic – partly caused by winds blowing paratroopers off course, while some drops are in the wrong location, miles away from their correct DZs. It will take some time to gather 7th Para Bn together and head for the bridges.

While it is needed over there, its sister 9th Para Bn is assigned to crack a tough nut: the Merville Battery. Those troops must destroy heavy guns that can fire on Sword Beach and potentially sink landing ships packed with troops and equipment as they come in to be offloaded. There are also five bridges over the Dives River, which are to be destroyed by troops of the 3rd Para Bde, including the 1st Canadian Para Bn, in order to cut enemy lines of attack from the east.

The sooner the 7th Bn arrives at Benouville the better, for Howard is acutely aware that his lightly armed force will be no match for panzers, with only a single working Projector Infantry Anti-Tank (PIAT) weapon. This uses a large spring to punch a spigot into the base of a dart-like armour-piercing bomb and trigger its propellant. It has a limited, flat trajectory range of just 115 yards. The British troops' rifles and machine guns will not be much use against armour either.

Maj Howard is at least finally able to order his radio operator at the company command post, by the pillbox, to transmit the agreed message for successful seizure of both bridges – 'Ham' for the canal bridge and 'Jam' for the river bridge. 'Ham and Jam... Ham and Jam,' L/Cpl Tappenden says repeatedly into the microphone.

This rapidly becomes wearisome when nobody on the 5th Para Bde command net acknowledges it. Exasperated, L/Cpl Tappenden growls: 'Ham and *bloody* Jam! Why the hell don't you answer!?'[22]

Unfortunately, the brigade's radio equipment has been lost during the drop, but Brigadier (Brig) Nigel Poett, commander of the 5th Para Bde, and a couple of paratroopers soon arrive, which is not quite the level of reinforcements expected.

—

Not long before 1.00am a German staff car, accompanied by a motorcycle outrider, races down the road from Ranville. They run into a hail of bullets, the motorcyclist losing control, and both he and the machine plunge into the river. The staff car hurtles drunkenly over the Orne bridge, its tyres punctured and coming to an inglorious end in a ditch. Three occupants climb out, with two killed, the third shot in the leg.

The survivor is Maj Hans Schmidt who is supposed to be in command of defending the bridges. As Captain (Capt) John 'Doc' Vaughan, the Ox and Bucks medical officer on the scene, tends to his wounds, Schmidt's mood turns defiantly ugly. He shouts in English about the sheer stupidity of the Allies thinking they can actually beat Germany.

Schmidt storms: 'You are going to be thrown back into the sea!'[23]

Then he lapses into moroseness, asking 'Doc' to shoot him, for he has lost his honour along with the bridges, and the Führer will be very upset with him. Vaughan refuses to oblige and instead 'shoots' him with a large dose of morphine. Schmidt is thereafter very relaxed and full of gratitude for the excellent medical attention he is receiving.

The British soldiers are amused and intrigued to find Schmidt's staff car full of empty wine bottles, dirty dinner plates, and wine glasses along with ladies' cosmetics and items of lingerie – but no female passengers.[24]

Maj Howard remarks it appears his troops' sudden arrival out of nowhere 'resulted in "Herr Commandant" being interrupted during a most intimate soiree with an obliging local lady in Ranville.'[25]

The good humour prompted by this somewhat farcical enemy intrusion is dispelled when, at 1.30am, three enemy tanks, with troops trotting alongside them, clank down the road from Le Port on a foray towards the western end of the Caen Canal bridge.

Sergeant (Sgt) 'Wagger' Thornton waits until the leading panzer is almost on top of him before firing the unit's PIAT, which nobody has much faith in stopping an enemy tank. On this occasion, it does the trick. Pte Edwards witnesses how 'this flaming tank literally blew up, exploded ... there were great spurts of green and orange and yellow as all the ammunition inside was exploding, making a hell of a din.'[26]

More British troops open fire, forcing the German infantry to retreat while the tank's crew are incinerated, except for one poor panzerman hurled out onto the ground, mortally wounded.

His cries and moans of agony upset the British soldiers, with one officer suggesting to another the German ought to be put out of his misery. Nobody has the nerve to do so, and it is clear the medics cannot save him, so he is left to die – such is the cruelty of war.

The two other panzers halt, turn around, and, along with the troops, withdraw, leaving behind the burning tank's wreckage blocking a crossroads and hence both approach roads. If only the Germans knew how poorly equipped the Airborne soldiers are for the job of seeing off panzers, they might press their attack with more vigour and manage to endanger the eastern flank of the invasion. Paratroopers of the 7th Bn, seeing and hearing the explosions of the ammunition cooking off inside the blazing tank, use it as a means to navigate across country to the scene of battle.

Their arrival causes a bit of rejoicing',[27] an Ox and Bucks soldier calling out to them: 'Where the hell have you been!?'

The paratroopers pat the Ox and Bucks soldiers on their helmets, saying 'good lads, well done' and pass through to clear the enemy out of Benouville.

—

By 3.30am, while the Germans are making determined attempts to penetrate the Airborne perimeter, it is considered secure enough for a mass of gliders to land, bringing troops, anti-tanks guns, and other heavy equipment. Also flying in by glider is the commander of the 6th Airborne Div, Major General (Maj Gen) Richard 'Windy' Gale and his headquarters, and the HQ is soon established in a nearby chateau. After walking to the Caen Canal bridge, Gale borrows a horse to ensure he gets to the chateau promptly, in order to begin organising the defence of the invasion's eastern flank.

The Merville Battery is taken, despite most of the attacking force and its assault equipment going astray during the 9th Bn's drop. The battery's guns – which turn out to be less powerful than thought – are damaged enough to stop the enemy from using them for a while.

The main event of the invasion starts shortly before 6.00am. A massive bombardment by 137 warships creates a wall of fire, smoke, and thunder across the Bay of the Seine, with hundreds of shells arcing through the air.

The Americans begin their landings on Omaha and Utah beaches at 6.30am, on the extreme right flank, and the British on Sword at 7.25am, with commandos of the 1st French Marines Rifle Bn given the honour of spearheading the assault into the port of Ouistreham at the mouth of the Orne. British troops land on Gold Beach, also at 7.25am, with Canadian units going ashore at Juno from 7.35am.

Commandos of the 1st Special Service Bde, under the suave and daringly aggressive Brig the Lord Lovatt, with bagpiper Bill Millin by his side playing a rousing skirl, storm across Sword Beach.

The green berets make it to the canal crossing – soon to be renamed Pegasus Bridge – not long after 2.00pm on D-Day, bringing Churchill tanks with them for heavyweight back-up. The commandos suffer numerous casualties going across the bridge – under fire from enemy snipers in woods by the canal. The sky is filled by more gliders, as the rest of the Ox and Bucks and other elements of the 6th Airborne Div arrive.

By the end of D-Day, despite heavy fighting at Omaha and other points along the 50-mile invasion front, more than 150,000 Allied troops and thousands of tanks and military vehicles are ashore.

Meanwhile, Germany's supreme leader, Adolf Hitler, refuses to release the panzer divisions that Generalfeldmarschall Erwin

Rommel – commander of Army Group B and therefore in charge of trying to thwart the invasion – begs for in order to push the enemy back into the Channel.

The Führer and other senior German commanders have bought into a carefully woven Allied deception that convinces them Normandy is a mere diversion. They feel the real invasion will soon be launched across the Channel against the 15th Army, which waits in vain around the pas de Calais.

Weeks of slaughter lie ahead in Normandy, especially with the stormtroopers of Waffen SS divisions thrown into the battle – most of them against the British to prevent the capture of Caen. It is the hinge around which the whole affair will turn. Take Caen, and the Allies can charge across open country – all the way to Paris.

Despite the grinding, blood-soaked nature of the Normandy struggle, the Allies remain resolute in their determination to liberate France and the rest of north-west Europe from cruel Nazi occupation. It is felt by many on the Allied side that if they can just smash through the ever-thinner wall of enemy divisions, they may even achieve the ultimate objective of capturing Berlin and ending the war by Christmas.

However, on D-Day heavy fighting lies ahead for the British and Canadian Airborne warriors as they and the commandos secure the eastern flank of the beachhead. Reinforced by British, Belgian, and Dutch units – bolstered by tanks and artillery – the 6th Airborne Div fights on into August. It participates in the great push to break out, itself heading for Le Havre and beyond. Once that job is done, if needs be, the mighty Allied Airborne divisions (and the British still have the 1st Airborne Div in reserve) can be used again, this time to kick down the door into Germany itself.

It is just a case of deciding when, and where, to unleash them in another equally daring mission. The combination of air supremacy, overwhelming material resources and highly trained elite troops looks likely to be decisive again, if used at the right time in the right place. How can the Allies not seek to capitalise on the ability of Airborne troops to strike suddenly from the skies, using them to carry out yet another *coup de main*?

It becomes a burning issue as the Allied armies surge towards the frontiers of the tottering Third Reich, which is also under pressure from massive Russian offensives on the Eastern Front.

To End the War

'Now these things befell at Arnhem.'

—By Air to Battle: The Official Account of the British Airborne Divisions

In early September 1944, following the breakout from Normandy the Germans in the West appear to have collapsed. Allied armies push a tide of broken enemy forces before them at a rate of tens of miles a day.

Except, now there is a pause at the Belgian-Dutch frontier.

The British 21st Army Group is low on fuel and ammunition.

Commanded by 56-year-old Field Marshal (FM) Bernard Montgomery,[28] its men are more than a little weary from the huge effort but jubilant too.[29]

It will take a few days to replenish and rest, especially as supplies are still coming all the way from the invasion beaches of Normandy and a few Channel ports. They are conveyed by a massive fleet of trucks, aircraft and what survives of the French rail network after prolonged Allied bombing.

The supplies are split between the British and Canadians in the northwest and American armies to the centre and south. General (Gen) George S Patton – commander of the Third US Army, which in late August 1944 charged over the River Meuse – feels he should be getting the bulk of them and not his long-time, and bitter, rival Montgomery. The fiery and daring Patton believes that he and his troops are the best option to slay the Nazi dragon. In the eyes of the meticulous Monty – careful to preserve Britain's rapidly declining[30] military resources and expend them only to achieve something truly decisive – this will be an error. Monty besieges Allied Supreme Commander General Dwight D Eisenhower with demands that the main Allied effort should be his proposed drive into the Ruhr – a killer thrust into the military-industrial heartland of the enemy war effort.

To achieve this, he wishes to launch a stunningly daring – and massive – operation into Holland, rolling up to the Ijsselmeer, pivot to the east and then make a narrow, rapier-like lunge into Germany. It will pass the northern end of the Siegfried Line, the much-vaunted concrete and steel ribbon of defences stretching from the Reich's northern frontier with Holland (at Kleve), almost to Basle in Switzerland.

If the British plan succeeds, the war really could be over by Christmas, such is the vaulting ambition of Monty's plan.

The springboard for it all is the proposed Operation Market Garden.

It envisages using the elite divisions of the newly formed First Allied Airborne Army – commanded by an American air force general, Lieutenant General (Lt Gen) Lewis H Brereton – to drop a carpet of paratroopers and glider-borne troops (the 'Market' element) that will pave the way for an armoured Corps (the 'Garden' part) to attack hard on a narrow front, linking up with the Airborne divisions en route. The Airborne warriors will be a means to seize and secure bridges over eight waterways, including three major rivers – the Maas, Waal, and Neder Rijn (Lower Rhine). Should the crossings be blown by the enemy, they may present serious impediments to a successful outcome.

In Monty's mind, capturing those bridges appears to be all that stands between the Allies and destroying Hitler and his evil regime. Yet it is a task 'as hard for the Allies [to pull off] as it was for Hannibal to get his elephants over the Alps.'[31] In order to stand any chance of success, the operation has to be launched while the enemy is still in a state of shock and disarray. That means – in contrast to the detailed planning and rehearsal for D-Day, which was spread over months – everything must be organised in days.

On 14 September Montgomery issues his orders for the audacious Market Garden – which will include the biggest Airborne assault in history – triggering frenetic activity not only in Britain, at the bases of various divisions of the Allied Airborne Army, but also in Belgium.

The 30,000 paratroopers and glider-borne soldiers in the aerial vanguard are almost twice as many as were sent into action on D-Day.

The main ground attack will be undertaken by hundreds of British tanks and armoured cars and, coming behind them, tens of thousands of ground troops aboard trucks, half-tracks and all supported by other vehicles and equipment. This mighty force belongs to the British Second Army's XXX Corps under Lt Gen Brian Horrocks. While XXX Corps will take the starring role – centre-stage for the drive on the Rhine up 64 miles of a single, two-lane highway – XII Corps and VIII Corps of the Second Army will protect the flanks, or try to.

The US 101st Airborne Div and US 82nd Airborne Div will be landed/dropped north of Eindhoven and south of Nijmegen respectively. That the final three crossings – the rail, road, and pontoon bridges over the Lower Rhine at Arnhem – will prove the sternest test of all in Market Garden is recognised. That is why the plan uses the British 1st Airborne Div for the trickiest part of the mission – if it goes askew at its most exposed end, then it is more politically palatable for British troops to take the pain.

The air-transportable 52nd (Lowland) Div – infantry recently switched from specialising in mountain warfare – is available for reinforcement of the 1st Airborne, should an airfield be taken that is suitable to bring them in via an additional airlift (or if territory is secured to construct advance airfields).

Breretons deputy in the Allied Airborne Army is 47-year-old Lt Gen Frederick 'Boy' Browning – also commander of Britain's I Airborne Corps. He will nominally be overall boss of Airborne troops for the initial phase, with 43-year-old Maj

Gen Roy Urquhart in command of the 1st Airborne. While its sister formation, the 6th Airborne, may have been sent into action to pave the way for the Normandy invasion, and took part in subsequent fighting, the 1st Airborne has been held back in reserve since returning from several combat operations in the Mediterranean theatre.

Like the 6th Airborne, the 1st Airborne is composed of two brigades of paratroopers of the Parachute Regt and an air landing brigade, the latter similarly composed of troops flown in aboard gliders piloted by the aviator-soldiers of the Glider Pilot Regt. The primary fighting units in the 1st Para Bde, commanded by 38-year-old Brig Gerald Lathbury, are the 1st, 2nd and 3rd Bns of the Parachute Regt. The 4th Para Bde, commanded by Brig John 'Shan' Hackett, also has three Parachute Regt battalions – the 156th, 10th, and 11th. The 1st Air Landing Brigade (Air Ldg Bde), commanded by 49- year-old Brig Pip Hicks, is spearheaded by infantry battalions too: the 7th (Galloway) Bn, the King's Own Scottish Borderers (KOSB); 2nd Bn, the South Staffordshire Regt; 1st Bn, the Border Regt. Attached to boost the power of the division is the 1st Polish Independent Para Bde, with its main constituent parts the 1st, 2nd, and 3rd Bns, under the command of Maj Gen Stanislaw Sosabowski.

Included in the 1st Airborne Div's order of battle are artillery, signals, engineer, and reconnaissance units – the 21st Indep Para Coy and the 1st Airborne Reconnaissance Squadron (Airborne Recce Sqn) – plus assorted others. The 1st Airborne Div has an overall strength of 10,095 men (including 1,126 glider pilots). The Polish brigade, and its support group, offers a further 1,680 men.

These, then, are the principal actors in this soon to unfold epic – all due to enter the theatre of war in the most dramatic fashion. Not only are these men distinctive due to the means by which they travel to war, their headgear is intrinsic to the fighting legend they have already established.

The soldiers of the British Airborne forces all wear the maroon 'red beret' because Browning's wife – the celebrated novelist Daphne Du Maurier – suggested it would be an inspirational touch to set them apart from other elite bodies. For such men – who soon forged a formidable reputation, earning the nickname *Die Roten Teufel* ('The Red Devils') from German troops they fought in North Africa – it seems no task is too hard.

When Montgomery asks Lt Gen Browning to hold the all-important Arnhem road bridge for two days, he suggests his troops can do it for twice as long – but adds a telling caveat about the wisdom of the plan's final objective. 'I think we might be going a bridge too far,' says Browning.[32]

The young men who will be the tip of the Airborne forces spear will soon enough discover whether or not Browning is correct in his analysis.

—

The epic story of being at the sharp end of Monty's bid to end the war by Christmas 1944 is told here by some of those plunged into the cauldron of battle. Much of the testimony about one of the most famous fights in history was gathered during a unique series of interviews or obtained from museum archives. The participants' experiences reflect the confusion and mayhem of war, seen from the point of view of ordinary soldiers caught up in extraordinary events. We go into battle not only with famous commanders in the thick of the action, including Lieutenant Colonel (Lt Col) John Frost of the 2nd Bn, the Parachute Regt, and Brig Hackett of the 4th Para Bde, but also those whose fate was settled by their decisions.

Capt Peter Fletcher of the Glider Pilot Regt will fly into battle at the controls of a Horsa glider, having already participated in the Normandy invasion. In the early hours of D-Day itself, Capt Fletcher only narrowly avoided death, when the nose wheel of his glider smashed through the cockpit, injuring his co-pilot. Hoping for a less hazardous landing this time, the 29-year-old will be attached to the 1st Airborne Div Headquarters throughout the coming fight. Royal Army Service Corps (RASC) L/Cpl Dennis Clay, aged 25, will narrowly avoid a grisly death under tank tracks, while Pte Stan Turner, aged 22, is to fight at Arnhem with a detachment of the Royal Electrical and Mechanical Engineers (REME). Like many soldiers in the division, this is his first battle. He is to become the victim of a final bitter twist.

Others in this story include Glider Pilot Regt SSgt Pat Withnall, aged 27, who will take Polish paratroopers into action. During the Normandy invasion he flew a glider carrying Airborne troops in on the first wave, his Horsa landing in the middle of an enemy minefield, fortunately without detonating anything. Then there is eager young Lt Jeff Noble, aged 20, of the 156th Para Bn who will let nothing stop him getting into action and 19-year-old anti-tank platoon soldier Pte Frank Newhouse of the 10th Para Bn who will receive a painful baptism of fire and find himself betrayed by a Nazi.

Corporal (Cpl) Harry Tucker, aged 25, is an ace marksman, serving with the 1st Bn of the Parachute Regt. Tucker was a regular soldier in the Duke of Cornwall's Light Infantry (DCLI) on the outbreak of war in September 1939, seeing action in France with the British Expeditionary Force (BEF). Caught up in the retreat to Dunkirk in 1940, he subsequently put himself forward for the British Army's new parachute forces, to get the earliest possible opportunity to hit back at the enemy. Tucker has already fought his way through North Africa but did not take part in the drop on Sicily of July 1943 that saw so many casualties among veterans of the 1st Airborne. The Dakota parachute aircraft he was in suffered several hits from AA fire and turned back before it could disgorge its paratroopers. Following further combat in Sicily and Italy, Tucker, like the rest of the 1st Para Bn, returned to the UK to endure a long wait for action.

There could hardly be a more different theatre of war from the comparatively parched, sparsely populated and rugged Mediterranean than the flat, water-logged Netherlands and especially the pleasant, tree lined avenues of towns and villages the Airborne troops will soon be contesting with the enemy.

The fact that it will be waged in neighbourhoods where thousands of people reside means there is another side to this story that must not be overlooked. That is of the civilians who find themselves at the mercy of the brutal, vicious battle waged in Arnhem and the neighbouring village of Oosterbeek. The civilians' perspective is provided via the remarkable testimony of a teenage boy and an anxious father – Jan Loos and Frans de Soet – whose families are trapped by the fighting. They give us graphic insights into their experiences, often imprisoned in cellars below their homes at the very heart of the conflict. This is the story of a battle that will be described by the official history of Britain's Airborne Forces in the Second World War as 'a feat of arms which will be remembered and recounted as long as the virtues of courage and resolution have power to move the hearts of men.'

Sunday

17 September

*'It was a still, lazy day – and the sun was shining...
Our arrival was deceptively peaceful.'*

—Maj Gen Roy Urquhart, Commanding the 1st Airborne Div[33]

The 1st Airborne Div has been straining at the leash for much too long but now – at long last – its men are about to take off into the wide blue yonder. At airfields across eastern, western, and southern England, British paratroopers climb into twin-engined Dakota transport aircraft, the glider-borne troops settling in aboard Horsa and Hamilcar gliders. The latter is a big, ugly monster carrying heavier vehicles and equipment, including 17pdr anti-tank guns.

Waiting for take-off, the Airborne soldiers taste a heady cocktail of apprehension and excitement. The virgins are concerned about what lies ahead, but veterans of previous fighting know more than a little of what to expect. Most battles are hard, but, as some of the British Army's toughest soldiers, their *esprit de corps* is second to none. With 15 proposed 1st Airborne operations cancelled since June 1944, it is no exaggeration to say the division's troops are at a high pitch of readiness. They have been held in reserve so long, they are in danger of going off the boil.

According to the 33-year-old boss of the 4th Para Bde, 'for three of them [the cancelled operations] we were already in the aeroplane...'

Brig Hackett's men had already written their last letters to loved ones and relatives, leaving them behind to be mailed out if they did not come back; they had put their affairs in order in case they were killed. Hackett recalls they were sat in the Dakotas, engines roaring, preparing their minds for combat when...

> 'Chap comes around, hammers on the outside of the aircraft and says "alright, dismount, it's all off boys" and [we then have] everybody going on three days leave. Well, you can't keep on doing that to really first class troops without endangering morale, and I longed to get this lot into battle.'[34]

In Hackett's view, 'there wasn't a better division in the whole British Army at that time', but its men are referring to it as the 'Stillborn Division' – a sign of contempt for their recent inactivity and cancelled ops.

Pub brawls with personnel from other military formations, especially Americans, are not uncommon. Sometimes, when the military police try to restore order, the Yanks and Brits unite to give the MPs a good battering for daring to intervene.[35]

The most recent cancelled operation was dubbed Comet, which would have seen the 1st Airborne Div and the Poles alone attempting to seize all eight key crossings for the thrust north. It made both Brig Hackett and the 52-year-old Maj Gen Sosabowski deeply unhappy. The Polish brigade boss asked Lt Gen Browning after being briefed on the Comet plan:

'But the Germans, general – the Germans!?'

In Hackett's view, the planners were gravely underestimating the likely reaction of the enemy, whose ability to bounce back from defeat he had come to deeply respect when fighting them elsewhere. Some of his colleagues had not received the same kind of baptism of fire, which perhaps explained their optimism. Hackett knows the Germans may appear to be lightly holding an area initially but 'the moment you threaten something really vital there, their reaction would be swift and violent' with reinforcements poured in to stiffen the fight back. 'Comet – thank God – was called off.'

While they wait for an operation that will actually go ahead, there are numerous absences without leave among the 1st Airborne Div's troops – the men heading off for a spot of rest and recreation in towns and cities, taking advantage of all the dubious attractions, or simply going to see loved ones. As news of an operation somehow filters out – despite blanket secrecy – many of the AWOL troops slip back into base, so they will not miss out.

The 31-year-old Commanding Officer (CO) of the 2nd Para Bn, recognises his troops walk a fine line between being ready for battle and losing their edge. Lt Col Frost feels morale among his men is 'terrific' but there are bound to be a few troops who have 'absented themselves...'

> '...but they had a sort of grapevine, which seemed to tell them wherever they were that an operation might be pending and they made certain that they turned up. In fact, one party of men turned up in a taxi from London.'[36]

One paratrooper in the 21st Indep Para Coy is so determined to take part, he doesn't care about a broken wrist and will parachute into action with his right arm in plaster and wearing a sling.[37]

Being supposedly confined to barracks on a Gloucestershire airfield ahead of the operation does not stop Pte Stan Turner and his mates going for a final night out in an old Roman town that boasts its share of ancient pubs. As he reveals in his diary, getting back to base calls for military initiative.

> 'We were briefed about the Arnhem operation and told it will be a success because there are only remnants of German divisions there. Some of our unit, including me, go out for a drink in Cirencester.

We found we could not get a lift back and so we "borrowed" an RAF lorry.'

And now – on this day of days, 17 September 1944 – accessories of war weigh many of the paratroopers down so much they hobble to the waiting aircraft. Each man carries in excess of 70lbs of equipment.

There is no cast iron guarantee of resupply, so he takes as much as he can manage in pockets of his camouflage smock and backpack, the latter worn on the chest during the jump. He also wears a disposable 'jump jacket' (aka an oversmock) on top of all this to prevent things snagging on the parachute harness, the rigging lines or just falling off.

Many parachutists also have a Leg Kit Bag, containing *additional* ammunition and possibly mines, grenades, rations, explosives, detonators, entrenching tools – whatever else might come in handy. The kitbags containing all this material – adding up to 100lbs extra – are strapped to the paratroopers' legs. After they jump from the aircraft, they release the kitbags to dangle 20ft below, leaving them able to focus on steering their parachutes.

The famous Sten sub machine gun can be carried when jumping, secured on the man's chest, under parachute straps, with its stock and magazine removed. The Lee Enfield infantry rifles and Bren light machine guns are too long and cannot be broken down so are slipped inside a felt valise that, likewise, can dangle on the end of a strap during the jump.

The bigger items of equipment, including the Brens and also 2-inch mortars plus associated ammunition, can also be put in containers and dropped under their own parachutes.[38] The theory is that the kitbag lands a few seconds ahead of the paratrooper, ensuring nobody suffers broken bones due to landing awkwardly – that is the theory, anyway. Once the kitbags touch earth the parachutist also receives a welcome break in his rate of descent, which (hopefully) assists an injury free landing. If luck is not on their side, however, Leg Kit Bags can break free in the descent and are never seen again by their owners.

A vast airborne armada composed of several thousand parachute aircraft, gliders, their tugs, and escorting fighters fills the skies above England, carrying the troops of the 1st Airborne and 101st and 82nd US Airborne Divs to their rendezvous with destiny.

For this first lift alone, the 1st Airborne Div requires 157 Dakota parachute aircraft of the United States Army Air Force (USAAF) 314th and 61st Troop Carrier groups along with RAF Albermarle, Halifax, and Stirling bombers on tug duties and 358 gliders of the AAC.

As it passes over England, below the massive air fleet worshippers run from churches in which sermons and hymns have been drowned out by the din of aircraft engines; they gaze skyward in wonder, open-mouthed at the awesome spectacle overhead.

The noise is so great, horses bolt in the fields while car drivers pull their vehicles over to the side of the road to watch. Passengers on trains leap up to press their faces against grimy carriage windows to get a better look.[39]

The parachute aircraft, gliders, and their tugs along with escorting fighters sweep over the North Sea and English Channel as Holland basks in a lazy summer's day, the Allied air armada splitting into three.

Those carrying the American divisions head for the DZs and LZs around Eindhoven or Nijmegen, while the British are soon approaching theirs outside Wolfheze and Heelsum, two villages in the country to the west of Oosterbeek. There has already been frantic air activity over Holland, with hundreds of Allied bombers attacking targets and fighters on strafing runs, prompting a furious response from German AA guns. The Netherlands is thickly sewn with anti-aircraft batteries, some of them located right next to peoples' homes, even in their gardens.

Earlier, Frans de Soet – an engineer by trade – sat in the garden of his home, the Vredehof villa, in Lower Oosterbeek, enjoying the fine weather. De Soet's abode is near the Rhine and close to the village's Oude Kerk (the Old Church), which dates back to the 10th Century.

He watches the usual routine of 'people going to church in little groups'[40], but, from 10.00am, the roar of aircraft and crack of AA guns shatters the customary Sunday peace. Though their colleagues elsewhere may be busy, the crews of AA guns nearby seem unperturbed. Even when bombs are dropping on Arnhem, several miles away, at Oosterbeek the laid-back German gunners carry on with their little game of throwing sticks at pear trees to knock down the fruit.

—

Jan Loos is a 14-year-old pupil of the secondary school at the Zaayersplein in Oosterbeek, living with his mother Margarethe, father Martinus, and 11-year-old sister Gini in a modest house at De la Reyweg 7.

It is just 600 feet from the plush Hartenstein Hotel and its expansive grounds, which is currently host to German military staff officers.

Early on the morning of 17 September, Martinus leaves home and heads for Arnhem where he is employed in the offices of the Provincial Food Commissioner, near the northern ramp of the Rhine road bridge.

Jan, along with his mother and sister attend the Sunday morning service in the Dutch Reformed Church at the Toulon van der Koogweg, amid 'noise and activity with many planes flying over and – in the distance – explosions… The minister stops the service, and everyone goes home quickly. Things quieten down…'[41]

There is a bomb hit near the Vredehof villa, forcing Frans de Soet and his family – his wife Ann and 18-month-old daughter Roelinde – to take shelter in its large cellar. Above ground, he notes, the 'German flak [now] shoots like mad.' People flee from the Oude Kerk, some seeking shelter in de Soet's cellar. They reveal that, initially, 'during the bombardment the congregation sang the Dutch national anthem, standing erect.'

They will not do that for some time, thinks de Soet.

'Who could have imagined that the last prayers had been said in that ancient little church...'

—

Dutch civilians out on Sunday strolls close to the DZs and LZs gaze up at a dark, thunderous mass of approaching Allied aircraft.

Jan Loos goes outside to watch 'hundreds of low-flying aircraft. In the direction of Wolfheze and Ede ... planes, gliders and innumerable parachutes in different colours, which is beautiful to see. Everyone is on the street cheering: "The English are coming!" We watch until the last parachute has gone down and then go inside.'

But what of the Germans who also stare at the parachutes filling the skies? How will they react?

A German account records a sky filled with many aircraft and thousands of troops tumbling from them or landing in gliders, adding:

> 'In those first few minutes it looked as if the down-coming masses would suffocate every single life on the ground.'[42]

From his house, Jan sees 'a German patrol, sticking close to the boundary hedge of the house opposite ours, heading towards the Steijnweg with their weapons at the ready. After they disappear, we hear shooting in the distance from time to time but we sleep peacefully that night.'

The German high command is not likely to do so. The Allied Airborne divisions are a big stick poked into a wasp's nest, bound to provoke a furious reaction. The precursor to striking back – once they get over the immediate shock at the sheer scale of the Allied assault – is for the Germans to start 'searching the countless forests and large parks ... cut by numerous small streams' in order 'to ascertain where the enemy intended to concentrate his forces: only then could a basis for our counter attacks be established.'[43]

Maj Gen Sosabowski of the 1st Polish Bde had wondered, when the Market Garden plan was outlined for him, by Maj Gen Urquhart, about the wisdom of the chosen LZs and DZs. Surely, he thought, the Allies realise Arnhem is 'the gateway to the Germany' and that means they are not going to 'leave it open.'[44]

This is true, for it lies on the main avenue of retreat back into the Reich for enemy forces in north and west Holland – and there are up to 150,000 German troops still in The Netherlands – while the area around the Haagse Bos (Hague Forest) has since early September been a key launch point for V2 ballistic missiles. The Nazi leadership is betting on turning the tide of the war in the west via such *Vergeltungswaffen* (retaliatory weapons).

The V2 blitz of Britain is underway, threatening to create a state of terror in London. The ballistic missiles arc 60 miles above the Earth before plunging down on the British capital. The supersonic bang and terrifying *whoosh* seconds before impact are the only warning given, with 1,400 of them exploding in London and eastern England between September 1944 and late March 1945.[45] The V2 launch sites are bombed by Allied air forces to try to protect England and liberated cities, such as Paris and Antwerp, which are likewise facing a missile barrage, but Montgomery is also under pressure to overcome them as soon as possible. The thrust towards Arnhem will enable him to cut off and destroy them. Even so, the chosen direction of the Market Garden attack will, after the event, be viewed as colliding with the law of unintended consequences. That's because, for all its value to the Germans – as a base for V2 launchers and an exit route to the Reich – it is still more by accident than design that the opposition in the Arnhem area will be so strong. With three major rivers between themselves and the British Second Army, battered Waffen ('Armed') SS[46] combat formations sent to refit in locations around Arnhem no doubt hoped they were far enough behind the front line to relax and lick their wounds. South-east of Arnhem are the recently arrived 9th SS 'Hohenstaufen' and 10th SS 'Frundsberg' panzer divisions, or what is left of them – collectively the II SS Panzer Corps under 50-year-old Obergruppenführer Wilhelm Bittrich.

Among the various other units is a *panzergrenadier* training battalion, commanded by Sturmbannführer Sepp Krafft. It is settling into a camp in the woods north-west of Oosterbeek, between the British DZs and LZs and Arnhem, having arrived just five days earlier.

The 9th SS is due to begin a move to Germany on 17 September while the 10th SS is to remain in Holland, restoring itself to fighting order. These formations still retain many survivors who are among the toughest and most dedicated fighters of the Third Reich. They received their baptism of fire on the Eastern Front against the Soviets before being switched to the West to try and hold back the Allied armies in Normandy. That campaign was a harrowing experience, with the scale of equipment and people lost during the fighting and subsequent retreat horrific.

Narrowly escaping total destruction in the Falaise Pocket – the slaughterhouse for so many German formations – these Waffen SS troops were among those who held open a gap for others to escape through.

The normal strength of an SS panzer division is meant to be 9,000 troops. Now, under the temporary command of 31-year-old Obersturmbannführer Walter Harzer, the 'Hohenstaufen' has 6,000 men left, while the 'Frundsberg', under Standartenführer Heinz Harmel, aged 38, is even more depleted, with just 3,500 men. The 'Hohenstaufen' has only around 20 Mark V Panther tanks left but does possess dozens of armoured personnel carriers and self-propelled guns (SPs), though the 'Frundsberg' has very few vehicles of any kind. It does have anti-aircraft weaponry

– including guns mounted on half-tracks or tank chassis – and artillery.

While both Waffen SS divisions would fare badly against Allied armoured formations, their residual strength is more than enough – in conjunction with SS training units and other formations lodged around Arnhem – to give the lightly armed 1st Airborne Div serious problems.

But it is the arrival *in the very place* where the British are to land of the battle-hardened Waffen SS divisions – no matter how weakened – that will prove the worst news of all for the Airborne warriors.

Photo-reconnaissance missions by the RAF pick up evidence of their presence in the Arnhem area while decrypts of German military signals also indicate significant SS units are there. Based on this, warnings are issued by the 1st Airborne Div's intelligence staff, but the British top brass take the gamble anyway. They persuade themselves that, no matter who they are, these enemy troops will not be a significant problem after their supposed evisceration in Normandy.

–

In the calm before the storm, at an airfield in England, Capt Peter Fletcher sips a mug of hot, sweet tea as he waits for the Halifax bomber towing his glider to start heading down the runway. Once the Halifax begins rolling, Capt Fletcher carefully brings his Horsa up first, to ensure there is enough slack in the tow rope to avoid the glider being torn apart.

The cargo carried by Fletcher's aircraft is vital to the division's wellbeing: Colonel (Col) Graeme Warrack, the senior medical officer, accompanied by medics. They are all squeezed in around a jeep – one of the division's casualty evacuation vehicles, displaying a red cross emblazoned on white square.

Even after the cargo has been safely delivered to the LZ, the story is not over for Capt Fletcher. Unlike their American counterparts, who immediately head home to base after landing their own Waco gliders, most of the Glider Pilot Regt soldiers will, during the forthcoming battle, be expected to fight on as infantry, at least for a short while.

Fletcher sees it all as 'good fun', and, besides, he loves flying – even if the gliders exhibit a tendency to break up on landing or, sometimes, even in mid-air while being towed. Once it is cast off from the tug, the Horsa will – depending on the skill of the pilot, and prevailing weather conditions – fall to earth like a brick, or swoop like a graceful pigeon.

In a similar fashion to Maj Howard of Pegasus Bridge fame, 1st Airborne Div troops who ride to war in a Horsa frequently exhibit their opinion of its flying qualities by covering the floors in vomit.

Unlike his D-Day touchdown, Capt Fletcher's landing this time is smooth, the glider staying in one piece.

> 'My main worry was being brained by one of the paratroopers dropping around my glider. I thought they were going to come crashing through the plane's fragile sides.'

In Lt Col John Frost's Dakota, the men of the 2nd Para Bn occupy themselves with the usual things paratroopers do to keep themselves at ease before leaping into the great unknown. 'I remember we had all the Sunday papers,' he recalls, 'which we all used to read avidly … and of course one could smoke and eat and so on.' As the aircraft takes off from an airfield at Grantham in Lincolnshire, Lt Col Frost is 'very optimistic' because the enemy seems to be in no fit state to put up much of a fight.

> '…the German Army had taken the most tremendous hiding in Normandy and all the information was that they were a beaten force,

> retreating more or less in disorder back to the Siegfried Line and back into Germany. So, I was expecting a fairly easy battle.'

He can see 'absolutely no reason why the thing shouldn't go according to plan'. There is 'a great feeling of elation in the British Army after the Normandy campaign and I think that people began to think there was going to be a bit of a walkover.'

The flight is smooth, with hundreds of escorting fighters and fighter-bombers attacking enemy flak positions and suppressing them with rockets and cannon fire. Keen to get on with it, Lt Col Frost is the first man in his aircraft to see where they will fight.

> 'I always used to jump number one and I was in the door and [so] could make quite sure we were going to land where we expected – and we did.'

In another Dakota transport, Cpl Harry Tucker of the 1st Para Bn shuffles to the door and hurls himself into the air, 400ft over the DZ at Wolfheze. The 'chute is pulled open two seconds later by the static line, giving him a violent jolt. Swiftly recovering as he swings under the oscillating canopy, Tucker calmly looks around – thankfully unmolested by German gunfire. Below he spots a Dutch couple out for a Sunday stroll beside a railway line. They are shouting and waving, so he waves back and then makes a perfect landing.

As he comes in to the LZ aboard a Horsa, the perennially air sick commander of the 1st Airborne Div is horrified to see a Hamilcar glider – carrying jeeps and other heavy equipment – somersault as its nose digs into sandy soil. The sight of a Horsa crashing into the trees, its occupants spilling out, their limbs flailing, is equally appalling.

Once safely down, Urquhart is deeply satisfied to see paratroopers landing safely, quickly regaining their senses and bearings, then arming themselves and heading for assembly points.

Less pleasing is the discovery that signallers in his tactical headquarters, in a wood by the LZ, have reported the radios needed to co-ordinate the operation are not working properly.

Establishing contact with units now moving off towards their objectives is difficult, and it looks like contacting anyone further away will be impossible. It is a problem that will bedevil the British throughout the battle.

The wheels have already begun to come off the Market Garden wagon and Urquhart had been far from happy with the plan even before he left Britain. The fact that his troops face a march of between four and eight miles from their DZs and LZs to the bridges has caused particular anxiety.

It is true that, on exercise, the parachute brigades are expected to handle a march of more than 30 miles in 24 hours, but, during Operation Market, not only are the 1st Airborne Div's troops heavily laden, they must fight their way through any enemy they encounter. The chance to achieve total surprise has been discarded by not landing any troops on top of objectives.

Not only was a *coup de main* carried out with notable success on D-Day, but Urquhart also has examples from his own division's recent exploits. During the invasion of Sicily in July 1943 some of its glider-borne troops captured and held the Ponte Grande at Syracuse, suffering heavy casualties.

Elements of the 1st Airborne a few days later also attempted to seize the Primosole Bridge, near Catania. During three days of heavy fighting, the troops at Ponte Grande were saved from being overwhelmed by the timely arrival of British units that had landed on beaches just a few miles away. The battle for the Primosole Bridge was equally bitter, and the 1st Airborne's men were forced to yield it, but, in the end, it was secured by troops from the main invading force.

Those *coup de main* assaults, while successful, were rather costly, with troops also drowned in gliders that crashed into the sea or aircraft shot down, while many of the Airborne warriors were scattered far and wide.

Fourteen months later a similar ploy – to simultaneously take both ends of the road bridge at Arnhem – was rejected by planners. This was due to fears of enormous casualties in transport aircraft: from heavy enemy AA fire and fighters based near at hand.

Maj Gen Urquhart has still tried to inject a *coup de main* element into the final plan. He has tasked the 1st Airborne Recce Sqn, commanded by Maj Freddie Gough, with racing ahead of the 1st Para Bde in its armed jeeps to, hopefully, occupy both ends of the road bridge simultaneously. Even Gough is not confident it is the best way to use his outfit of 205 seasoned veterans who parachute in or go by glider with their vehicles. He favours sending three of its four Troops down each of the routes chosen for the 1st, 2nd, and 3rd Para Bns, to scout out the line of least resistance rather than gamble on one route.

The jeeps are open-topped and thin-skinned, their Vickers machine guns unlikely to be a match for enemy armoured cars or tanks, or even heavily armed infantry trying to block their way. The squadron is also, by its nature, sparsely manned. It does have some Polsten 20mm anti-aircraft guns, but these cannot be used on the move as they are towed.

The whole idea starts to go wrong from the off. One jeep does not arrive, several others are missing or trapped inside damaged gliders and the squadron's assigned assault engineers end up on the wrong LZ. Some of the Squadron's vehicles are on one LZ while the men meant to take them into action are on another. Nonetheless the Recce Squadron manages to assemble 28 out of its 31 vehicles, though getting everybody and everything together delays the departure of its HQ Troop along with C and D Troops for the bridge until 3.30pm. A Troop is held in reserve at the divisional HQ.

L/Cpl Dennis Clay does not have a good landing, his Horsa crashing so badly in a wood that he is the sole survivor. On clambering free of wreckage, he is confronted by a Dutch civilian gesturing wildly from the front door of a nearby house.

After making sure he has suffered no serious injuries himself, Clay grabs his rifle and goes over. The Dutchman informs him in perfect English, 'I have five Germans in my home who want to surrender.'

Still a bit dazed, L/Cpl Clay merely nods and follows the man inside.

> 'I was scared to death at what he was landing me with, but the Germans were co-operative because they were just that bit more scared than I was.'

Clay points his rifle at the enemy troops and tells them to put their hands up, marching them out of the house and in the general direction of what he hopes are British positions.

—

Having taken cover in his cellar in Oosterbeek for some hours, Frans de Soet ventures out to find that the Germans manning the anti-aircraft guns in his street are in a panic. 'They are leaving. The English have dropped paratroops near Wolfheze. We shout for joy. It is 2.00pm.'

Telephoning a friend in Heelsum, de Soet is told British paratroopers have landed there too, and it was 'a magnificent sight.'

> 'My friend in Heelsum tells me that he is surrounded by soldiers, who are anxious to learn where the Germans are, how many of them and where they are going. I tell him that in Oosterbeek they are retreating...'

Learning where some German guns are positioned nearby, de Soet again rings his friend in Heelsum, passing on the information, 'which the English mark on their staff maps.'

Hearing that Airborne troops are marching in the direction of Oosterbeek, de Soet tells some Germans standing by a big truck in the road outside his house about the landings. One of them replies defiantly: '...they will be surrounded and finished.' Nonetheless there are no Germans hanging around outside the Vredehof villa by 3.30pm.

—

With the first wave of the Airborne divisions being delivered, it is time for the ground element of the offensive to be launched. The XXX Corps attack begins at 2.00pm, with 600 Allied artillery guns pummelling German positions either side of the road to Eindhoven.

Even as the 1st Airborne troops are forming up on their DZs beyond Oosterbeek – to make their long march to the bridges over the Rhine – the Guards Armoured Division begins rolling forward from its start line on the Albert Canal, three miles south of the frontier with Holland.

A column of tanks and military vehicles 50 miles long is lined up behind the Irish Guards who follow creeping artillery fire moving at eight miles an hour.[47]

The enemy soon give notice they are not going to be a push over. German troops concealed in woods open fire with hand-held *panzerfaust* anti-tank weapons and brew up nine Sherman tanks, one after the other. These burning wrecks easily block the main highway, which is only wide enough for two vehicles to pass each other.

If one, and then another, is knocked out, it becomes impassable, especially if ammunition is cooking off. It is the first of many such halts that will curse the push up the single main highway. RAF Typhoon fighter-bombers armed with armour-piercing rockets are called down from where they circle overhead, blasting the enemy out of the way. Forty minutes later, the advance gets rolling again.

As that problem is being tackled south of Eindhoven, the Airborne advance on the Arnhem bridges almost immediately runs into small groups of surprised Germans. Cpl Tucker is among those caught up in one fight as the 1st Bn finally gets moving. For the paratroopers of the 1st Bn it has already been a case of waiting around, for a couple of hours – watching sister units move off towards Arnhem – while their own orders are finalised. Now the 1st Bn experiences mortaring by Wolfheze railway station and is subjected to heavy machine gun fire.

Advancing towards the Ede-Arnhem road,[48] enemy armour is encountered, with the battalion forced to take a diversion south into woods 'There was an outbreak of shooting on the road just the other side of the woods we were creeping through,' recalled Cpl Tucker.

> 'We hit the ground, then after a few seconds got up and moved forward again. On the road was a German staff car and its occupants were firing at us, so we fired back and killed them. We then set off down the road in the direction of Arnhem.'

While some attempts to interfere might merely be temporarily inconvenient, Sepp Krafft's trainee SS *panzergrenadiers* are not so easily eliminated. Krafft soon has his troops out on fighting patrols that prove a much more effective hindrance to the British, including the lead elements of the Recce Squadron, which at 4.00pm run into an ambush by the railway track near Wolfheze. The jeeps are shot up and the men pinned down, courtesy of Krafft's *panzergrenadiers* and armoured cars.

Attempts are made to try and get around them, but these also hit trouble. In the middle of all this Gough is called back to see Maj Gen Urquhart who wants to know if it is true many of the jeeps have not even arrived. He supposedly wants to formulate an alternate plan. While Gough is away, the Recce Squadron becomes even more entangled with the enemy and some of its men are even forced to surrender.

Back at his LZ, after Col Warrack and the medics speed off in their jeep, Capt Fletcher gathers himself together. He ensures his personal armoury – Sten gun, revolver, commando dagger and some grenades – is all properly stowed away in the multitude of pockets in his battledress and the camouflage smock he wears over the top of it, or hung around his webbing straps. Fletcher pats his glider on the fuselage, murmuring 'thanks and farewell' then strides off in search of Lt Col Iain Murray, CO of the No1 Wing Glider Pilot Regt. Fletcher is to be his aide and trouble-shooter. They head for Arnhem behind lead elements of the 1st Para Bde, which are again hitting trouble. 'It became a case of stop-start, stop-start,' said Capt Fletcher, 'and because of the problem with the radios all we got were rumours coming back down the line.'

> 'Sometimes the delays lasted half an hour and some of us took that as an opportunity to pop into a Dutch house for a shave, or a chat. The Dutch were very friendly, offering us chocolate and drinks to toast their liberation.'

By 4.00pm British troops are marching through Oosterbeek, with de Soet going out to see and thinking they look incongruous on the town's streets.

> 'They creep stealthily up the road, their Bren guns ready... Some of them carry a radio set on their backs, the antennae sticking a yard above their heads... Many of them already have orange ribbons[49] on their khaki uniforms... It is like a dream. These soldiers dropped from the skies, coming from another, free country. Many of them wear dark

red berets instead of helmets. More people are now gathering. They have pears, tomatoes and pails with fresh water. The soldiers are tiring and sweating. Some of them rest a little... Now they come also on bikes and small cars. Even German trucks, just captured, loaded with British soldiers. Presently we see field guns pulled by German prisoners. Oosterbeek rejoices.'

De Soet sees the British are especially interested in the local girls, trying to chat them up before they are hurried along by their officers and NCOs. De Soet takes some snaps of the Airborne soldiers, one of them joking: 'That's nice of you, send me a copy.'

The Dutch, who have repressed their true feelings for years under German occupation, cheer and clap. The national flag is raised on the Oosterbeek church tower and displayed on homes, while Dutch Nazi wall posters are torn down. If caught doing that by the occupiers and their fanatical collaborators it could be punishable by death – but the arrival of the British troops makes people giddy and daring.

'People shake hands,' reports de Soet, 'everybody laughs and tries to express their joy one way or other. Just imagine, suddenly to be liberated on this Sunday afternoon. Free, after long gloomy years of ever-increasing oppression.'

—

The further away from the divisional HQ troops get, the more spread out they are along the lines of advance – and fragmented by various actions with the enemy – and the more the radio problems assert themselves.

With so many operations cancelled and a desperate eagerness at all levels for the superb 1st Airborne Div to be used, there was a tendency to overlook likely reality in some of the fine detail that might, on the ground, make the difference between success or failure. One such is radio communications, but back home nobody wanted to rock the boat.

Maj Tony Deane-Drummond, aged 27, of the Royal Corps of Signals is a veteran parachutist. He jumped into action behind enemy lines for the first time in 1941, part of a team dropped on southern Italy to blow up an aqueduct. Captured, he escaped twice and returned to join the 1st Airborne Div. For Market Garden, he is assigned to the divisional HQ as the deputy to the officer in charge of radio communications.

Not long after landing, a nagging foreboding about how things will unfold once again pushes itself to the fore. On being briefed on the plan back in England, Deane-Drummond feared everything 'will be fine for communications on the Dropping Zone, which was about two, two or three miles across ... but as soon as we go off into Arnhem itself it is unlikely that we will be in communication with the brigades. Well, this unfortunately turned out to be what, in fact, happened.'[50]

Here they are on the day of the match, and Maj Deane-Drummond has watched as 1st Para Bde HQ 'on the way to Arnhem was rapidly [rendered] out of contact ... as we'd all predicted.'

It happened as the spearhead brigade got to 'about half way through this very large forest ... between the Dropping Zone ... and the very large town of Arnhem.'

At the very tip of the spear, Lt Col Frost with his 2nd Para Bn is becoming acquainted with the same problem at the other end of the command and control chain.

> 'One became aware of how badly the wirelesses were working... Quite a lot of them had been packed away for some time because we'd been expecting to go [on so many operations] and they'd been netted [networked] in England.'

It is apparent that 'netting' for the terrain in England will not suit the terrain of Holland with its water-logged polders, woods, and urban areas like Arnhem, which are so unlike Salisbury Plain where much British Army training is carried out.

The Airborne troops have various types of radio sets, and this is the very devil to sort out on the ground in action. The 18 Set is used within a battalion for inter-Company communication and has an effective range of a mile-and-a-half, while the walkie-talkies for communicating between platoons and a Company HQ possess a half mile range.

For longer-range communication – Division to Brigade – there is the 22 Set, with a range of six miles, and the 19 Set, with a range of 12 miles. Both need a jeep equipped with battery chargers to carry them. Then there is the 68 Set, which is used for battalions to talk to each other, but with a range of three miles and so-called 'dry' batteries that are small and easily replaced – provided you have an adequate supply.[51]

Frost reflects wryly that his battalion's radios almost need visual contact to work. It is obvious that it will be impossible for the divisional headquarters to exert effective command and control of the various units advancing on Arnhem as they move beyond effective radio range of each other – unless some quick fix is found. The radio frequencies being used are also subjected to jamming by the enemy and possibly being used incorrectly by the British operators.

Attempting to get a grip on what is happening, Maj Gen Urquhart sets off in a jeep to try and establish contact with the advancing units, coming upon rear elements of the 2nd Bn. With a fierce battle raging up ahead, he decides Lt Col Frost, is too busy for a chat and so leaves a message to be passed on. 'I tried to impart a sense of urgency to them which I hoped would be conveyed to Frost... Even so, I knew that Frost of all people would press on rapidly if it were humanly possible...'[52]

Frost's progress is at times seriously impeded by ecstatic civilians, including people cycling alongside his soldiers saying how lovely it is to see them. One of these cyclists waves a bottle of gin, which he offers to the paratroopers, while drunkenly weaving down the road. This infuriates a British officer who threatens to shoot any of his men who take a swig.

Elsewhere, Lt Col Frost encounters other well-meaning encumbrances.

> 'The route given to me to get to the bridges was obviously along the north bank of the river and as close as possible to it And along that route were little villages and settlements and the Dutch all came to their gates to give us what they could – mostly milk, apples etc.'

Frost feels this is 'very nice but it became a little bit of an embarrassment in a way. I think one felt the whole thing seemed a little incongruous.' He is even offered use of motorcars by some of the locals, which he politely declines.

Hearing from Brig Lathbury during a roadside conference that the Recce Squadron is not going to be able to mount the planned *coup de main* by road with its armed jeeps, Frost feels it is more urgent than ever to maintain a fast pace. His troops will deal as briefly as possible with any enemy interference. After one firefight, the paratroopers dash forward, past two dead Germans in the blue-grey uniform of the Luftwaffe lying alongside each other in the gutter. Looking down, 19-year-old Pte James Sims sees one of them is a girl, who has been feeding a belt of bullets through a light machine gun operated by a boy. Both of them are about his own age.

He reflects: 'The girl's blonde hair was stained with blood; they had died quickly and violently.' He wonders if they were brother and sister, or even lovers and feels it is one of those things in war that makes 'a mockery of fiction.' Earlier, amid crowds of jubilant Dutch, Sims had raised his gaze to find a 'dark-haired and beautiful girl' looking down from the upstairs window of a house. She mouthed 'goodbye' to him as he made off down the street, the fleeting encounter sending a shiver through him.[53]

Lt Col Frost has no time for such musings on dead Germans or exchanging glances with pretty girls. He hurries his men on, eager not to deploy his battalion in full fighting stance, which could see them dispersed off the main route to deal with the Germans in detail. One tactic employed to make sure the enemy is rapidly cleared out the way is bringing a pair of 6pdr anti-tank guns forward.

They are usually at the back of a column, being towed by jeeps, but are now covering the road ahead, in case enemy armour turns up.

Frost finds this is 'very effective against prowling enemy armoured cars.' These are either destroyed or chased away with a few well-aimed shots from the 6pdrs.

During his mad dash around, Maj Gen Urquhart also comes across Maj Tony Hibbert, the chief of staff to the commander of the 1st Para Bde, who is making his way down the same route as Frost's battalion. 'A jeep came up from behind, and, in it, I was amazed to see General Urquhart,' recalls Hibbert of this salty encounter.

> 'This was definitely Indian territory, with Germans all over the place. And just, to have your commander with no protection [turn up] seemed a bit odd. And he stood up in the back of his jeep and said: "Hibbert! For Christ's sake get your bloody brigade moving faster or the German tanks will be on the bridge before you!" And I said: "Yes, Sir!" Then he disappeared…'[54]

It is indeed highly unconventional to have a divisional commander racing about in a jeep. With himself behind the wheel, he is accompanied by a signaller and no substantial protection, except for, at various stages, two junior officers and the Regimental Sergeant Major (RSM) of the 3rd Para Bn. The Maj

Gen is disconnected from his HQ at a crucial time, but what else can Urquhart do in such circumstances?

He could pick up the phone, like the enemy does.

Throughout the battle, the local telephone system functions, with occasional interruptions. In addition to being used by local residents to swap information on how well the British are doing, it is utilised by the Germans to organise their reactions. The British rarely use it, despite their chronic radio problems.

Bittrich's staff officers actually have to rely on the telephone system, because much of the II SS Panzer Corps' radio equipment was destroyed in the Normandy battles. Sometimes, in a gesture of defiance, the Dutch civilian operators put the Germans through to the wrong numbers.

Frustrated by this, the II SS Panzer Corps HQ sends out messengers on bicycles and motorcycles to convey orders to various units that are forming up. The 'Hohenstaufen' is ordered into Arnhem to destroy the British while the 'Frundsberg' is told to head for Nijmegen to block any enemy advance from the south.

While the 'Frundsberg' gets itself organised, shortly before 7.00pm, the 9th SS Reconnaissance Bn – a mixed force that includes armoured cars plus half-track armoured personnel carriers and lorries carrying *panzergrenadiers* – races across the Arnhem road bridge to scout out the situation at Nijmegen. An hour later, Lt Col Frost's paratroopers are creeping through streets approaching the road bridge.

Under the original plan, C Coy of the 2nd Bn was to seize the railway bridge – about four miles west along the river from Arnhem town itself – and then move along the south bank of the Rhine to take the other end of the road bridge. The majority of the 2nd Bn was to remain on the north side, reinforced by the rest of the brigade to create a perimeter and keep the Germans out, while the Poles were to be dropped on the south side of the Rhine to reinforce the force holding that end of the road bridge.

That plan hits the buffers now, for as the paratroopers move across the rail bridge, charges are detonated. 'The centre span of the bridge exploded,' according to Lt Peter Barry, '...the metal plates right in front of me heaved up into the air.'[55] No casualties are suffered due to the explosion, though some are harmed when the enemy opens fire and the paratroopers withdraw.

Having made it to the northern end of the road bridge, Lt Col Frost ensures his soldiers waste no time. 'We quickly as possible occupied those buildings which dominated the north end and the approaches to the north end.' These include a large government building and a factory on the approaches to the north end.

By the next morning, there will be around 740 British troops in various positions around the bridge, including later arrivals, some of whom have to fight their way through the town. Approximately half of them are paratroopers from the 2nd Bn, alongside C Coy of the 3rd Para Bn, but also glider pilots, a substantial number of Royal Engrs, an anti-tank battery with four 6pdr guns and assorted others from a variety of units. The latter include the 1st Para Bde HQ, under Maj Hibbert, including its defence platoon, and Maj Freddie Gough the commander of the Recce Squadron, with a handful of his soldiers.

After finding Maj Gen Urquhart had departed his headquarters to try and find out what was happening with the 1st Para Bde, Maj Gough chased around in his jeep, accompanied by another as escort, for the rest of the day. Failing to make contact with the boss, Gough gave up his quest and headed for the road bridge. In doing so he got further away from the Recce Squadron, which would fight the rest of the battle at Oosterbeek without him.

Among the other odds and sods at the bridge are two officers of the so-called Jedburgh Team Claude, a hybrid special forces unit whose purpose is to make a link between the Dutch underground and the 1st Airborne Div.

There are justified fears about local civilians who are Nazi sympathisers, but plenty of Dutch loathe the occupiers and want to fight back, so it is worth parachuting in the Jedburgh operators. Team Claude consists of an American officer, Lt Harvey Todd, from the Office of Strategic Services (OSS), and a wireless operator, Technical Sgt Carl Scott, another American, along with Capt

Jacobus Groenewoud, a Dutch soldier in the Special Operations Executive (SOE). Scott has been separated from the other two and, after searching for missing radio equipment for a few days, ends up fighting with the Airborne troops in Oosterbeek.

Todd and Groenwoud will be in the thick of it at the bridge. The Dutch officer uses the telephone system to talk to trusted contacts in order to identify those in the neighbourhood of whom they should be wary.[56]

Capt Eric Mackay, in command of the 1st Parachute Squadron Royal Engineers (Para Sqn RE), has installed his 75 men in school buildings overlooking the northern ramp, alongside soldiers from C Coy of the 3rd Para Bn. Mackay's men settle in for the night, trying to make room for themselves and their weaponry in classrooms 'furnished with desks, blackboards, etc,' as he describes it.[57] Not long after moving in the Germans attack, throwing grenades into an exposed side of a building Mackays engineers are in, so they decide to withdraw from it.

As Frost and his troops are completing their march to the road bridge, Dennis Clay makes it to the positions of the 2nd Bn South Staffordshire Regt. Sentries greet the approaching Clay with the codeword challenge: 'Red!' His use of the correct reply – 'Beret!' – ensures that he and his German prisoners are not gunned down. Such procedures are designed to ensure the enemy cannot fool the British and so change each day. For 18 September the challenge word will be 'Uncle!' with the correct reply 'Sam!'

As he gets closer, the Staffordshire Regt men warn Clay the surrounding woods are full of Germans. 'I know,' he replies, 'I have just found some of them.'

—

Having failed to get troops across the river to capture the southern end of the road bridge, Lt Col Frost still feels it is worth having a go from the north end. As the last daylight fades, a platoon from the 2nd Bn's A Coy makes the first bid. 'It is a horribly dangerous thing to do this, even in the half-light,' reflects Frost who watches what unfolds through binoculars. 'You only require one machine gun on the far end of the thing like that to cause very heavy casualties.'

The paratroopers are not far across when machine guns positioned at the far end, or half way across the bridge – Frost isn't sure – open fire, with 'bullets spattering off the road and onto the girders'.

The valiant paratroopers must retreat.

Frost realises any major attempt to get across with the resources he currently has risks 'unacceptable casualties.'

There is sporadic firing throughout the night. Trying to think of how else to get one of his companies across, Frost orders some of his men to go down to the river and see if any part of the pontoon bridge, which has been broken up, can be used. The pontoons are too heavy to be moved without tugs and Frost reluctantly concedes 'we had few enough people as it was to hold the north end, never mind bothering with the south.' He decides to 'make as tight a perimeter as we could to hold that north end' – to thwart moves across the bridge by the enemy. Nonetheless, there is one more attempt that night to charge across the road bridge, but the enemy lights up the night with flares and there is very heavy machine gun fire.

There is another spate of violence when three lorries full of ammunition and *panzergrenadiers* try to speed across but are hit multiple times and also set on fire by British flamethrowers. Waffen SS soldiers become flaming torches and fall screaming from the bridge into the black waters of the Rhine. The heat and explosions from those vehicles makes it impossible get on the bridge for any further crossing attempts by either side. The pyrotechnics increase when British engineers create a hole in a house by the bridge, which enables a flamethrower team to target a pillbox, but they miss and instead set fire to an adjacent ammunition store, which explodes.

Blundering into the scene just north of the bridge is a truck loaded with 17 Luftwaffe personnel who have been firing V2 ballistic missiles at England and whose unit is being withdrawn from the Arnhem area. Attempting to leave the town, these stragglers are instead taken prisoner by British soldiers.

Among those bundled out of the truck and into a house is Lt Joseph Enthammer, who is amazed to be spoken to in German by a paratrooper sergeant, who, so it transpires, was born in Vienna.

The British NCO jokes that it is just as well they had not fallen into the hands of the Polish paratroopers who are also taking part in the operation, for they have vowed not to take any prisoners.[58] Lt Enthammer decides, all joking aside, that it will be best not to reveal what he and his men have been doing, for fear of reprisal.

Down by the bridge, Lt Col Frost gazes out at the burning wreckage and thinks it may well be possible to hold on until the vanguard of the Second Army arrives. After the war, much will be made of the fact that the Airborne troops were expected to hold the bridge for 48 hours before XXX Corps arrived, but in fact, at the time, it was thought possible it might even be half that. 'We were told [in England] that the British Army would be up with us within 24 hours,' according to Frost.[59] The 2nd Para Bn's success in getting through where other units have so far failed will indeed soon be rewarded with the sound of military vehicles racing across the bridge from the south.

Monday

18 September

'At dawn we stood to our arms and we didn't have long to wait.'

—Lt Col John Frost, Commanding 2nd Bn, the Para Regt[60]

For a teenage boy, the arrival of liberators from the skies is exciting, and Jan Loos is eager to see the fighting men who have dropped in to kick the Germans out of Holland.

> 'I wake up early, get dressed quickly, then go out and up the street, in the direction of Utrechtseweg and there I see for the first time English soldiers, who are going in the direction of Arnhem. One of the boys from the neighbourhood tells me that on open ground not far away there are dead Germans. I want to see that. It will be the first time in my life that I have seen fallen soldiers. What strikes me when I do are the strange postures in which they lie there. I see two German soldiers who were killed while one was, apparently, trying to help the other to safety. That isn't a pleasant sight. More and more English soldiers pass by – the mood is joyous, with flags waving and cigarettes and chocolate being given out by the troops. Amid all this celebration, we also hear that three men from the neighbourhood were arrested by a German patrol the previous night and executed.'

At the Arnhem bridge, the Germans by now have a machine gun on the southern end, shooting straight down the road. It can hit anyone trying to get across the northern bridge ramp – from British positions on one side to those on the other – so good use is being made of a road tunnel running underneath.

While the Airborne troops are keen to respect the property of townsfolk, they have ostensibly come to liberate – it must not prevent them from fortifying their positions. This inevitably means making houses less of a death trap for defenders by ruthlessly using whatever furniture is available to block doors and windows. The Airborne engineers are asked to help enact this process. 'Civilians protested at us breaking their windows,' reports Capt Mackay. 'They were terrified; just gaga. We cleared them out. Then all [the local residents] went north back into the town. We [by now] held a ring about quarter of a mile round the bridge.'[61]

Other civilians depart their homes with less fuss, the men, women, and children packing up a few belongings and 'gradually they took themselves off ... they more or less seemed to seep away,' according to Lt Col Frost. The British are braced for determined counter-attacks, Frost remaining optimistic about 'bringing fire to bear on the bridge if the enemy tried to come across it.'

The early morning sees an unfortunate driver of a refuse truck killed when he brings his rattling, rumbling vehicle into streets by the ramp. Just following his normal rounds, he is greeted in the dim early morning light by dozens of gun flashes, as keyed-up Airborne troops fire at what they fear is the enemy. Three lorry loads of Germans also pull up, totally unaware the British have taken possession of surrounding buildings, climbing down to stretch their legs and wondering what comes next. The answer, for all but two of them, is death. They are mown down by bullets and their vehicles destroyed by grenades.

The Germans do make several probes with their infantry and light Mk III tanks early in the morning but are seen off, and the lull lasts until just before 9.00am. The next player to try his luck is a Waffen SS hero who, until now, has enjoyed a charmed life, escaping death and serious injury.

During reckless acts of bravery under fire in Normandy, Hauptsturmführer Viktor Gräbner came through unscathed while many of his comrades in arms were maimed or killed. Only the day before, as the British landed on the outskirts of town, Gräbner received the Knight's Cross from Obersturmbannführer Harzer by way of tribute to his exceptional valour in Normandy. Having that same evening been ordered to take the 9th SS Recce Bn to scout out the situation on the road to – and around – Nijmegen, Gräbner has handed over duties to a unit of the 10th SS. He is returning with his unit to obtain new orders from the divisional HQ, It is the Recce Bn's deep misfortune to encounter the eager killers of the British Airborne who have devised a zone of death.

Forewarning of what is to come is given as motorcycles and armoured cars approach the southern ramp. The 75mm light howitzers of No 3 Battery of the Light Regt – firing from a field by the Oude Kerk at Oosterbeek – have been preregistered on key fixed points and now lay down a barrage, hitting some motorcycles forging ahead, killing or wounding their riders. While a few armoured cars manage to speed past the British positions around the northern ramp – due to their sheer cheek and fire being withheld in the mistaken belief they may be from XXX Corps – the vehicles and troops that follow are not so lucky.

The British let rip with everything they've got: rifle and machine gun fire; PIATs; gammon bombs[62] but, doing most damage, are 6pdr anti-tank guns sited to fire on the ramp. The crew of one of these uses rounds to blast a large v-shaped notch in the parapet of the bridge and then fires as 9th SS Recce vehicles pass by, shells screaming through it and ripping into their vulnerable sides. Mines laid on the bridge detonate under German vehicles and there is horrific chaos... burning lorries crash into each other, spilling out dead and wounded troops. Capt Mackay relates his unit's part in this close quarters fight: 'You could shoot down into these half-tracks at a range of 10 to 70 yards. It was easier for us, for we fired at the driver and the co-driver and the thing would crash into the house. Then the bloke in it would try to get out, but we killed them all.'[63]

As desperate SS drivers try to shunt their way through the mess, British mortar bombs also crash onto them, hitting the twisted wreckage, spraying hot shrapnel everywhere. Some damaged vehicles career down the ramp's embankment. Any Waffen SS troops who clamber out of them and try to escape are cut down by British fire.

With things quietening down momentarily, Capt Mackay hears the comparative silence broken by a clanking sound and looks out of a window. He discovers a half-track just below – he reckons less than six feet away.

> 'I looked straight into its commander's face. I don't know who was more surprised... His reaction was quicker than mine, for with a dirty big grin, he loosed off three shots from his Luger [pistol]. The only shot that hit me smashed my binoculars around my neck.'[64]

As Mackay staggers back, his soldiers leap forward and spray the half-track with bullets, hurling in grenades for good measure, killing everybody aboard. A similar reception is given to more Germans 'trying to run the gauntlet', as Mackay puts it.

Up to a dozen 9th SS Recce vehicles are destroyed over the course of the 90-minute battle, with 70 *panzergrenadiers* killed, including Gräbner.

Capt Mackay gazes at the carnage strewn all around the school building, counting half a dozen destroyed half-tracks, along with 'a lot of burnt-out transport on the bridge ... Bridge absolutely blocked by 11 o'clock...'[65] Frost judges it a good morning's work: 'We were able to do really quite good execution of this squadron...'[66]

At one point during the action, in which every man capable of firing a weapon took part – including signallers, drivers and clerks in the 1st Para Bde HQ formation – Frost could hear men actually enjoying themselves, infected with the euphoria of battle. 'Amid the din of continuous fire and crash of falling burning buildings, laughter was often heard.'

It puzzled him that what sounded like German machine guns could also be heard 'firing from immediately below our windows.'

Lt Col Frost decided to take a look.

'By craning out, one could just see Freddie Gough in action behind the twin K-guns [Vickers machine guns] mounted on his jeep, grinning like a wicked uncle.'[67]

German survivors retreat to the southern side of the bridge but subsequent attacks from Waffen SS units in Arnhem town itself are increasingly vigorous. They are learning from their errors and soon apply classic urban combat tactics to flush the British out – bombardment by tanks and self-propelled guns, along with mobile AA guns to dismantle buildings and rip apart people, followed by flamethrower and infantry assaults.

The storm of bullets in the air is often so thick the glittering hands of the massive clock mounted on the tower of the Church of St Eusebius are pushed around.[68]

As the battle intensifies, it is not easy for Frost to exert the kind of face-to-face direction he desires as the different elements of his force are isolated from each other. Moving between the various buildings to see them is a very risky affair, 'for to cross a street in daylight was to draw fire from the Germans.'[69] The burning buildings mean full darkness is banished and, amid the flickering half-light, Frost feels anyone moving around in the open, even at night, risks being shot by friend or foe. The Germans have now also made sure that 'to move under the bridge to see people on the eastern side was suicidal.'[70] To avoid taking such risks, a radio is a useful command and control tool – if it works.

After several engagements overnight, on the morning of 18 September, the 1st Para Bn is seeking a way to thread itself through enemy blocking forces. It gives up on getting through via one of the higher roads and tries its luck further south, nearer to the river.

The commander of 6 Platoon, in the battalion's S Coy, is 24-year-old Lt Richard Bingley, who was wounded during fighting in Sicily and only recently returned to the unit. For him, the new day starts off in an unfortunate fashion.

> 'At dawn, S Company became leading company and my platoon was at the rear as company reserve. At 05.20 hours, we emerged from the trees and total darkness and came to a crossroads, where we turned at Oosterbeek. There were large fields on either side of the road – the field to our left sloped towards higher ground, with a house at the top. The field on our right was level. Suddenly, without warning, the company came under heavy fire from heavy machine guns, rocket propelled mortars and a tank. My company commander ordered me to take my platoon left flanking, to deal with the enemy. This I did and some 20 minutes later the Germans withdrew, having lost two machine gun crews. My platoon sustained four dead and three wounded and Company casualties were some 40 in all. A tragic start, as we were still many miles from our objective – Arnhem Bridge.'[71]

It was only the beginning of the 1st Bn's struggle to break through, as Lt Bingley notes: 'Throughout the day, we twisted and turned, to find a way through German tank positions.'

Sent ahead by his CO to find out what is happening at the 1st Para Bde HQ Maj Deane-Drummond has been told to 'sort out some solution' for the communications problems. Deane-Drummond thinks this will 'probably mean an intermediate radio which could then retransmit the calls from the brigade back to the division.'

He sets off in a jeep with his batman/driver, L/Cpl Arthur Turner, and heads into Arnhem. Deane-Drummond makes contact with the CO of the 1st Parachute Bn, Lt Col David Dobie, who is confident his men will soon reach the road bridge. Deane-Drummond learns the 1st Para Bde HQ has gone forward with Frost's battalion to the bridge.

At around this time Cpl Tucker's platoon, in one of the 1st Bn's companies, is probing for a route down towards the Rhine.

> 'At first there were trees lining the road which made good cover, but then we came to an opening. As we crossed it, a German popped up from this hole where a paving slab had been removed and sprayed us with bullets.'

Five paratroopers in the leading section are hit, including Tucker.

> 'I was lucky and just got a graze across my side. The platoon Lieutenant got a bullet across his knuckles, and I think a couple were killed. While our platoon Sergeant charged forward and sorted the German out, I made an attempt to help a poor beggar who was making a hell of a fuss after being hit in the leg. He was babbling away with shock and his leg was a terrible mess. I stuck my hand on his wound to stop the blood while I got hold of a field dressing. I jabbed him with morphine[72] to help with the pain, did what I could to make him comfortable and told him we'd have to leave him behind.'

Cpl Tucker is later sent down nearer to the Rhine to help a nervous young sniper armed with a .303 rifle try and take out the crew of a 20mm AA gun firing on the advancing British troops.

The Germans have put it down to its lowest elevation and are blasting away whenever they see movement.

If there is one type of weapon truly hated by infantry it is AA guns – known in German military lingo as *Fliegerabwehrkanone*, or Flak – which can be used to devastating effect against human beings.

With their high rate of fire and explosive shells, they can mow troops down by the dozen, chopping heads and limbs off those unfortunate enough to be caught by their fire-spitting sweep. Even paratroopers under cover in houses on Arnhem's lovely residential streets are ripped to shreds as shells spewed by AA guns shatter masonry and tear through walls.

While many of the Flak weapons may be mounted on a half-track or on a tank chassis, such vehicles offer little protection for their own crews (who are generally forced to expose themselves in order to operate them).

They can be easily eliminated by British tanks, but unfortunately 1st Airborne has none. The division's anti-tanks guns are thin on the ground, while the few AA cannons that made it to the LZs safely with the Recce Squadron are not available. In fact, these weapons will be put out of action by mortar fire while parked up near the divisional HQ after helping to repel enemy attacks.

It leaves more precise, but potentially less effective, counter-measures to be used against the hated Flak, such as Cpl Tucker and the nervous kid with the sniper rifle.

> 'I was there to cover the lad's back, but he couldn't hit the people firing the gun, so I suggested he let me have a crack, as I had qualified as a marksman before the war. I took a shot at the German in the firing seat of the AA gun and he dropped down. Another jumped into his place, so I shot him too. The third one decided to train the gun on us, so we scarpered back to the platoon.'

The 1st Para Bn is now just over a mile from the bridge, with the 3rd Para Bn also pressing hard along other routes. However, casualties are rising inexorably, and, by Monday afternoon, the 3rd Bn's strength of fully able fighting men (in the town) has dropped to around 140, while the 1st Bn is reduced to 100. Maj Deane-Drummond is seeking to establish contact with the 3rd Bn too, and, in doing so, follows troops edging down towards the river. He and L/Cpl Turner are caught up in heavy fighting by the Rhine Pavilion, a hotel. Pushing forward to around 1,400 yards short of the bridge, the company Deane-Drummond is with suffers major casualties.

The unit has lost all its officers and has, in effect, fallen apart, divided up into small groups of men fighting for their lives. Deane-Drummond and L/Cpl Turner stick together, and the Major rallies some of the 3rd Bn soldiers and heads for a small river harbour, where other troops are also taking cover. Deane-Drummond realises it is only a temporary reprieve:

> 'Clearly by this time, the Germans were in strength, with machine gun positions and so on, preventing any further movement. And so one was in a rather tricky situation, perhaps a slight understatement.'[73]

It won't be long until the enemy makes the harbour a killing zone, too, so Deane-Drummond orders the survivors to make a dash for some nearby houses. As they do this, men around him are 'literally dropping like flies'[74] amid a storm of grenades and bullets, until about 20 of them are left, splitting up into three groups as they escape into the houses. Deane-Drummond and L/Cpl Turner, along with two 3rd Bn paratroopers, choose one and 'rushed in through the door, opened the windows, used that as a place from which we could start firing…'[75]

In Oosterbeek, Frans de Soet has been asked to help translate captured German documents in a British headquarters established by a small barn not far from his home. While he is there, a swarm of aircraft flies over and the Dutchman assumes they must be Spitfires, but, when he looks up, de Soet sees 'the hated swastika on the planes…'

> 'In years I have not seen so many German fighters together. There are at least 30 or 40 of them. Why are they there just now? The English have no flak. The Germans circle around but they don't shoot.'

The enemy aircraft fly away. They were sent in anticipation of destroying an incoming airlift,[76] but, due to bad weather in England, it has been delayed, so they miss their chance. The hold-up gives the Germans time to prepare their response on the ground around the LZs and DZs, while, elsewhere, strafing German aircraft have caused casualties.

–

Lt Jeff Noble is the 20-year-old commander of the Medium Machine Gun Platoon of the 156th Para Bn and is very keen to get into action. At one stage, there were high hopes that his unit might be involved in the Normandy drop, and he had relished the training.

During an exercise in English countryside similar to the bocage of Normandy – with sunken lanes topped by thick hedgerows – Noble came up with the ingenious idea of putting one of his Vickers machine guns on top of a haystack (as he was playing the part of the defending 'enemy' at the time). This aroused the ire of Brig Hackett who remonstrated with the eager young officer that it was a daft thing to do, pointing out that the hot cartridge cases of the machine gun rounds ejected into the hay could set it on fire.

Noble responded that in such a situation he would have taken the precaution of ripping doors out of a nearby farmhouse to put the guns on. He would also wet down the hay to prevent it catching light. Infuriated by the cheeky answer, Hackett told Noble to shut up and remove the machine gun from the haystack.

Putting the disappointment of not being allowed to fight in Normandy behind him, Lt Noble is nonetheless delighted to finally head for combat under the leadership of Brig Hackett, who is worshipped by his men. Hackett is 'very much revered,' he says. 'We respected his intelligence. We respected his ability, and he treated his subordinates very well.'[77]

During briefings for the Arnhem mission, at a platoon level in the 156th Para Bn, there is huge confidence it will all go well.

> 'We had this strong impression the war was virtually over and had been given the impression that the enemy resistance would be not very strong. We had tremendous faith in the air support that the Royal Air Force could give us. We were [though] a little worried about it being a long approach march…'

Taking off from Saltby in Leicestershire, the whole airlift around three hours later than planned, Lt Noble's platoon of 39 men is split across two Dakotas of the USAAF. Crucially, there are containers under Noble's aircraft to be released over the DZ. These contain spare ammunition and machine guns, but, not long after take-off, the parachute on one container deploys.

Efforts by the American air crew to ditch it fail, and the parachute catches on part of the Dakota, while the container ends up being towed along behind.

This is an absolute menace and means Noble and his stick cannot jump without serious risk of their own parachutes getting tangled up in it. Applying the same sort of ingenuity that he proposed for machine guns on haystacks, Lt Noble supervises his men in radical measures.

One of Noble's soldiers is dangled out of the Dakotas door, with several men keeping tight hold of his feet. He attempts to use a bayonet fixed on the end of its rifle to cut away the parachute and container. This fails, so they put a bayonet on the end of a broom – somewhat easier for a man buffeted by the slipstream of an aircraft to wield. That doesn't work either.

The Dakota drops out of formation, the pilot saying that, with regret, he will have to turn back and do an emergency landing at the nearest available airfield. Noble and his men brace themselves as the Dakota touches down at an American bomber base in South Yorkshire, with the container 'crunching and banging' along behind.

Once out of the aircraft, the paratroopers cut the 'chute and container away, with Noble watching his 'merry men', as he calls them, divide it into small strips, which they use as scarfs. Less amusing is the attitude of the Dakota pilot, who refuses to take off again and head for Holland.

In Noble's view the aircraft is not badly damaged, but the pilot shakes his head and says: 'No way can I fly with it in that condition'.

Lt Noble thinks this is not a good enough answer, especially as the last of the massive air fleet is currently passing overhead.

> 'We watched the tail end of the armada sailing away towards Holland and we didn't want to be left out of it and we said "we've got to go because we couldn't miss this".'

A jeep carrying some air force engineers who work on the air base's Flying Fortresses swings in by the Dakota. These robust characters are used to getting battered bombers in the air for repeated missions over Germany. They are more than happy to help the British get on their way, hammering and banging until the Dakota is back in shape.

Then the transport pilot suggests that, as the navigator for the drop is in 'the lead ship' of the formation – by now long gone – he doesn't know the way to the DZ. Noble knows he flew paratroopers to Arnhem the previous day, so isn't buying it, thinking 'surely it's not that difficult… we can catch up… After a lot of persuasion [of the pilot] we finally got back aboard and took off.'

Fortunately, the Dakota is only about half an hour behind and can fly faster out of formation, as it does not need to keep station on anyone, though it does become the centre of attention for enemy AA gunners.

'Being the only aircraft in the sky, to some extent, we got all the flak that was available and also the fighter support which had been supporting the main armada had tended to go home.'

With the other transport aircraft now visible ahead, spotting the DZ isn't a problem as parts of it are burning.

> There was a lot of smoke on it and we jumped … unfortunately half the stick then dropped late into the woods which were occupied by the Germans. I was hit by a bullet after I landed. I stood up and promptly got hit on the right thigh. Fortunately, it didn't penetrate. It hit my map case and went through my trousers and all I got was a mild scratch. There was one officer who was hit through both legs, one of our rifle platoon commanders, and found himself surrounded by burning gorse and shot himself because he didn't want to, obviously, be burnt to death.'

The other stick of Lt Noble's platoon, which had managed to stay with the formation, suffered a cruel fate.

> 'My platoon Sgt's aircraft was hit in the air by flak and crashed in flames just south of Arnhem. All the men were killed except one. And one [other] was thrown out and broke his back and died that night in a local farmhouse… I can imagine [the men] were … as

the aircraft went down ... thrown to the front of the
aircraft. The pilot apparently did make a reasonable
landing but hit a dyke which flipped the aircraft over
onto its back and they were all wiped out.'

Among those British troops now flying into the battle aboard a glider is Pte Stan Turner who records his perspective in a private diary.

'Our take-off is 11.30am and everyone is sat silent for
a while, all having thoughts of their own. At 2.30pm
we cast off from our tug plane and make a steep dive
to land. There is a mass of gliders on the ground,
some on fire, some overturned.'

As the Dakotas of the 4th Para Bde arrived over the DZs, Brig Hackett jumped first from his aircraft, which had been hit more than once by small arms and AA fire. Landing safely, despite all the lead and shrapnel flying around, he realises it could actually have been far worse were it not for the tenacity of British troops clearing the enemy off the DZs and LZs.

'In the event when we did get in there our dropping
zone was being cleared by a bayonet charge by the
King's Own Scottish Borderers... We were in the
battle from the word go.'

Hackett jumped grasping his favourite walking stick, but lost it during the descent and while looking for it in the gorse, comes across ten Germans who want to surrender. Suppressing the fear that they might change their minds and instead overwhelm him, Hackett stays outwardly cool. In perfect German, he tells them to hang on for a few moments. Having located the walking stick, he marches the Germans away and hands them over to someone else to take care. Hackett then concentrates on gathering together his brigade HQ team, which he achieves with 'some difficulty'.[78]

Lt Pat Glover, aged 35, of the 10th Para Bn leaps into all this mayhem with an unusual companion in a canvas bag affixed to his left shoulder. This is Myrtle, a so-called 'parachick'. Back home in England she has completed the required six practice drops to earn her Para wings, which are displayed on an elastic band[79] around the chicken's feathery neck.

During training Myrtle was initially released to flap to earth from 50ft above the ground. Latterly managing it from 300ft, she always makes a safe touchdown to wait for Glover, pecking and clucking happily until he scoops her up. Those were not combat drops, however, and Glover decides it will be best this time to keep her in the bag all the way down.

In the rattling, juddering Dakotas as they fly over the North Sea on the afternoon of 18 September, the paratroopers of the 4th Para Bde – sitting on seats along the sides of their respective aircraft – occupy themselves in various ways.

Some have a snooze while others stare out a window – at the air armada, or down at the undulating waves – or scrutinise the Spartan interior of the aircraft. Some read newspapers with headlines about Hitler's armies being on the run and on the brink of collapse. In his Dakota, Glover soothes Myrtle, whose head and neck poke out the bag.

Now the aircraft are approaching the DZ – a heath to the south of a road between Ede and Arnhem – and all is not calm below.

As he stands in the open door – red warning light showing – the roar of the engines and rush of air drown Glovers thoughts. He waits for the green light to come on, signalling him to lead the stick of paratroopers out.

He is horrified at the vista daubed across Ginkel Heath. It is on fire, with shells and mortar bombs exploding amid a carpet of smoke. Glowing tracer bullets and anti-aircraft gun shells criss-cross the sky, in which are dotted explosions. Flak hits his Dakota a few times, sounding to Glover like sledgehammer blows on a dustbin.

From the door of his Dakota, 24-year-old Maj John Waddy, CO of B Coy of the 156th Para Bn, is fascinated at being able to see the pale faces of the enemy anti-aircraft gunners as they go about their deadly work of trying to shoot his aircraft down.

Even worse is seeing a Dakota in the same formation hit by AA and turned into a fireball, passing under Waddy's aircraft 'ablaze from nose to tail… I watched it crash in a great ball of white flame, as two carthorses [in the same field] galloped off in fright.'[80] He sees instant vengeance delivered from on high as two Typhoons swoop in to blast an enemy AA gun with rockets. Anxious to be out of the aircraft and on the ground, Waddy thinks: 'Never was the green light more eagerly awaited.'

When it finally appears, there is a great shout in unison from all the paratroopers behind him in the stick: 'Go!'[81]

Waddy leaps out, the air crackling and snapping with bullets as his 'chute opens. Dutch and German SS troops are taking careful aim with their rifles, shooting at the doorways of the aircraft, hoping that by felling the first man in a stick they will stop the others jumping.[82]

From Oosterbeek, Jan Loos watches over the rooftops and trees as the grim spectacle unfolds, with 'large numbers of paratroopers and gliders landing again in the direction of Ede, but now there is a lot of firing by German guns and we see planes being hit, crashing and burning.'

—

In his Dakota as the light turns green, Lt Glover pushes Myrtle the parachick's head back into the bag, fastening it, and jumping.

As he descends under the silk, numerous bullets zip past and below are many broken, shattered gliders, several on fire; he watches horrified as some unlucky paratroopers drop right into the flames. Glover steers his parachute to land safely, making sure to roll onto his right shoulder to avoid crushing Myrtle.

A few damaged aircraft come in way too low, with one stick of 11th Bn paratroopers jumping from a Dakota whose cockpit is an inferno.

It is less than 200ft – though the minimum needed for the 'chutes to open is 96ft – while the normal height to jump is somewhere between 400ft and 700ft.

In a matter of seconds after exiting the aircraft, these paratroopers hit the ground, but only two men go missing. A few Dakotas overshoot, sprinkling paratroopers widely across the countryside, with some landing amid woods bordering the DZs. Pte David Dagwell, a paratrooper of the 156th Bn, finds himself hanging above the ground 'like a trussed chicken',[83] legs entangled in the rigging lines with the parachute itself caught on the tops of fir trees. Below him German troops search for British soldiers to kill.

Spotting three of the enemy on the path directly beneath, Pte Dagwell stops struggling and freezes, breathing a huge sigh of relief when the SS troops move off towards the DZs. Dagwell finally manages to get his knife out, cutting himself free and plummeting to earth, the impact cushioned by a springy carpet of pine needles and the soft, sandy soil.

Despite all the fighting during the drops and landings, Dutch people are still keen to go out and greet the Airborne troops, with Lt Noble of the 156th Para Bn finding 'quite a lot of civilians had come out to the DZs, waving Dutch flags … giving out drinks of water and wine.'

Such is the bizarre nature of war that day, with one set of locals (the Dutch SS) trying to kill British paratroopers before they can even jump from their Dakotas, while another (oppressed civilians) turn up to toast their arrival as liberators.

That same afternoon, the commander of the II SS Panzer Corps, Obergruppenführer Bittrich holds a heated discussion with Generalfeldmarschall Walter Model, commander-in-chief of the German armies in the West, about the bridge at Nijmegen.

Bittrich believes it should be blown as soon as possible, to stop the Allied ground assault dead in its tracks – clearly the enemy are going to attempt a link with their embattled troops at Arnhem.

The Germans are giving the British Airborne a nasty shock, but Bittrich is keenly aware of the massive Allied strength overall compared to his own threadbare and battle-worn resources. He fears reinforcement by air could decisively tip the balance in favour of the enemy.

'If the Allies succeed in their drive from the south and if they drop one more airborne division in the Arnhem area we're finished,' the SS general tells Model.[84] To make things crystal clear, Bittrich adds: 'The route to the Ruhr and Germany will be open.'[85]

Yet Model refuses to budge on blowing the Nijmegen bridge. His orders stand.

Furthermore, he tells Bittrich, the Arnhem road bridge must be 'captured within twenty-four hours.'[86]

When the first wave of British troops landed the previous day, Model, famously suspected the whole objective of the enemy was his capture. He abandoned his plush HQ, at the Hotel Tafelberg in Oosterbeek, close to the equally well-appointed Hotel Hartenstein, which was being used by his staff officers. In an ironic twist, from late afternoon on 18 September the Hartenstein will become HQ of the 1st Airborne Div. No 1 Wing, of the Glider Pilot Regt sets up its own nerve-centre in the Hartenstein and tries to locate its scattered men to weld them into a fighting battalion. Capt Fletcher hears two particularly unwelcome pieces of news.

> 'The Divisional boys bagged the best-protected rooms, so we had to make do with a side room but we were alarmed to hear General Urquhart was missing and either dead or captured. I also remember

feeling absolute terror when I heard we were facing the Waffen SS and not the old men and bits and bobs that had been forecast by the planners.'

—

In fact, Maj Gen Urquhart safely spent the night of 17 September with Brig Lathbury and the 3rd Para Bn. In the morning he goes forward with the brigade column, worried about the constant stops and starts along the way as enemy resistance is encountered. Happy Dutch people – greeting Lathbury's men with flowers and kisses and even offering pots of coffee – are another hindrance that niggles Urquhart.

Later, in the maze of streets that is Arnhem town, heavy fighting sees Urquhart and Lathbury taking cover in a house not far from the St Elizabeth Hospital. Even the brigadier is at one of the windows using a rifle to exchange fire with the enemy.

Moving on, Urquhart encounters an officer who has been sent forward from the HQ at Oosterbeek to find out if he is wounded, dead or captured. Apparently, things are not going well, with the LZs and DZs being contested, but Urquhart feels he cannot yet go back. He is keen to find out how far the paratroopers have got with their bid to reach the road bridge.

As Urquhart, Lathbury, and two other officers – Capt Jimmy Cleminson and Capt William Taylor – make their way towards the hospital, going over fences and through back gardens, they are spotted by German troops who pursue them, opening fire and hitting the brigadier in the back. Dragging him between them, the Airborne fugitives find refuge in Alexander Straat 136.

It is while Lathbury's wound is being tended to – the brigadier laid out on the floor of a front room in the terraced house – that a German passes by, making the mistake of pausing to peer in.

Without even a second's hesitation, Urquhart pulls out his 9mm automatic pistol and sends several rounds the enemy soldier's way. As Urquhart explains, he could not miss at 'point-blank range at a range of a few feet; the window shattered and the German dropped outside.'

The official history of the battle, published in late 1945, will observe of this moment (with typical British understatement): 'It is seldom in modern war that the Commander of a Division has an opportunity to fight the enemy at such close quarters.'[87]

In fact, Cleminson and Taylor also open fire. With their ears no doubt ringing from having weapons discharged in such a confined space, Urquhart allegedly remarks: 'You know, I am the only serving general who has shot a German soldier with a pistol in a battle.' Cleminson responds: 'You weren't the only one who did – we all shot him. He was riddled with bullets!'[88]

Dashing in on hearing the firing, the owners of the house persuade Urquhart and his comrades to leave, saying they can take care of Lathbury and ensure he gets to the St Elizabeth Hospital.

Going across back gardens again, Urquhart and his two bodyguards duck through the kitchen door of Zwarteweg 14, where the middle-aged homeowner warns them German troops are approaching in the street outside. He points towards some stairs, which take them up to a front bedroom.

The British soldiers spot an entrance to a tiny, open-ended attic – more of a large shelf really – and quickly squeeze themselves up a ladder onto it. Expecting the Germans to come rushing up the stairs at any moment, they lie there with pistols drawn and hand grenades primed, ready to give any intruders a hot reception.

The voices of German troops shouting as they search the streets below are drowned out by the noise of a self-propelled gun coming down the road and parking right outside the house.

While he ponders what to do, Urquhart pulls out chocolate and boiled sweets he had earlier traded his cigarettes for and shares them around.

A cautious survey through the bedroom window reveals the Germans settling in for the night.

Feeling rising anger at the situation, and that he must get back to the divisional HQ without delay, Urquhart announces:

'There's no future in this. We're contributing nothing.' He suggests 'lobbing a grenade' at the self-propelled gun so they can 'make a dash for it.'[89]

His companions are not convinced it is a good idea and recommend waiting. Cleminson suggests that the likelihood of them all being killed in the act is very high and so Urquhart bows to the aggravating reality of their predicament.

Attempts by the Divisional HQ to find out where Urquhart is by using the radio net fail, as it is still not functioning. Even when the radios do work, the 1st Airborne is spread out across far greater distance than any of the planners envisaged.

'Not being able to establish proper radio contact with anyone was a terrible business and absolutely crippling,' observes Capt Fletcher.

> 'It played a major part in sealing our fate. Urquhart had been faced with no other choice but to go and find out for himself what was going on. Towards the end of the day I was sent out on my own scouting missions, amid the mortar shells and bullets, to make sure our own chaps were settling in at various places in Oosterbeek. I soon learned it was best not to be second across a road or garden. The first one stood the best chance of making it but by the time the second man made his dash they had his range and so down he went. Several times during the battle the man coming after me never made it.'

Among those positioned close to the Divisional HQ is Stan Turner. 'We are told to dig in near the Hartenstein Hotel where firing can be heard in every direction.' As yet, the storm seems some way off and he hopes there might yet be a chance that things will work out alright.

For XXX Corps, straining every sinew to reach the embattled 1st Airborne Div, air power is less in evidence on this day. There are fewer RAF Typhoons or USAAF Thunderbolt and Lightning fighters available to be called down and destroy enemy strongpoints. Consequently progress is slow.

The 101st Airborne has Eindhoven secure, but there is a major setback when the bridge at Son is blown up. Fortunately the 82nd Airborne manages to take bridges at Grave and also over the Maas-Waal Canal, though its units have yet to take the crucial road bridge over the Waal at Nijmegen, with SS troops rushed south from Arnhem to stop them doing so. The rail bridge to the west of that crossing is also still in German hands.

Working throughout the night, British engineers put a new bridge across at Son, hopefully allowing the advance to resume in the morning.

Monty's idea that the 1st Airborne need only hold the Arnhem bridge for two days before the ground troops arrive is already looking hopelessly optimistic. The blithe suggestion that the Germans will offer only old men and kids to fight back has proved catastrophically wrong.

For Dutch civilians, in the middle of a rapidly escalating battle on the north bank of the Rhine, there is thankfully one means of swiftly checking on a friend or relative's situation that still functions efficiently. Jan Loos watches his mother dash out of the house to use a telephone to find out how her husband is faring in Arnhem.

> 'Ma talks with Pa by using the only phone in the neighbourhood, located at the butcher's house across the road. Pa tells her that the top-floor of the office-building he is in near the northern ramp of the Arnhem road bridge is used by English soldiers to provide supporting fire for the troops that are engaged in fierce fights while trying to get across the

bridge. He also says that he does not know if, and how long, he can stay where he is, because there are several buildings on fire in the neighbourhood. He says he will try to get back to Oosterbeek, if possible, tomorrow.'

In the meantime, records Jan, with the shooting in Oosterbeek 'getting more and more intensive, we will stay inside that night and sleep on mattresses on the kitchen floor.'

Desperate times call for desperate measures and that evening, the 1st Bn's CO, Lt Col Dobie, and the commander of S Coy, propose a mission for Lt Bingley to undertake. They hope it will provide an important boost to the troops at the bridge. If the battalion cant get through on foot, perhaps a motorised dash will prove so unexpected it will succeed?

'Lieutenant Bingley, I want you to take your platoon, with as much ammunition as possible, in three Bren Gun Carriers,' explains Lt Col Dobie, 'and join the chaps at the bridge, as fast as you can.'[90]

The 1st Airborne Div's only tracked vehicle on Operation Market is the small, lightly armoured Bren Gun Carrier – more properly named the Universal Carrier. It is a maid of all works that does what its name says.

Transported to Holland aboard Hamilcar gliders, the carriers are dubbed 'baby tanks' by the Dutch who see them whizz by on their streets at up to 30mph. The Bren Gun Carrier's main armament is – self-evidently – the Bren, though in different guises it can also mount mortars, anti-tank rifles, and even 20mm AA guns, in addition to carrying supplies and a few people. The 1st Airborne also utilises the carriers to recover supply containers from DZs, casualty evacuation, and towing 6pdr and 17pdr anti-tank guns.

With a two-man crew – a soldier in a gunner's position to the left of the driver in the open-topped front compartment – each of the Parachute battalions have two or three of the carriers. Sixteen in all were successfully offloaded at the LZs. Devoting three carriers to an ammunition run through enemy territory thick with tanks and anti-tank guns is a very risky proposition, but any gambit is worth a try.

As the first of the vehicles trundles up, Lt Bingley observes it without enthusiasm, not entirely delighted at being awarded the mission: 'as we advanced to load ammunition, so the wretched thing blew up from an [enemy] 88 mm gun [hit], and the same thing happened to the second carrier.'

Stunned by these shattering blows – each carrier turned into smoking scrap metal, killing whoever was in it – Lt Col Dobie says: 'I am not risking my third and last carrier.' The bid to get through to the bridge will have to be made on foot after all, and it is decided to wait until the early hours of the morning.

It is therefore imperative that as many as possible of the 1st Airborne Bde's scattered troops – currently taking cover in various places in the neighbourhood – are gathered together. A senior S Coy officer orders Lt Bingley: 'Take a couple of chaps with you and search for some of our missing soldiers in the nearby houses.'

An hour of searching finds a dozen 1st Bn soldiers, and Lt Bingley sets off again with two bodyguard soldiers to gather a few more, this time finding 14. Bingley is asked to hunt down more stragglers before the battalion makes its bid to get through to the bridge.

> 'With that my two escorts asked permission to remain behind and clean their rifles and I agreed. As I approached the Rhine Hotel, I realised how stupid I had been in venturing forward on my own.'

Lt Bingley starts to climb a hedge about four houses down from the hotel but then pauses.

> 'I sensed danger, opened fire with my Sten the very instant that a German soldier leapt from the doorway ... and struck my Sten gun out of my hand, smashing both [gun and hand], by wielding his rifle butt. This was the hand through which an Italian bullet had passed – through the four metacarpals – the previous year, so I really was in trouble.'

The two men engage in a grapple to the death.

> 'Fortunately the burst from my Sten severely wounded him[91] but we still had a few unpleasant moments before I was able to kill him with my Very [flare] pistol...'

Having narrowly avoided being killed by making his opponent into a fiery mess, Lt Bingley heads back to his battalion positions. He feels drained by 'the effort I had used wrestling with him and my hand by then had taken an awful mauling because it had hit the ground umpteen times as we wrestled furiously.'

His hand is now in such a state he cannot even unbuckle his pistol holster. On his return fellow officers remark on how terrible he looks, so he explains what has just happened. Lt Vladimir Britneff, the battalion's Russian-born intelligence officer, remarks:

'I will give you the very thing you need – a brandy.'

Bingley says that will be great, but when he takes a swig discovers it is cherry brandy, which makes him feel even more nauseous.[92]

—

At the bridge, Lt Col Frost receives a radio message that the rest of the brigade has given up trying to get through and will renew its efforts in the morning. This, he feels, is a terrible error and they should have pressed on.

'During the night the enemy made quite certain we were sealed in and anybody that tried to get through in daylight would find it much more difficult than trying to continue to get through at night.'

This was especially so in light of the blood-chilling discoveries Frost is making about the calibre of their opponents, who are likely to severely punish such errors. 'We had been given absolutely no information at all about the presence of SS panzer troops of any kind.'

Yet enemy troops captured the previous day by the 2nd Bn of the Parachute Regt on its march to the Arnhem road bridge wear SS lightning flashes on their collars. Finding Waffen SS troops per se is not that much of a surprise. After all there are many thousands of them still fighting hard for Hitler – and it was known there were SS trainees in the Arnhem area – but some formations are to be dreaded more than others.

During the afternoon of 18 September Lt Col Frost is informed troops captured and now held in the cellars of British occupied houses around the bridge – where SS wounded are being treated alongside the Airborne's – are from the 9th SS Panzer Div. This surprises Frost, as this renowned unit of battle-hardened fighters was assumed wiped out in Normandy, along with the 10th SS. These are not trainees, 'and of course it was at this stage that we realised that these were the troops from an SS panzer division, from their badges.' He asks for an English-speaking Waffen SS officer to be brought to him for more questioning, so he can confirm the bad news for himself.

A Hauptsturmführer is duly produced and Frost enquires politely: 'What are you doing in these parts?'

The German replies that his unit has been 'resting, re-equipping and getting reinforcements'. With the terrible significance of this twist absorbed, Frost ruefully observes: 'Well, there it was.'

He realises the lightly armed 1st Airborne Div faces formidable opponents with 'its back to the Rhine'[93] and the chances of success are now very slim indeed.

-

The nature of modern war is for much of the killing to take place at a distance. Bomber crews do not see those they pummel on the ground, artillery batteries hurl shells at targets miles away, while U-boats rarely, if ever, glimpse the human beings aboard the craft they sink.

This struggle between the British Airborne and *panzergrenadiers* is by contrast a brutally intimate one, with a German report making clear the close quarters character of the fighting.

> '…between the railroad tracks and the Rhine, in the residential suburbs of Oosterbeek, the struggle for each building continued for hours. In the narrow streets, hand-grenades were thrown from one side of the street to the other.'

Of the fight for the northern end of the road bridge, the same SS report observes: '…the fight for the buildings from which the enemy dominated the bridge with his guns had continued since dawn. Hand to hand fighting raged on each floor of the houses.' In one building German troops 'mounted to the first floor and exchanged hand-grenades with the British on the floor above.'[94]

To emphasise the Germans' determination to winkle the British out, Luftwaffe fighters strafe the road leading to the bridge, though cause no casualties. Worried the British have placed artillery observers in the nearby church towers, the Germans send bomber aircraft to blitz it, destroying the roof. After dark, the Waffen SS mount a series of 'fierce attacks on individual houses,' according to Capt Mackay, who watches buildings consumed by flames as the enemy tries to burn British troops out of their positions. At least this time the fires are extinguished.

The Germans reserve flamethrowers and phosphorous shells and Panzerschrecks, a German-style bazooka, for the school buildings by the bridge, firing in shells and rocket after rocket, which, so Mackay reports, 'went on all night and killed a few blokes.' British troops have to be on their guard, as an enemy infantry assault could come at any moment. 'We had no sleep,' reveals Capt Mackay. 'We had benzodrine [sic], with which some people get double vision. Some of the men got to sleep in shifts, but the officers had none.'[95]

Sleep is also a stranger for Maj Deane-Drummond and his three companions hiding in the house not far from the bridge. Down to around ten rounds each for their weapons, after dark – keenly aware they are surrounded by enemy troops – they withdraw from their positions at the windows of the house into its middle. There is a large lavatory, which they decide will become their refuge.

'We found ourselves in this loo,' reports Deane-Drummond, 'with a stairway going down to a cellar'. It contains 'a number of piles of apples, which again was useful as we were able to eat a few... We were there in fact for three nights ... the Germans also came into the same house and put a machine gun post on the roof, threw away the tiles ... and another one on the pavement just outside. So, we were in a rather difficult position.'

As was the entire 1st Airborne Div, trapped in a fight to the death with elite enemy troops not supposed to be there, directed ruthlessly by generals who are, unlike Urquhart, not missing from their headquarters.

In his absence at the top, there is strife between senior commanders.

Brig Hicks has taken over as divisional commander, at Urquhart's verbal request before he embarked on his wild goose chase, but Hackett is senior to him (though lacks the same level of Airborne/infantry experience). Faced with the problem of guarding the DZs and LZs while trying to reinforce the effort to capture the Rhine road bridge, Hicks decides – once the 4th Para Bde arrives – he will order the 11th Para Bn into Arnhem, along with two companies of the 2nd South Staffs.

Now, Hackett is furious at his brigade being broken up. He has deep misgivings about the plan, which he feels lacks achievable objectives, though he is to be given temporary use of the KOSB to bolster his efforts once the final landing of Polish gliders occurs the following day. After supervising the assembly of his remaining battalions, Hackett heads for the Hartenstein to have it out with Hicks – who has, anyway, asked to see him as soon as he is available.

Arriving at midnight, Hackett makes it clear, during a heated exchange, he is rather aggravated by losing the 11th Bn. On hearing that there is no overall commander of the battalions trying to reach the bridge – that they are all acting independently of each other – he is even more perturbed. He feels these 'do not appear to represent the best arrangements.'[96]

Hicks explains he is doing the best that he can and realises it is 'clearly unsatisfactory'[97] but that helping Frost in any way possible overrides normal command structures. Hackett later reflects that he was 'prepared to do what Hicks said if it were the general plan, provided it made sense, but it did not completely. My Bde was being ordered about as a collection of individual coys. I was given no Bde task and no boundaries on both of which I insisted.'[98]

Hicks proposes that Hackett's brigade should push up into north-eastern Arnhem in the morning, to give the troops at the bridge an outer perimeter, as in the original plan.

Hackett finds this rather vague and suggests the more realistic objective should be to take high ground to the north and west, around Johannahoeve Farm, beyond the railway line. Only after that should he try and assist Frost's troops at the bridge. Hicks accuses him of trying to place himself in command of the division, but Hackett protests this is not his intent.

When things calm down, they agree a plan that will see the 4th Para Bde – the remaining 156th and 10th Para Bns plus support units – driving forward through the woods beyond the railway line, swinging south and east towards Koepel, then down into Arnhem, following the route alongside the Amsterdamseweg.

However, the delayed second lift – with the late entry of the 4th Para Bde – has given the Germans time to strengthen their blocking forces on the proposed line of attack.

On paper, it appears that, across the battlefield British and Germans are, at that moment, fairly evenly matched – nine Airborne battalions versus 14 Kampfgruppes (battalion groups) the latter of variable quality and rapidly thrown together, drawing on numerous sources. The British, at most, have light artillery and anti-tank guns while the enemy is being bolstered by panzers and self-propelled guns, plus heavier artillery.

The territory through which Hackett's brigade will attempt to advance, will bring it into contact with SS Kampfgruppe Spindler, commanded by 43-year-old Obersturmbannführer Ludwig Spindler, a Waffen SS artillery officer and veteran of combat on the Eastern Front and Normandy. He has self-propelled guns, four SS *panzergrenadier* companies, and some flak guns plus various other troops, including air force and naval personnel alongside additional Wehrmacht and Waffen SS units.

If the British are to stand a chance of breaking through the gathering strength of this formation especially, and also other enemy units, they must not linger long. 'We were in quite high spirits [though] a bit worried about the slow progress,' admits Lt Noble of the 156th Para Bn, who has managed to scramble together around 20 men and two Vickers machine guns. News from the fight in Arnhem is not encouraging. There were already rumours flowing through that some things weren't going so well with the brigade that had dropped the day before,' states Lt Noble.

Despite this, the 4th Para Bde 'halted that night, which gave the Germans time to consolidate, which they did very rapidly and very brilliantly in my humble opinion…'

Tuesday

19 September

'...the enemy tried with great determination to break through our lines ... fighting that raged from house to house – from garden to garden, yes, even from flat to flat, man against man...'

—Hauptsturmführer Hans Moeller, Commander, 9th SS 'Hohenstaufen', Division Engineer Bn[99]

In the early hours of Tuesday, September 19, the remnants of the 1st and 3rd Bns, the Parachute Regt, along with the 2nd Bn, The South Staffordshire Regt and 11th Para Bn, fix bayonets for another attempt to push through.

An unsettling silence blankets the streets and open spaces as the British surge forward. The Germans soon cotton on to what is happening. They are well positioned to counter the enemy's lines of attack and with a murderous fire. The air is filled with shrapnel and lead; the streets are carpeted with the corpses and bloodied bundles of wounded Airborne soldiers.

The 1st Bn, now reduced to only 40 men capable of fighting, is pressing on along a road that runs parallel to the Rhine. It is no easy task, as the Germans have put machine gun nests at the base of trees – digging holes into which are dropped 40-gallon kerosene drums, with machine gun teams placed inside them, and all disguised by camouflage netting. There are even snipers lurking in the treetops. 'After advancing some 600 yards, my excellent Platoon Sergeant, who was next to me, was suddenly killed by a sniper,' Lt Bingley notes bitterly. As he takes one of the sergeant's ID tags – so the NCO's death can be recorded later – and also the man's ammunition, Bingley is shot in the ankle but limps on.

> 'So the Colonel decided we should advance from this river road up to the middle road. Accordingly "T" Company swept all before them and cleared German SS from a large, white, three-storey house: whereupon "S" company then joined "T".'

There follows a superhuman effort to prevent those soldiers left from being slaughtered in the streets – they will try and reach the bridge by smashing through buildings. Lt Bingley is to the fore despite his latest injury.

> 'It was impossible to move along the roads, so, in order to advance to the next house, it was necessary to mousehole, that is knock holes through the wall to the adjacent house.[100] This happened some 20 times, until we came to the end house, where German tanks and tank [self-propelled] guns, were swarming around, firing at our houses point blank.'

The enemy are even ramming their tanks into the houses while seeking to finish the job with flamethrowers.

> 'Eventually they overwhelmed us, when we were in sight of our objective, but still 1,000 yards away. Three days to travel eight miles, with almost total casualties. It was a bitter pill to swallow.'

Knocked unconscious, Lt Bingley comes around to find 'that I had been a prisoner for five hours and was lying in a builders' yard.'[101]

Urquhart is released from his confinement very early on the morning of 19 September by the renewed British push for the bridge, which sees the self-propelled gun parked outside make an exit.

Dashing out of his refuge, he finds troops from the South Staffs, who are amazed to see their commanding general in the thick of it. Maj Gen Urquhart immediately commandeers a jeep, climbing behind the wheel, with Capt Taylor in the passenger seat. He speeds off in the direction of Oosterbeek, to find the Hartenstein Hotel, which is apparently where the divisional HQ has been installed. During the course of the dash, the jeep is fired at several times by the enemy, with Urquhart at one point advising Taylor to 'duck and hold tight.'

> 'I put my foot down hard ... bullets pinged around us... We were untouched however and the jeep held the corner...'[102]

Reaching the Hartenstein at 7.25am, Urquhart is a remarkable sight, in filthy clothes and unshaven, while demanding to be told exactly what is going on. The appearance of the Maj Gen after 39 hours missing – seemingly risen from the dead – does boost morale considerably.

The same cannot be said for Urquhart, his heart sinking into his boots when he realises how desperate the situation is. He decides that a senior officer must be sent into the town to try and co-ordinate the attacks.

He chooses Col Hilaro Barlow – temporarily commanding the air landing brigade while Hicks is in charge of the division – and sends him forward in a jeep. To reconnoitre the situation more closely, Col Barlow gets out of the vehicle and with his batman/driver, L/Cpl Raymond Singer and accompanied by Capt John McCooke, of the 2nd South Staffs, edges into Arnhem's tightknit streets.

As they run from one house to another, with Capt McCooke leading, German mortar bombs fall. One of them lands in the middle of the street, with shrapnel hitting McCooke in the leg. Collapsing into the doorway of a house, McCooke manages to get inside and then looks out into the street from an upstairs window. He sees 'a mess on the pavement – which I presumed was Colonel Barlow – and a dead body behind that which must have been his batman.'[103]

—

During the attempt to reach the bridge, Harry Tucker's band of half a dozen paratroopers initially avoids the worst of it, creeping along a side road, which enables them to bypass several German positions unchallenged. It looks for a moment like they might get through to the Arnhem road bridge.

Cpl Tucker realises their luck has run out when, up ahead, he sees several paratroopers taking cover in doorways and front yards or flattening themselves against walls. Looking further down the road, he notices smoke emitting from a side street.

> 'It was really black and oily. We were naturally very cautious and came to a halt, to see what the next few seconds revealed. We could hear the engine revving up and then it emerged…'

It is a former French tank – captured by the Germans in 1940 and converted into a self-propelled flamethrower – spewing fire and smoke as it comes on, the growl of engines and squeal of tracks putting the fear of God into the paratroopers.

> 'It was a terrifying moment and some blokes ahead were caught by this thing and roasted alive – so we thought better of using that route and slipped down another road.'

Tucker and his men can finally see the massive on-ramp and the bridge itself. Ugly and brutal in its concrete and steel modernity, it looms beyond the rooftops. The percussive chatter of guns and explosions signifies that battle is raging there too.

> 'The bridge could not have been much more than 500 yards away. There was a lot of fighting going on ahead, including Germans firing down from the girders of the bridge.'

It is so tantalising – the ultimate objective seemingly almost in touching distance. Getting to the bridge will enable Tucker and his men to feel their comrades have not died in vain, but it is not to be.

> 'Suddenly some of our soldiers up ahead broke and started to run back towards us, chased by German tanks... For a few seconds we just crouched there and watched our men running by with little thought to fleeing ourselves. An officer stumbled by me clutching a shattered arm and so we decided to get out of there.'

Hopes of getting through to Frost's beleaguered force are fading fast – the Germans have built walls of steel on routes to the road bridge. With every hour, they are growing stronger while the British get weaker and weaker, despite fresh troops being thrown into the contest on Arnhem's streets.

They are frittered away, with Frost's force at the bridge aural spectators to the intensive fighting to the west, while also straining to hear something reassuring coming from the south. 'The worrying thing was although we could hear quite a lot of fighting going on from where we expected the division to come from,' recalls Lt Col Frost, 'we could hear absolutely no fighting at all from the area of Nijmegen where we were expecting the

Guards Armoured Division to debouch from. Whereas our own town was a great flames and smoke going up into the heavens…'

It might be that the continuous noise of their own battle means the British simply cannot hear the Nijmegen fighting – or that is what they hope.

–

The prime 4th Para Bde objective on 19 September is for the 156th Para Bn to seize and consolidate a position at Koepel, as a precursor to taking high ground at Lichtenbeek. It is then to press on down to the south-east, parallel to the Amsterdamseweg and through Arnhem town towards the road bridge to support Frost's embattled force.

On the way, they pass through 7th KOSB, already at Johannahoeve Farm and protecting LZ 'L', awaiting gliders carrying the third lift, which are coming in that afternoon. The 7th KOSB will send two of its companies to follow 156th Para Bn and take over and secure any objectives the paratroopers achieve in order for them to continue their advance.

In the early hours, the 156th Para Bn attacks as planned but fails to get beyond Johannahoeve, with Lt Noble and his medium machine guns among those in action, trying to see off the enemy.

Nobody can get through the wall of German troops, while to the north, attacking towards a pumping station on the other side of the Amsterdamseweg, the 10th Para Bn also runs into strong enemy forces. It is during one of these episodes that Lt Glover of the 10th Bn loses track of Myrtle the parachick. She has been kept in her bag for safety's sake in the custody, in turn, of Glover and his batman, Pte Joe Scutt who are now sharing a slit trench. During a pause after an intense phase of combat, and while having a brew of tea – Lt Glover asks Scutt what's happened to Myrtle, realising she was left in her bag by the trench when they were digging in. Finding the bag, Glover opens it to find Myrtle has been hit by more than one bullet and is dead. Taking her over to a nearby bush they give Myrtle a proper burial, still wearing her parachute wings on the elastic band around her neck. Scutt observes that Myrtle was 'game to the last'.[104]

One of the younger soldiers in the 10th Para Bn, assigned to its Anti-Tank Platoon, is 19-year-old Pte Frank Newhouse, who is charged with one of its most dangerous jobs – taking on panzers with a PIAT.

Landing without a hitch the previous day, he became immediately acquainted with what the enemy looked like, but shrugged it off with the callous nonchalance of youth. 'My first sight on the DZ was a dead German and I thought that's not a bad start...'[105]

In reality, he is a frightened young lad and that night, dug in with his platoon in some woods, he suspects people who are not likely to be friendly are creeping past his slit trench. The rustling of leaves, cracking of twigs, and other unsettling sounds of things moving about in the dark is terrifying, but somehow Newhouse keeps a lid on his fears.

The next day Newhouse gets his first call to action, to deal with some tanks that have turned up, which, it seems, is 'a bit of a problem...' When he gets there, he finds out it is not, after all, enemy armour but rather 'some trouble coming from a house.'

Pte Newhouse lobs a shot high over the house, which plunges through its roof and explodes deep inside. He then puts another shot through a window, and the enemy's interference with the advance ceases.

Then enemy armour does turn up – probably a panzer Mk IV – and Newhouse is called forward again. His mission will definitely be very dangerous, as effectiveness of a PIAT against a tank depends on getting as near as possible to the target.

> 'Our platoon Sgt insisted you got within 25 yards and underneath the trajectory, if you could, of its machine guns. So that you could hit between the turret and the tank, the weakest bit. No good firing at the front as it would just bounce off...'

His first attack is not spectacular but still does the trick: 'I never claim to have knocked a tank out, but I do claim to have been near enough to hit one which went back again…' Newhouse think his efforts won't be 'so effective against the Tiger tank we heard of but which I never saw.'

The call to action comes for a third time, and Newhouse is sent up with another soldier, carrying PIAT ammo, to sort the tanks out. Full of cockiness, Newhouse tells his fellow paratroopers not to worry: 'we'll go and get them!'

It doesn't turn out well, for, half an hour later, Newhouse is brought back down the line badly wounded, hit in the head by shrapnel thanks to an air burst of an enemy shell.

While he can walk, he is slipping in and out of consciousness a lot of the time, and the next several hours pass in a haze. He will recall being in a house with other wounded soldiers, which catches fire. They are evacuated, and he is put in a jeep and taken to the asylum at Wolfheze, where the nurses and doctors are looking after a few wounded Airborne soldiers.

At 2.00pm, with the so-called Battle for the Woods north of the railway line in full swing, Maj Gen Urquhart and Brig Hackett have a conference. They decide the 4th Para Bde should, after disengaging with the enemy – a very tricky manoeuvre to pull off without it becoming a rout – then advance into Arnhem along an axis further south. Hackett's brigade will insert itself between 1 Airlanding Bde (to its west) and 1st Para Bde (in town to the east), whose progress is, at that point, decidedly uncertain, its evisceration not yet known to Urquhart.

In fact, to the west of the Arnhem bridge the retreat to Oosterbeek of the 1st Para Bde's harrowed soldiers is in some instances frantic and chaotic, unit cohesion gone.

These are but the remains of five battalions swallowed by the unequal fight in Arnhem's streets, with more than 1,700 casualties suffered – 120 soldiers killed, with the rest wounded and/or captured, though some have gone to ground in enemy territory. Around 500 men committed to the vain struggle to reinforce Frost's force at the bridge reach Oosterbeek to re-join the rest of the division.[106] They straggle back in ones and twos, sometimes in groups, running in panic occasionally, discarding weapons and other accoutrements of war to hasten their flight.

It is a sight that distresses many Dutch civilians who not long before hailed them as liberators, but of course many of these soldiers are just boys and have never been in combat before. Offering the retreating troops cups of water and fruit, some civilians hear from the British that the Germans have decisively gained the upper hand. Freedom from Nazi occupation it seems was but a dream and the *Moffen*[107] are coming back with a vengeance.

The painful futility of it all doesn't mean the British troops will give up the fight – far from it. Those who retreat from Arnhem town are rallied, organised, and will, for the most part, acquit themselves well in the battle to come. Typical British bloody-mindedness exerts itself and, besides, the edge the enemy holds is not necessarily in the quality of his infantry.

Many of the Germans are hardly trained and some units arrayed against the 1st Airborne Div include a motley collection of sailors and Luftwaffe personnel who no longer have a role in their own services. There are also units that are a mix of teenagers barely out of school and middle-aged men. These are troops previously thought too young, on the one hand, and too old, on the other, to be conscripted. Then there is the Dutch SS who shot at the British on the LZs and DZs – turncoats loathed by the majority of people of the Netherlands who have not collaborated with the occupiers. Alongside them, however, are units that include many Waffen SS and Wehrmacht veterans who have seen action in Russia and in Normandy – the hardcore of Bittrich's fight back.

As time goes on, despite Bittrich's fears of being overwhelmed, reinforcements such as assault engineers with flamethrowers and more powerful tanks are ordered into the fight, coming from the Reich itself. The German superiority resides, above all, in tanks and self-propelled guns, in the artillery and anti-aircraft weaponry – the kind of firepower against which the Airborne troops can only resist for so long. The British, and soon also Polish, anti-tank teams will fight to the last of their shells, while the Light Battery's 75mm pack howitzers will be lowered and fired over open sights at panzers. Incredibly courageous tank-hunting squads armed with PIATs, gammon bombs, and mines will fight on until they too are spent, or wiped out.

It is about hanging on for as long as possible.

A good way of surviving to fight is to get under cover in a house or in a trench as deep under the ground as possible. Where possible, the latter are covered with doors ripped out of sheds or other solid overhead protection against scything shrapnel and plunging fire. With houses and their gardens in Oosterbeek being taken over, Jan Loos watches as 'paratroopers begin to dig into our back gardens, and around noon our house is requisitioned to set up a defensive position.'

> 'Fighting gets fiercer in the direction of Arnhem and the Oosterbeek-Hoog railway station. It is clear that the violence of war is getting closer. Together with our neighbours – an elderly, single lady named Rika, and a young married couple called Walter and Annie, in their late twenties living with Rika – we make preparations in the cellar of their house, so we can use it as a shelter when necessary.'

All the way from Normandy, the Allies have held one ace card that devastates the enemy's ground forces – almost total air superiority. German divisions have been torn to pieces by Allied aircraft and especially the rocket-firing Typhoon fighter-bombers of the RAF and Thunderbolt equivalents of the USAAF. No German tank, no matter how tough, can survive a hit from an anti-tank rocket. Such flying artillery, descending like Thor's hammer on the enemy, could easily wipe out the advantage held by the panzers in the struggle for Arnhem. The Airborne troops pray for such salvation from above and, finally, it seems to have arrived. 'At 10am fighter planes appear overhead,' records Stan Turner, 'around 30 of them.'

> 'At first it is assumed they are ours, then one dives down to machine gun a position and we can see the black crosses. Suddenly Bren guns all around me open up but cannot hit the planes.'

The lack of close air support from their own side mystifies the soldiers of the 1st Airborne Div throughout their struggle in Arnhem and Oosterbeek. Allied air supremacy is supposed to be a fact of life and should, as in other recent battles, confer a decisive advantage over the enemy. It certainly did, and to decisive effect in the struggle for Normandy, where the enemy suffered terribly from strafing, bombing, and rocket salvoes. Yet, for those fighting for their lives in Oosterbeek and Arnhem, there is a dispiriting lack of aerial artillery assistance.[108]

—

With the number of wounded men growing inexorably amid the fighting at the bridge, Lt Todd and Capt Groenewoud of Jedburgh Team Claude volunteer to make a dash to visit a doctor whom the Dutch officer has been in touch with via the telephone. They intend to then establish contact with the St Elizabeth Hospital, to try and get an ambulance sent to pick up the most seriously wounded. As he runs across a road, Groenwoud is killed, a sniper bullet through his forehead. Todd carries on but, on telephoning the hospital from a house he takes shelter in, learns the Germans are threatening to shoot anyone who tries to help the British. Realising his mission has failed, Todd heads back to join his comrades at the bridge.

In Oosterbeek, the British are warning Dutch civilians of German snipers at work, but Frans de Soet still ventures out with a friend from the Dutch Resistance. Rather than being shot down by a marksman, they are caught in an artillery barrage, hearing 'an awful whistle of a gun shell...'

It explodes not far away, but more shells are coming in, fired by German guns located somewhere over by Arnhem.

> 'We lay flat against a house... The hits are coming quite close to us.
>
> 'We cannot stay where we are. Pieces of debris hit my hat, and shell splinters hit the iron railings of the gardens. We run towards another house. We want to cross the main road, to take shelter in the cellar of the police station. The shrieking [of the shells] keeps on, quite a barrage. We arrive at the road opposite the police station, more crawling than running. We signal to them that we are going to cross the road there. From the police station they wave back at us, indicating to us that we [should] stay where we are and lay flat. My friend stays there and I venture to cross the road and arrive safely in the cellar of a house occupied by a number of scared people. I am thirsty and eat an apple. After a few minutes the gunfire ceases. I realise the difficulties for Oosterbeek and the English have begun.'

By the afternoon refugees from Arnhem are arriving, bringing news that 'heavy fires are raging' there. Nevertheless, de Soet is told by a British soldier entrenched outside his home: 'Everything is going O.K.'

The British soldier gives de Soet and one of his neighbourhood friends all the cigarettes he has, as if a smoke will help calm their nerves. They are reluctant to accept them, but he insists, saying: 'It doesn't matter – more supplies will be dropped and with them fresh cigarettes.'

During the next supply drop, de Soet watches Allied aircraft 'having a hard time in this hell of German flak-fire'. Much of what they drop falls to the enemy, the planes 'lavishly dropping rows of coloured parachutes' with canisters and baskets swinging underneath – straight into the eager hands of the Germans.

Outside the Vredehof villa that afternoon there is another worrying sign the relative peace so far enjoyed by Oosterbeek – even while vicious fighting has raged elsewhere – may soon end. 'The English are expecting German tanks and are making tank-traps,' says de Soet. One takes the form of 'a chain consisting of tins with dynamite, [stretching] from our fences to the fence across the road.'

> 'They explain that when the tank drives over it, it is blown up. Our house is only fifteen yards away from it. The English assure us, though, that we will be safe in our cellar, however we should not sleep in the front rooms. The house of our neighbour, across the road, is in an even worse position. This family of seven, amongst them a paralysed man, is given room in our cellar.'

As more fleeing Arnhem residents stream through Oosterbeek, de Soet and his neighbours warn them away from the tank trap. He hears from people living in east Oosterbeek that they have been forced to leave, due to their homes catching fire, while other parts of the town are also now being affected.

> 'A married couple, friends of ours from Oosterbeek-high, want to pass the night with us. Their house is destroyed. They thought with us it would be quieter. Their little son has contracted scarlet-fever. The lady expects a second baby within a few weeks.'

De Soet takes them to a neighbouring house, as there are already 13 people sheltering in his own cellar. On the other side of

Oosterbeek, the time has arrived for the Loos family to leave their home.

> 'With the shooting getting worse and worse, we decide to move in with the neighbours, taking our bags and going down into their cellar at De la Reyweg 9. When we then try to fill a few buckets with water it turns out that the supply has been shut off, as well as electricity and cooking gas. Walter therefore suggests that he and I should go to a hand-operated water pump located near a butcher's shop at the Paul Krugerstraat, which is not too far away.'

Walter and Jan discover that 'everywhere the paratroopers are digging in, and they make it clear to us that we would be better off going home.' Walter and Jan nevertheless carry on, filling their buckets with the much-needed water and make it to safety.

Peter Fletcher is ordered out from the Divisional HQ, leading a patrol of local streets to assess the situation. As he prepares to set off, Capt Fletcher is surprised to see a woman in German uniform being escorted through to tennis courts at the back of the hotel where enemy prisoners are being kept.

> 'I asked who she was and was told that she was a clerk who had come back from leave and somehow managed to pitch up at the Hartenstein. She was totally unaware the German HQ had moved on or that there was a battle on.'

Grabbing his Sten gun and chuckling to himself, Capt Fletcher gathers together his squad of glider pilots and sets off down the road, entering Stationsweg. They proceed very cautiously because the German and British positions are interwoven.

> 'We were searching allotments and gardens and then going into homes and placing troops. I remember sneaking around one garden when suddenly we were ambushed by a little girl. She announced she had watched us peering through the bushes.'

This is 12-year-old Ans Kremer, whose mother, Anlu, comes out to talk to them.

> 'We felt proper Charlies because it showed that, had the house been occupied by Germans, they could easily have gunned us down. She told us not to worry because the Germans were on the other side of the road.'

Even as bullets cut through the air overhead – the enemy shooting at other British troops – Capt Fletcher and his group are asked to pose for pictures by Mrs Kremer.

> 'She then handed us a guest book and asked me to sign it. I wondered what on earth I could say, so wrote some stupid message like "glad to have been able to liberate your country." Sadly, their home was to be destroyed during the fighting.'

At the Arnhem road bridge, there are high hopes the rest of the 1st Para Bde and other units will fight their way through – and within a matter of a few hours. But, as the morning draws on and nobody makes it, Frost's force has to accept that it will get no reinforcements. Frost is impressed with the reaction of his troops, whose morale does not collapse. They just get 'annoyed that nobody else came.'

That afternoon Frost manages to speak with Maj Gen Urquhart on the radio. Urquhart isn't able to hold out much hope of any relief. Frost reveals that ammunition is getting low, but is otherwise deliberately light on detail.

'I couldn't say too much because, you know, the Germans would have been listening in. If we started whining ... they would have said "hooray".'[109] The primary concern is not actually ammunition, but food and water, especially as the latter is cut off by the enemy. The troops at the bridge had arrived in Holland with their own 48 hours ration packs, which they are eking out well, but the only supplementary food they can find in any quantity is apples stored in the Dutch houses. Feeding around 60 German prisoners is also a bit of a challenge. Water is the greater problem and some of the captives do not help by trying to sabotage water tank reserves. Lt Col Frost feels there is no point in retaliating, except to point out they will suffer too.

> 'Once or twice we caught them turning on the tap and leaving it running full blast. There was nothing you could do. You couldn't shoot them out of hand. All you could say is "we will do nothing to help you…".'

Some water is still available via taps, though getting to them is often a perilous process. Pte Sims is sent out to fill two mess tins with water from a tap fixed on the end of a 4ft-high pipe in the centre of a backyard, which is the scene of furious exchanges of fire between the Germans on one side and British on the other. The objective for Sims is getting enough water to make a meal for himself and his platoon commander, Lt Reginald Woods.

Somehow, he manages to dash across and then crawl to the tap without being killed. Crawling back to the British side, pushing the mess tins in front of him, Sims receives a great cheer from Airborne soldiers.

After slaving over a small cooker, creating a steaming concoction out of biscuit fragments and crumbled dehydrated meat cubes, Sims hands a mess tin to Lt Woods. He finds it revolting and discards the contents. Pulling out a bar of chocolate, Lt Woods shares it with Sims.

—

The appearance of more and more enemy armour is not reassuring.

While these are older, lighter tanks, their actions are very aggravating, though the easily portable PIAT proves an effective countermeasure. 'They waltzed round the whole area,' reports Capt Mackay, 'about 30 at a time. We disposed of about five or six of them by climbing over the roofs of houses to where the tanks were and letting them have it.'

Another boost to morale is provided by the incompetence of a Luftwaffe fighter pilot. A Messerschmitt Bf 109 comes in very low, endeavouring to kill British troops on a strafing run. Mackay notes with satisfaction that it 'crashed onto the church steeple while trying to avoid being fired on, and was wrecked.'

That morning Standartenführer Harmel had asked for a British Airborne NCO to be brought to him. The chosen man was Lance Sgt Stan Halliwell, only recently captured while trying to make an ammunition delivery. The 10th SS 'Frundsberg' division commander is, as he will later confess, 'beginning to feel damn foolish'[110] at his failure to so far wipe out the lightly armed British. Bittrich has already made his displeasure clear, so Harmel tells the 25-year-old Halliwell to go and ask the British commander to surrender. He should point out that it is impossible for any relief to reach him through the town and so pointless to carry on resisting while the alternative to capitulation is death. Harmel puts Halliwell, who is one of Mackay's combat engineers, on his honour to return with the response. Under a white flag of truce the SS troops take Halliwell to a point where he can cross safely to the British side. Message delivered, Frost responds furiously:

'Tell them to go to Hell!'[111]

Looking a little worried about conveying that message back to the SS commander, Halliwell enquires: 'Do I really have to go back to tell them that, Sir?' Frost shakes his head and says he can either return with the message or stay to fight. The enemy 'will get the message anyway.'[112] Lance Sergeant (L/Sgt) Halliwell returns to the fray.

Halliwell's news that the Germans are getting increasingly dismayed at their high rate of casualties and low level of success, actually encourages Frost to think it is worth fighting on, just in case XXX Corps does get through.

Over at the school, Capt Mackay gives a rude response to a German emissary in the form of a nervous SS soldier standing in the street with a grubby handkerchief attached to his rifle.

'Surrender!' the German calls.

Mackay wonders if the enemy want to surrender… but there is absolutely no room for them in the school, so he yells back: 'Get the hell out of here! Were taking no prisoners!'[113]

Airborne troops hurl more abuse at the forlorn looking enemy, one shouting: 'Bugger off! Go back and fight it out, you bastard!'[114]

—

At 3.00pm, before the agreed plan for the 4th Para Bde's attack can be enacted, strong enemy forces are detected coming up hard from Heelsum and probably aiming to go through Wolfheze and attack LZ 'L'. Even worse – to lose the railway crossing at Wolfheze could trap the 4th Para Bde on the wrong side, isolated from the rest of the division. It forces Hackett to order the 10th Para Bn to disengage and withdraw under fire, so it can head across the LZ to meet the enemy attack. It must ensure there is still a means to quickly and safely get vehicles across the railway line. Sending jeeps and anti-tank guns up and over the embankment will be suicidal under intense enemy fire and the only other crossing is already firmly in German hands.

Hackett's brigade must extricate itself from extreme peril. It is engaged in a vicious fight in the woods – fending off enemy self-propelled guns and infantry attacks, trying to protect the LZ while being subjected to forays from armoured cars and under heavy mortar fire.

The 156th Para Bn and 7th KOSB carry out a fighting withdrawal, with the former also heading for Wolfheze and the latter seeking a way to join the rest of the division to the south of the railway line.

'We received dramatic orders to withdraw within the next 15 minutes,' recalls Lt Noble of the 156th Para Bn, 'back down to the railway line ... to Wolfheze crossroads.'

> 'At the same time there was a German attack coming in and we had already been strafed by German aircraft, which rather took everybody by surprise... so, we went back and in some confusion.'

At 4.00pm the chaos increases. Gliders carrying elements of the Polish brigade, including its own vehicles and anti-tank guns, land on the contested LZ, just as the 10th are heading across it to meet the enemy. Observing this from his house, de Soet sees 'the sky is suddenly clouded with planes...'

> 'The weather is splendid. Over our heads cables of gliders are loosened. Stately they glide down. Scores of them. There is terrible flak coming almost horizontally from Arnhem, exploding with terrific force low above our heads. One plane is on fire but it flies on... One glider crashes on the river bank causing heavy smoke columns. [sic]'

The original plan was for the entire Polish brigade to be sent into battle in the third lift but fog covering central England meant the Dakotas of Sosabowski's parachute troops could not take off. Clearer skies in the south of England saw tugs and gliders carrying anti-tank guns, vehicles, and accompanying troops going ahead.

Sosabowski and his paratroopers are left fuming on their airfields, the delay deeply upsetting the Poles. They yearn to kill Nazis as revenge for their nation's brutal subjugation by Germany. They would actually far rather jump into action to save the uprising then raging in Warsaw than go to Holland. The Poles console themselves with at least being able to vent their fury on the Germans somewhere else. Urquhart did send a message to divert supply aircraft to DZs and the Polish landings to an LZ still firmly controlled by his troops, but it did not get through. The 1st Airborne Div's after-action report will record of the moment the gliders touch down: 'The enemy reaction was violent; pressure and volume of fire immediately increasing.'[115] As they clamber out of their gliders the Poles find themselves caught in the crossfire between the Germans and British. In the mayhem on the LZs British troops and Poles even fire at each other, causing numerous casualties. Glider Pilot Regt SSgt Pat Withnall is lucky enough to land away from the worst of the fighting, though his journey to battle was not without incident.

> 'On the flight over we were hit three times by flak but no-one was injured. I did a perfect landing and although there was a lot of small arms fire it wasn't coming up at me. Together with my co-pilot, Sgt Ken Travis-Davison, I watched the six Poles off-loading their two jeeps by the usual method – driving the vehicles out through the side of the glider. They went off without so much as a goodbye. There again, there was a communications problem – because we couldn't speak any Polish and they couldn't speak any English. They drove off into some woods and there was a terrific amount of firing. The two of us grabbed our rifles and scrambled off towards the woods where the Poles had gone. There was a great deal of firing ahead of us and lots of screaming. Something nasty was going on. We inched our way

> forward to see what was happening. There were one
> or two corpses lying around.'

Withnall and Travis-Davison are unsure which side the dead are from and there is no sign of the Poles or their jeeps. 'It wasn't until years later that I discovered they had all been killed at that moment, so it was just as well they didn't offer us a lift.'

As bullets are sprayed through tree branches above them, the glider pilots duck down into a ditch for cover. 'After about 15 minutes I poked my head up to take a cautious look but couldn't see any sign of Ken. I was alone and pretty frightened.'

SSgt Withnall sits down and ponders what to do next. After an hour or so, he decides to follow the railway, which he knows runs right through the middle of the DZs and LZs.

> 'Our general orders were to make our way back
> across the Rhine and head back to England so we
> could fly another wave of gliders in. I walked along
> at the bottom of the railway embankment to make
> sure I wasn't silhouetted for snipers. I was still very
> nervous and in a state of shock about being deserted
> and left to fend for myself.'

As Pat Withnall wanders forlornly, the British at the Arnhem road bridge are fending off ever more determined German attacks. The Battle in the Woods remains intense, with heavy casualties on both sides. The 7th KOSB carries out the withdrawal, with its C Coy disengaging in concert with the 156th Para Bn. The rest of the 7th KOSB finds it a gruelling process, subjected to several enemy attacks, which are only thrown back at great cost.

These are actions in which Maj Alex Cochran and Drum-Major Andrew Tait have 'particularly distinguished themselves each killing at least 20 Germans with Bren guns, mowing down Waffen SS troops who exposed themselves in the open on LZ 'L'. Provost Sergeant (Provo Sgt) Andrew Graham 'was outstanding throughout the whole operation [and] inflicted enormous casualties with a Vickers...'[116]

It is not until 6.00pm that 10th Para Bn, along with some of the 156th Para Bn reaches the Wolfheze railway crossing, which the enemy squat on, strongly resisting attempts to kick them off. The British assault is disorganised. According to Lt Noble: 'We got to the railway line, we were under attack ... it was really quite a rabble...'[117]

In the meantime, efforts are being made to get vehicles and, crucially, the anti-tank guns, through a tight little tunnel under the railway embankment, to the south-east of Wolfheze.

Some are even being sent over the railway embankment or finding other ways across, while a few do manage to slip through via the Wolfheze crossing. Getting over the embankment is not easy even for people. The wise roll over the top, while the unwise who show a higher profile are taken down by a sniper's bullet.

As darkness comes on, the main body of the 156th Bn is down to 270 men, Lt Noble recording, 'by end of the second day the battalion was very weak...'[118] The 10th Bri has only 250 men.

The 7th KOSB has also suffered heavy casualties, and, by the time it has consolidated itself around two large houses to the south of the railway line, it is down to 300 men. Its CO, Lt Col Robert Payton-Reid, remarks bitterly that it is against the military textbook 'to break off an engagement and withdraw from the battlefield in broad daylight', which in this case meant his battalion 'was reduced, within the hour, to a third of its strength...'[119]

Though as Maj Geoffrey Powell, CO of C Coy in the 156th Para Bn, will point out 'there was no question of Hackett being able to postpone the move until nightfall.'[120] Powell will concede that the withdrawal during the day was too disorderly.

What remains of 4th Para Bde then repeats the error of the 1st Para Bde when trying to reach Frost's force at the bridge, namely of staying put overnight to recuperate and reorganise after its ordeal. It would be much better to join the division immediately, before the Germans can tighten their ring. But, rather than making the move back to Oosterbeek during the night – with the attendant risk of another exchange of fire between friendly units mistaking each other for the enemy – Hackett's brigade remains around Wolfheze. He has agreed during a radio discussion with the 1st Airborne Div HQ that he will move the brigade to Oosterbeek at first light.

For some troops dug in at Oosterbeek, arrayed in slit trenches around the Hotel Hartenstein, hearing the cacophony of battle but unable to do anything about it means their overactive imaginations fill in the gaps. Maj Gen Urquhart sees this manifesting itself as 'wild, fantastic rumours with no basis in fact.'[121] From the operations room in the Hartenstein Hotel, he observes small groups of soldiers hurrying around the grounds. They appear to not be under anyone's control. Then a large group runs across the grass, accompanied by an equally panic-stricken officer.

Urquhart hears them shouting: 'The Germans are coming!'

Along with some of his staff officers, he rushes out to restore order to 'young soldiers whose self control had momentarily deserted them.'

Urquhart bellows at them and physically restrains some, threatening serious consequences if they do not return to their positions. He has a special word with the young officer about setting a proper example of leadership.

Showing admirable empathy, Urquhart reflects later that it takes a special kind of courage to face an enemy in combat. It requires control of the willpower and the strength of character to handle 'the unknown, the unexpected and the unsuspected'. He is keenly aware that certain units under his command are more battle hardened than others – and that even some of the veteran units have a lot of new blood.

The nature of the Airborne Div's missions means that its soldiers, regardless of combat experience, are plunged in at the deep end rather than being gradually acclimatised to combat. He hopes they will settle down but knows that 'a flash of panic' such as he has just witnessed 'could have been contagious.' Urquhart is determined to prevent that happening and, in particular, to clamp down on 'indiscriminate shooting' that shows shaky control, which is also a waste of ammunition.

The Germans are not without their own problems, seeming to control their less effective troops by excessive shouting of orders as they go forward into action. It does not always work, as one Airborne soldier notes when he observes reluctant enemy troops being berated after 'whining' about whose turn it is to go forward first. He watches in amused astonishment as a German officer becomes so enraged with frustration that he takes his hat off and stamps on it.[122]

These are not Waffen SS and Wehrmacht veterans who have been blooded in combat but, as is admitted by the Germans themselves, men who in some cases only 24 hours previously were 'not known to each other'. They were aircraft technicians, or had been second line troops guarding military bases, naval coastal artillery crews and even teenage auxiliary labourers. 'Only a few of them were familiar with the principles of fighting in forest and hedgerow or street fighting,' notes an SS combat reporter.[123]

Even some of the Waffen SS soldiers are over the hill: one group of glider pilots are taking prisoner new recruits who are in their forties, and even they are convinced that, for the Reich, the war is over.[124]

The Germans are, however, renowned for their genius in welding together formidable units out of unpromising material. One battalion sent into the fight saw 'as many as 28 different units [that] fought side by side.'[125] The better units that engage the 1st Airborne Div in the woods and streets have proved extremely proficient in the art of killing.

The British advance up the highway from the south is discovering much the same. Just 15 miles to the south, troops and tanks of XXX Corps and US Airborne divisions are finding it hard-going, though the enemy is still barred by orders from taking the most obvious course of action.

Generalfeldmarschall Model remains hopeful the Nijmegen road bridge can be used for counter-attacks and so must remain intact. Despite this, Heinz Harmel, who goes south from Arnhem to supervise that fight too, vows to blow it should the situation appear irretrievable.

He instructs his combat engineers to prepare the charges and resolves that, if he spots a British tank crossing, he will order them detonated, regardless of Model's orders.

Desperate to keep the momentum going, the Guards Armoured and 82nd Airborne plan an assault they hope will take the bridge. Lt Gen Browning tells Brigadier General (Brig Gen) James Gavin, commander of the 82nd Airborne, the Nijmegen road bridge 'must be taken today or tomorrow at the latest ... we must get to Arnhem as quickly as possible.'[126]

Had Americans made their assault on the bridge on 17 September, it is reckoned they could have taken it due to weak enemy forces. Many of Gavin's troops have been occupied with securing the Groesbeek Heights first, to protect the main DZs and LZs, and to ensure an attack from Germany cannot be launched through them. This task absorbs the 82nd Airborne to the detriment of seizing the road bridge at a time when, perhaps, the task would have been easier. Now the Americans and British are locked in vicious street fighting with Hamel's SS *panzergrenadiers* in Nijmegen. Browning contemplates speeding things up by landing another parachute brigade to the north of the road bridge, in order to storm it from that end but that idea is axed.

—

In Oosterbeek a sentry has been put on the tank trap outside the Vredehof villa. He sits against the wall of a house across the street. Engaging him in conversation, de Soet discovers he is a Scottish soldier. He has not had more than two hours sleep since landing in Holland and gratefully receives water and bread. The Scot seems resigned to his soldier's lot and de Soet asks if losses have been heavy in the fighting. According to de Soet 'with tears in his eyes he answers: "We lost more than a thousand".' Even so, the Scots soldier believes the Second Army will arrive within three days.

At 10.00pm news is conveyed by phone of German tanks approaching and it is claimed the Nazis are once again in control of Wolfheze. De Soet tells his friend on the other end of the line the Vredehof villa and its immediate environs remain 'solidly English.'

An hour later, a soldier rings the front door bell. He says not to be afraid when the British guns located in fields around the nearby church – 75mm pack howitzers of the Light Battery – start firing.

The soldier advises: 'When you hear a boom and whistle it is ours; when you hear a whistle and a bang it is theirs.'

The encroaching tumult of combat strikes fear into more and more people around Oosterbeek, who venture out on desperate bids to find shelter underground. Jan Loos and the others are joined by 'two old ladies from the neighbourhood. With six adults and two children in there it is pretty full in the narrow cellar. In the late afternoon an older couple arrive, who are acquaintances of our neighbour.'

> 'There are so many people in the basement now that Walter has to sit on the stairs and me in a corner on the floor. There is not much sleeping going on that night – everyone is scared and tense. There is no room to lie down and the noise of battle outside becomes worse.'

Some Waffen SS troops pay a heavy price for dropping their guard. Having blasted the school buildings by the road bridge with everything they have – including phosphorus shells and using flamethrowers – a large group of Germans takes a break from their exertions. They think all enemy resistance has been snuffed out.

Unfortunately for them, Capt Mackay and quite a few of his stubborn engineers are still alive amid all the carnage. One of them tells Mackay it appears they are surrounded by enemy troops.

When Mackay takes a cautious look through a window, he is astonished to see dozens of Waffen SS troops relaxing on the grass.[127] Whispering orders to those of his men still capable of fighting, they silently gather up their Sten guns, Brens and primed grenades, going to various windows. Mackay yells: 'Fire!'

Roaring the blood-curdling 'Whoa Mohammed' – battle cry of the British 1st Airborne since North Africa – they unleash a withering fire, with dozens of the enemy felled.

'The Germans weren't good troops,' Mackay judges. 'They came 'round the school talking... Every one of us just went quietly to the window and killed the lot of them.'[128]

With the Germans again trying to force the British around the bridge to surrender – via continued use of fire and bombardment – the night sky is alive with sparks and ash, set against a devil's chorus of explosions, gunfire, walls crashing down, shattering glass, and splintering wood.

With classic understatement, Capt Mackay thinks this makes the situation 'difficult for everybody', but things take a turn for the worse with the arrival of Tigers to reinforce the Mk IV panzers.

With their large 88mm guns, the Tigers 'can shoot through buildings,' relates Mackay. 'They came up the main road to the bridge and sat there,' and while the 6pdr anti-tank guns were ordered to engage them 'it was no good. The whole area was by then blazing, and these two Tiger tanks just sat on either side of the road and fired.' In the eyes of the Waffen SS the British Airborne had stupidly refused to surrender and so now must accept death.

That night, as he and Maj Gough peer out from the battered house that is the 2nd Bn's headquarters building, Lt Col Frost takes in an unearthly vista. He remarks to Gough: 'Well Freddie, I'm afraid it's not been a very healthy party and it don't look like getting any healthier as time goes by.'[129]

The two 'great churches' of the town are an inferno and 'for a while the shadow of the cross which hung between two towers was silhouetted against the clouds of smoke rising far into the sky...' It is as bright as day, and the sound of the night is as terrifying as the vision. 'The crackle of burning wood and strange echo of falling buildings was almost continuous.'[130]

Wednesday

20 September

'I am now going in with bayonets and grenades.'

—Capt Bernard Briggs, HQ 1ˢᵗ Para Bde[131]

The 75mm pack howitzers of the Airborne artillery at Oosterbeek open up at 3.00am, determined to give the enemy an early alarm call.

The recoil of the guns – jumping back as shells are sent on their way in rapid succession – sends tremors through the earth, shaking dust from the timbers and walls of the Vredehof villa cellar.

De Soet and the others have endured a fitful night and he listens with trepidation for the next development in this strange new world of war they have been plunged into. 'Between the gunfire,' he notes, 'the silence is broken by the rattling of machine guns. Another day dawns.' In the cellar in which Jan Loos, his family, and assorted other locals are sheltering, there is an early morning 'moment of relative peace.'

> 'Walter arranges the sequence in which we can go up the cellar steps to pay a short visit to the toilet. The old gentleman has bad luck, because, just as he sits there, a grenade goes off outside with a thunderous bang. He stumbles down the cellar stairs in a hurry with his underwear and trousers around his ankles. Despite all the misery, everyone laughs. There will not be much laughter in following days.'

At the Vredehof[132] villa, de Soet finds even mundane morning tasks in current circumstances are hard to complete without risking death.

> 'Breakfast becomes a problem. No gas, no electricity, no water. Even the telephone is now cut off. German shells come whistling in. There are many hits and fires range in the surrounding houses ... our house still stands erect, but for the window panes.'

Two German shells plough into the garden, just six feet from the house. The tank trap has its explosive power increased and paratroopers come down into the cellar to ask how the civilians are faring with all the firing around them. De Soet puts a brave face on it, telling them he only worries about German guns. A paratrooper expresses grim determination to find a solution to that problem. He promises de Soet: 'We are going to find them, and then destroy them.'

Five soldiers use the kitchen for a morning wash while de Soet deals with a family from a neighbouring house, covered in dust and plaster, who have turned up seeking sanctuary.

> 'They received a hit ... and had to climb over the debris ... through the windows. A girl has a slight wound in her leg. We take them in too. Shellfire continues.'

Many of the Airborne troops who failed to get through to the bridge now rally at Oosterbeek after their flight from the onslaught of enemy armour. They take up a defensive line in the south-eastern corner of the perimeter, some of them digging in on the polder just north of the river.

Heavy German attacks develop that morning. It is hard to tell friend from foe due to mist coming off the Rhine, especially as it is thickened by smoke and dust.

Taking cover in a ditch filled with around three feet of water, some 3rd Para Bn paratroopers are assailed by tank fire. A shell explodes right next to them, concussing Pte David Warden and mortally wounding L/Cpl Walter Stanley. Seeing his friend in danger of sliding under the water, Warden holds him upright.

> 'He appeared to be in deep shock but, nevertheless, he knew he was dying and spoke of his wife. He then sang five or six lines of the song "I'll walk beside you in the years to come". When it was obvious that he was dead I left his body leaning against the side of the ditch.'[133]

—

At the Hartenstein, Maj Gen Urquhart contemplates the situation laid out before him, and it is not a pretty picture. As an official history will relate, in addition to the 'virtual destruction of the 4th Para Bde in woods north and north-west of Arnhem' there is the 'virtual disappearance of the 1st Para Bde in the town itself while the Air Landing Brigade has also suffered heavy losses. It all leaves Urquhart with 'no choice' but to 'form a perimeter round the suburb of Oosterbeek and there hold out until the long-expected relief from the 2nd Army arrived, using for this purpose the remains of the 4th Bde together with any other troops available.'[134]

On the morning of 20 September, Urquhart issues formal orders for what remains of the division to form a perimeter in Oosterbeek, with its centre on the Hartenstein and its base on the Rhine.

—

A little more than thirteen miles to the south-east of Oosterbeek, at 5.30am, the Grenadier Guards take the lead in another assault on the southern end of Nijmegen bridge. After five hours of heavy fighting they are in a position to launch a final push to get across.

The need to do so with all haste is painfully clear following news by wireless direct from Maj Gen Urquhart at Arnhem – the first such contact. Urquhart has informed Lt Gen Browning: 'Fighting intense and opposition extremely strong. Position not too good.'[135] Browning's premonition of Market Garden reaching 'a bridge too far' seems to be coming true, though on landing in Holland he had persuaded himself things were going well.

–

At 6.00am, the enemy forces closing the vice on the 1st Airborne Div unleashed a heavy artillery and mortar bombardment, just as 4th Para Bde was beginning its move to Oosterbeek. According to Hackett at around 7.40am, Maj Gen Urquhart 'came on the blower [radio] ordering me to Div HQ… I gave him the situation. We were completely engaged and free movement from us to him was impossible.'[136] Every man was required to do his bit to save the brigade from being overwhelmed, with Hackett's own HQ under constant fire. The brigadier greatly admired the signallers' composure as they received and transmitted radio messages.

'This was however nothing compared to their stout handling of rifle and bayonet when we were really put to it for a few hours…'[137]

The rump of the 156th Para Bn – already divided the previous day, with one part on the Wolfheze side of the railway line and the other successfully over it – manages to weather the bombardment but is then engaged in intense fighting. By 10.00am, it is down to 90 men, while elsewhere the 10th Para Bn is heavily engaged too. It is ordered 'to break through to the main Div position at all costs…'[138]

By 12.15pm, even more pressure is being exerted by a very heavy push from the enemy, with tanks entering the fray alongside self-propelled guns. 'The third day was a bit of a catastrophe for 4th Para Bde,' observes Lt Noble, who has been at Wolfheze overnight. He adds: 'Officer Commanding B Company said "right abandon the position every man for himself" and we scattered into the woods...'

Noble gathers 20 men with him from of all sorts of units, but mainly parachutists and including a fellow officer from the 156th Bn, Lt Dennis Kayne. They get away by slipping between houses, clambering over garden fences and hedges in 'a mad scramble'. They are harassed throughout by the enemy firing from houses and elsewhere.

Once in the cover of the trees, Noble and the others 'lay low for a bit to see if any more people came...' After gathering a couple of stragglers it is decided that, as nobody has any idea what is happening, they should 'make for the river.' It is as Noble leads his group to the south that B Coy of the 7th KOSB, under the command of Maj Michael Forman and which has been guarding the LZs and DZs, enters the scene. While it has seen plenty of action, Forman's company is largely intact but lost contact with its battalion. Maj Forman decides to take his men south-west towards the river, in a bid to link up with other British units. Lt Noble's group attaches itself to this KOSB company, acting as scouts.

'We very soon ran into German opposition,' says Noble. The Germans have stealthily trailed the British and wait until they are in the middle of a clearing before revealing themselves by opening fire.

Lt Noble realises his men and the KOSB are 'completely surrounded...' During a lull in the firing, a German officer calls out for the British to surrender. Maj Forman ponders the offer, estimating he is facing two companies of enemy troops who he can see are assembling their heavy mortars to unleash a merciless barrage.

Forman mulls over the idea of a charge across 200 yards of the heather-covered clearing to try and break through and escape. A check on ammunition levels across his company and the paratroopers reveals it has virtually all gone. He feels the chances of losing half his men are high and also 'with the prospect of heavy hand-to-hand fighting with the Germans if we did get across...'[139]

Forman decides he will not order 'every man for himself' and instead tells his men to surrender and that he will take the full responsibility.

Lt Noble decides he won't be following suit.

'I personally didn't agree with that and took to the woods again with some of my parachutists,' but, in the end, he doesn't think badly of the KOSBs. Noble judges that 'probably it was the right decision ... because some 130 men lived to see the end of the war.'

> 'Whereas if we'd fought it out at that time most of them probably wouldn't and I don't think it would have affected the battle of Arnhem... I was subsequently wounded slightly and taken prisoner. I wasn't able to see very well because an explosion had taken place in front of me and I got a lot of stuff in my eyes...'

Once the muck had been cleaned out of his eyes, Lt Noble got a good look at the enemy, who appeared 'fairly well organised... quite well disciplined... quite well armed. They didn't look as though they felt they were on the losing side which we thought they should have been.'

In the final analysis of his own unit's performance at Arnhem, Noble feels the 156th Para Bn never had a chance to fight properly.

> 'Under different circumstances they'd have put up one hell of a fight ... there was no question that, if we had had time to consolidate, get into a position and get formed up, then do things, the men were very good indeed.'

The Germans never for a moment intend to give them an opportunity to do that. Capt R Temple in the 4th Para Bde HQ, himself wounded in action on 20 September, records that enemy attacks were constant and casualties on both sides heavy. 'At one stage we thought the Germans wanted to surrender, and they thought we did,' notes Capt Temple. By now, the main 4th Para Bde group numbers about 250 men and is 'practically out of ammunition and the Germans were still attacking.'[140]

A German shell hits a jeep loaded with ammunition. Next to it are two others, one of them towing a trailer on which lies a wounded officer, Lt Col Derek Heathcote-Armory. With the ammunition jeep bursting into flames, the driver bales out and runs for cover, the wounded officer seemingly doomed to a terrible death.

'We all waited in horror for the explosion,' says Maj Powell of the 156th Para Bn, 'then out of the trees a short spare figure ran to the burning vehicle – it was the brigadier! Springing into the driver's seat of the jeep with the wounded man he gunned the engine into life, and the jeep and trailer roared across the clearing.'[141]

-

At the Arnhem road bridge, the British position is getting ever more precarious, but a stiff resistance is maintained. Airborne diehards who have been chased out of houses reduced to smoking rubble are now in slit trenches in gardens. Others maintain a grip on the northern end of the bridge by shooting at the enemy from foxholes on its embankment. From positions in the road tunnel underneath the bridge, some paratroopers make determined forays against the Germans. The Waffen SS also sustain heavy casualties as they try to winkle out stubborn British troops hanging on to a warehouse and holed up in a few houses that remain standing next to the bridge.

During the day, Capt Mackay uses his unit's radio to listen in on the British net, trying to piece together what's happening beyond the ruined school buildings. He hears Capt Bernard Briggs in conversation with Frost, then in a house on the west side of the bridge.

The young officer is trying to make up his mind whether or not to hold a position in some houses to the east of the bridge with a mixed group of 1st Para Bde Headquarters men and other Airborne soldiers.

For two days they have fought off numerous infantry assaults, despite the enemy having excellent cover from which to attack provided by trees and shrubbery.

'The position is untenable,' Briggs tells Lt Col Frost over the radio. The buildings are ablaze after suffering constant attack from tanks and artillery.

'Can I have permission to withdraw?'

Frost responds: 'If it is untenable you may withdraw…'

'Everything is comfortable,' Briggs decides after thinking it over for a few seconds, deciding it is not yet time to retreat. 'I am now going in with bayonets and grenades.'[142] In hand-to-hand combat, Briggs and his men successfully root the enemy out.

Also hitting back is Trooper (Tpr) Cecil Bolton, a Reconnaissance Squadron soldier of Afro Caribbean descent. Another veteran of fighting in North Africa and Italy, he is an ace shot with the Bren gun. According to Maj Gough, Bolton goes out 'crawling all over the place sniping', shooting anything that moves on the northern ramp of the bridge. Every time he gets a German, Trooper Bolton, from Liverpool, gives a thumbs up, a broad grin and remarks in a thick Scouse accent: 'There goes another one of those bastards.'[143]

British and Germans do get to grips with one another in houses near the bridge, as Pte Steve Morgan, of the 2nd Para Bn relates:

> 'I mean, we could be in one house … we could be in one room and the Germans were either in the room below, or above or alongside. It was really savage fighting… Most of those we met were the 9th SS Panzer Division and boy were they tough troops.

> They were not afraid of us and we were not afraid of them ... you [just] imagine, two or three of our men [and] two or three of their men in a room ... fighting to kill one another.'[144]

Meanwhile, American special forces officer Lt Todd has his own go at sniping the enemy, targeting an enemy machine gun team who have set themselves up on a balcony directly opposite the building containing the 1st Para Bde HQ.

In the process of killing some of the enemy, Todd is spotted. German snipers open fire, one bullet hitting the butt of his M1 carbine. It causes Todd no injury, though he will later receive shrapnel wounds when a Tiger blasts him at point blank range.

Panzers venture in close to British positions to fire directly into houses, but it provides an ideal opportunity for Airborne soldiers to disable or even destroy them.

As a panzer lumbers along the road below, teams of British soldiers keep pace with it, being careful not to be seen as they use the mouse-hole tactic, knocking holes through walls on upper floors 'moving from room to room'.[145] PIATs and gammon bombs are the favourite weapons at such close range.

In one such case Lt Dennis Simpson, of the 1st Para Sqn RE manages to bring a Tiger to a halt. Peeping over the windowsill, he watches its crew bale out and try to escape by creeping along the wall of the house he is in. When they stop directly below a window, he drops a grenade on them, which he retains for two seconds before releasing it. This is to ensure they cannot scatter before it detonates, but such Canute-like acts of defiance cannot possibly hold back the growing tide of German forces whose firepower increases by the hour.

—

In Oosterbeek, Cpl Tucker is ordered to help clear out streets on the south-eastern edge of the perimeter. He takes a pair of privates with him called Lownes and Miller, along with a L/Cpl Smith.

'We went from house to house, searching for Germans who, in turn were looking for us. First part of the drill was to kick a door down and then go in very carefully, but not with guns blazing, as we had to conserve ammunition. However, if we saw anything move we would blast it. The Dutch people who lived in those houses had decided to shelter in their cellars and we would go down and ask them if they had seen any Germans. They thanked us for liberating them and were very happy. Of course, the way it turned ... we hadn't really liberated them. All we had done was start this battle that was destroying their town.'

Beyond Oosterbeek, SSgt Withnall decides to hide up in a copse during the day and continue his bid to cross the river when darkness falls.

'Sometimes I was terribly thirsty, so I sucked on grass blades for their moisture. It was while I was lying there that I suddenly heard this clanking noise getting closer and closer. It was a German tank and it started to crash through bushes all around me. I was terrified that I was going to get squashed.'

Elsewhere, Stan Turner can hear fighting, but has still not experienced it directly but then the enemy gives his position some serious attention.

'The noise is unbelievable and we are shelled for the first time. Orders are given for us to move inside the grounds of the Hartenstein Hotel to act as defence troops for the divisional HQ. This confirms our feelings that things are not going at all well.'

Using British boats, that afternoon – after air strikes by RAF Typhoons and a 15-minute artillery barrage to try and soften enemy defences up – paratroopers of the US 82nd Airborne's 504th Parachute Infantry Regt make a heroic assault across the river. The Americans suffer hundreds of dead and wounded. Despite the horrific level of losses, they succeed in taking the northern end of the Nijmegen Bridge.

Standartenführer Harmel watches as the first Sherman tank charges onto the bridge from the southern end, where his forces have been overcome by the British. Harmel waits until several enemy tanks are on the bridge then gives orders to blow it, expecting to see a massive explosion – but it turns out to be a damp squib. Nothing happens even when the SS commander orders his engineers to try and set the charge off again.

The Sherman and Cromwell tanks of the Guards Armoured surge across, with Harmel exclaiming: 'My God, they'll be here in two minutes!'

He tells his staff officers to issue orders for all available forces to block the road north, warning that if they fail now 'they'll roll straight through to Arnhem.'[146]

Capt T Moffatt Burriss, who has lost half his company in the assault across river, is ecstatic to see British tanks charging across the bridge, his men giving them a rousing reception. They clamber up onto the tanks to hug and kiss their crews whose heads are poking out of hatches. Capt Burriss also plants a smacker on the hull of one tank and shouts up to its commander: 'Head on to Arnhem!'[147]

If British infantry are not immediately available, the American paratroopers offer to go along with the Guards to help them take out enemy anti-tank guns and tanks. US paratroopers and British engineers have already pressed ahead around a mile, taking 17pdr anti-tank guns with them, but the British tanks soon come to a halt.

From the northern end of Nijmegen Bridge to Arnhem is just ten miles but the British need to refuel and wait for infantry to catch up – and they are still fighting their way through the town.

It enrages the American paratroopers who have paid such a heavy price to secure the northern end of the bridge. They are desperate to see relief get through to their fellow Airborne warriors and berate the Guards for not pressing on regardless. Lt Col Reuben Tucker, CO of the 504th, rages at a Major in the Guards: 'Your boys are hurting up there at Arnhem. You better go!'[148]

But the Guards stay where they are, fearful of the embanked road ahead, which not only makes their tanks and personnel carriers sitting ducks, but has marshy land on either side, severely limiting room for manoeuvre.

Up the highway, enemy forces, preparing to stop them getting any further, rapidly grow in strength, with Tiger tanks and 88mm anti-tank guns positioned to make sure of knocking them off the highway.

When he gets across the bridge with his unit that evening, 20-year-old Irish Guards infantry officer Lt Brian Wilson, is disgusted at the timidity shown by his own senior commanders. He observes angrily: 'The situation in Arnhem remained desperate. Yet the Guards Armoured Division did nothing.'[149]

—

Time is of the essence, not only in military terms in the fight for the bridges but also for civilians trapped in the cellars of Oosterbeek.

Some underground refuges are stocked better than others when it comes to food, but thirst is a universal problem. It requires the young and the brave, such as Jan Loos and Walter, to risk their lives despite the intensifying battle above ground. 'With 10 people now in the basement and eight to ten paratroopers in the house, our supply of water is diminishing rapidly,' reports Jan.

'In addition there is hardly anything to eat. Walter suggests he and I should once more try to get water from the pump by the butcher's shop. It is not a great distance, but from that direction we hear almost continuous shooting with machine guns and all kinds of other weapons. But we must get water, so we go upstairs, finding there is no longer glass in the windows of the house. In one room there are two paratroopers behind a machine gun, which is resting on the windowsill. From the paratroopers' remarks we understand they think it unwise for us to go outside. We pick up the buckets and go anyway. The noise outside is deafening. At the Stationsweg houses are on fire, there is debris on the streets and we see parachutes in the trees. Paratroopers are in trenches and foxholes here and there in the gardens. They are also taking cover in positions near the water pump. One of those paratroopers gestures us to be alert for German snipers shooting from the trees. With full buckets we return slowly – it seems to take forever and always with the fear that things could go wrong. We are almost home when I feel a slap against my left leg, but don't look and keep on walking back to the house. When the paratroopers see that we have water they come in turn to take a few sips. I see that my leg is covered in blood and I turn out to have a slight wound on my left shin. Grenade splinter? Bullet fragment? Luckily there is no damage to the bone – it is a flesh wound. Annie bandages it to stop the bleeding and that's it. There is no possibility of seeking expert medical assistance. At the end of the afternoon we cook some preserved meat on the wood-burning stove in the kitchen. The paratroopers use the stove to heat up their rations and brew up some tea – typically British.'

The remnants of the 10th Para Bn successfully linked up with the division by 1.30pm[150] but Hackett, his HQ and C Coy of the 156th Para Bn have not yet made it to join the nascent perimeter.

The enemy send in infantry with a tank several times, prompting Brig Hackett to galvanise his men by leading them in counter-attacks with 'rifle and bayonet in [his] hand'.[151]

Hackett has a close encounter with the enemy while looking for one of his senior officers, spotting what may be his corpse lying 30 yards from troops he thinks are Poles. Realising his mistake, Hackett tries to brazen it out: 'I told them to surrender but was alone and they saw me off.'[152]

Hackett calls Maj Powell over, explaining that he wants to withdraw south and find the division. The desired route passes through a hollow, which is around 150 yards away – the only problem being a load of German troops occupying it. What survives of Maj Powell's C Coy of the 156th Para Bn is the only cohesive fighting formation to hand, so Hackett asks him to take his soldiers and boot the enemy out. Powell gathers his men and suggests: 'We will charge the enemy – it will be better to be killed going for the bastards than lying in a ditch.'[153]

Powell leads the way, none of his men hesitating to follow. The Germans in the hollow flee, for, as Powell remarks: 'The sight of savage, screaming parachutists had been too much for them.' All that is left are German wounded lying on the ground.[154]

As enemy tanks and infantry roam among them, Hackett tries to rally the rest of the men and get them into the hollow but is forced to admit it is a case of 'all coherence lost.'[155]

Once the survivors are in the hollow – crammed into a space about 90ft across – the situation becomes even more desperate, the brigadier recording that there is 'no water or food, insufficient weapons, little room'. Many of his men are 'using German rifles',[156] not least himself, but Hackett soon replaces his enemy weapon with a Lee Enfield from a wounded officer who can no longer handle it.

The enemy seems reluctant to get too close – keeping their tanks out of gammon bomb range and preferring to apply a process of attrition on the British via bombardment, sniping and opportunity bursts of machine gun fire. Hackett decides, after a discussion with Maj George de Gex,[157] that they must all break out – their own ammunition is getting very low, a situation neatly summed up as facing 'annihilation or capture.'[158] Hackett suspects the enemy will soon try and 'liquidate posn [the position]'.[159]

Following a last word with wounded who cannot possibly take part in the mass charge that he plans, Hackett and Maj de Gex lead the escape bid.

What is left of the 4th Para Bde thunders out of the hollow, a snarling, shouting mass – with bayonets fixed – firing weapons from the hip and barging through the Germans who quail and scatter.

Hackett pauses for a second, rifle bayonet poised over an enemy soldier cowering on the ground, expecting death, but the brigadier gives him mercy and rushes on.

Covering 400 yards, losing only a few men along the way, the 4th Para Bde group reaches the divisional perimeter, passing through a section held by the Border Regt to the east of the Hartenstein. The Borders are shocked by the haggard, filthy appearance of Hackett's ragged band, some of them in bloody bandages and several still carrying enemy weapons. Alarmed at the potential for this mob to infect his own soldiers with disorderly conduct, a Border Regt company CO tells Maj Powell to take his men away, branding them 'a bloody shower'.[160]

At the Hartenstein, due to enemy sniper fire, it is decided to move the 1st Airborne Div HQ operations room from ground floor rooms down into the cellars. A table on which battle maps are laid out is put in the centre of the main cellar, with Maj Gen Urquhart sat in the right-hand corner between a wine rack and window grilles that have been blocked off.

Next to him is an officer of the intriguingly named Phantom reconnaissance unit which operates a very powerful wireless set. When it functions properly, the latter can be used to contact the War Office in London and other higher-level headquarters, including the Airborne Corps HQ in Holland. A BBC radio correspondent with the Divisional HQ also has radio equipment that proves useful to contact the UK.[161]

For those left behind upstairs, including Capt Fletcher, snipers carry on making life above ground rather risky.

> 'Things were getting a bit dodgy. There was this big door people kept leaving open, which enabled the German snipers to fire into the main HQ room. People often forgot to shut it, and then a sniper's bullet would snap over our heads, prompting someone to shout "shut that bloody door!"'

In one position on the perimeter held by men of the Recce Squadron, a dummy is created using a pillow with a helmet attached to it, stuck on the end of a broom handle. This is shown at various windows, in order to attract German sniper fire – with observers in a neighbouring house watching for the gun flash. This is replied to with a well-aimed single shot from a Bren or Sten. Fifteen enemy snipers are accounted for this way.

The 21st Indep Para Coy – the Pathfinders – who were the first of the 1st Airborne Div's troops to touch Dutch soil are now also doing their bit to hold the perimeter against enemy attack.

Commanded by Maj 'Boy' Wilson – an ironic sobriquet, given that, at 45-years-old, he is the oldest paratrooper in the division – its soldiers marked the DZs and LZs with smoke and high visibility panels, plus used special Eureka homing beacons to guide the air armada in. Among the 21st Indep Para Coy's men are 25 warriors especially eager to kill one-time fellow countrymen who have tortured, imprisoned, and murdered family members. Most are of German or Austrian origin and all are Jews who have already proved themselves in combat in North Africa, Sicily and Italy.

Having fled their native lands to find refuge in Britain, on the outbreak of war they were classified as potential enemies but, after passing a security vetting procedure, were accepted into the elite Airborne forces. They legally changed their identities, with fake birth certificates and even acquired pretend families, all to aid a potentially life-preserving deception should they be captured. Among those of them going into action at Oosterbeek are 22-year-old Pte Timothy Alexander (actually Adolf Bleichroder, son of a Hamburg banker); 24-year-old Pte Walter Langdon, a former chemistry student (real name, Walther Lewy-lingen, son of a German judge); Cpl Peter Rodley (in reality Hans Rosenfield, a 29-year-old one-time mathematician, originally from Dusseldorf).[162]

With the Airborne offering a home to soldiers who can be judged on their fighting abilities rather than their backgrounds, the 21st Indep Para Coy also includes two black soldiers: Joe Smith, the Platoon Sgt of 3 Platoon – son of an African American actor-singer who settled in the UK in the early 1900s – and Pte Ken Roberts, a Bren gunner with 1 Platoon, and a former boxing champion, from Stoke on Trent.[163]

Roberts is engaged in suppressing a troublesome German anti-tank gun. Along with 1 Platoon's other two Bren gunners, he places carefully aimed shots that force the enemy gun crew to take cover until mortar shells put them (and it) out of action for good.

There is a vicious spell of fighting that sees houses held by the 21st Indep Para Coy blasted incessantly, but they hold the line, kill a lot of the enemy, and knock out their armour. Sgt Smith and Lt Hugh Ashmore lead 3 Platoon in a desperate struggle against two Mk IV tanks and self-propelled guns.

Despite having made great efforts to hide their true identities from the hated Nazis, the 21st Indep Para Coy's Germans and Austrians cannot in the heat of battle resist taunting the foe in their own tongue, shouting:

'Fick dich selbst!'
'Go fuck yourselves!'

The retort is prompted by the Germans attempting to wear the 21st Indep Para Coy down by using loudspeakers to play Glenn Miller's 'In the Mood' and urging them to surrender.[164]

Another response to this is gunfire and grenades. Having endured and repulsed determined enemy attacks throughout the morning, and bombardment from mortars and self-propelled guns, on the afternoon of 20 September there is a lull for the 21st Indep Para Coy.

From the enemy positions in the woods comes a loud voice calling for the British to surrender. Cpl Rodley decides to reply in German and shouts back that perhaps *they* should come out of the trees and surrender.

Incredibly, dozens of enemy troops emerge, though with weapons at the ready rather than with their hands up.

1 Platoon section commander Sgt Ron Kent tells his men to hold their fire until the enemy are closer, as he is keen none should get away. When Bren guns belonging to glider pilots in a nearby position open fire, 1 Platoon joins in, dropping many Germans; any still capable of moving crawl for cover in the trees. A similar trick was used earlier that afternoon – but with the British as victims. Men of the 156th Para Bn were gunned down on a trail in the woods after being beckoned forward by mystery soldiers wearing Airborne camouflage smocks whom they mistook for Polish paratroopers.[165]

Unconventional tactics are also employed by Germans soldiers who seem reluctant to close with the troops of the Border Regt in woods on the western side of the perimeter.

Cpl Bill Collings, is in command of No1 Section in 10 Platoon of the battalion's A Company, waiting to see what will come down the various trails through the trees. On 20 September, Collings' position comes under attack from a panzer. During a failed PIAT bid to destroy the tank, his life is saved by a recklessly brave comrade.

> 'Jack Crawford stood up out of his trench firing his Bren gun from the hip giving me time to move position, then I saw a red flash and Jack falling back into his trench.'[166]

Crawford's burst of fire kills the tank commander who foolishly showed himself through a hatch in the turret. The panzer withdraws. The Bren has been wrecked by enemy fire, but fortunately Crawford survives. Looking down at his friend sprawled in the bottom of the trench Collings enquires incredulously: 'What the hell did you do that for?'

A grinning Crawford responds: 'I don't know'.[167]

Collings and his men are sent to watch over another path and this time see three German trucks approaching and disgorging troops, which provokes a brief exchange of fire. The silence that follows is broken by the sound of two trees being cut down. These are dragged over to block the path and provide cover, with enemy troops crawling behind them. Cpl Collings watches all this using his binoculars, and 'every time one came out I'd call to Jack and he would let go [shoot].'[168]

Having failed with their tree trunk ploy, the Germans change tactics and, out of sight, bring up some kind of loud speaker apparatus to broadcast messages in English to the British troops. They tell Collings and his comrades their mission is doomed, suggesting they should 'think about your mothers, wives and sweethearts.'

As Collings relates, when this fails the Germans have another bright idea. 'They then played some records of Vera Lynn songs to touch our hearts but it would not stop us from trying to do the job we all came to do. In fact, it gave our spirits a boost.'

That the Germans do not quite understand the psychology of their opponents in the Oosterbeek fight is further illustrated elsewhere on the perimeter. After broadcasting jazz music along with a long list of British senior officers allegedly taken prisoner, the Airborne troops are warned by the enemy that a heavy panzer attack is coming and they best give up.

Far from terrifying the Airborne soldiers, this news is 'greeted by abuse, catcalls, whistles and occasional bursts from a Bren gun,' observes Capt HF Brown, adding, 'we all felt it was a great joke.' A PIAT shot is fired in the direction of the speaker as it broadcasts another 'monologue' and, Capt Brown adds, with great satisfaction, 'there was a big bang and it stopped.'[169]

—

In the cellar of the Vredehof villa, de Soet considers fleeing with his family, telling others to do likewise, but then he realises there is probably nowhere better. By 3.00pm the phone is working again, so de Soet rings around his friends, discovering Wolfheze is now firmly back in German hands.

On calling a friend in a house 500 yards away he is shocked to find that area has been retaken too. Earlier that afternoon De Soet's friend took a look outside his front door only to have a German soldier snarl at him:

'Get inside man! I'll shoot!'

Ringing back at 5.00pm, his friend reports some Germans have not moved from taking cover pressed against the walls of his house. The British fire is too intense for them. De Soet passes this intelligence to the paratroopers. An hour and a half later an Airborne soldier shouts down to him: 'They are all killed!'

There are still plenty of German infantry left to worry about, and they mount a determined attack, with self-propelled guns providing fire support.

Even as this fight plays out in the streets, gardens and parkland, there is still great hope the Second Army will come to the rescue. News has reached British troops in de Soet's house of Polish paratroopers reportedly dropping on the other side of the Rhine. De Soet asks himself:

'Will the Second Army cross the river? Where are they?'

—

The process of forming the divisional perimeter throws up a brutal moment of confusion in the lines. Lynchpin in the northeast corner of the perimeter is the Dreyeroord Hotel, or White House, as it is known to the KOSB, where there will be an utterly brutal contest between them and the Waffen SS. A foretaste of that is given shortly after the KOSB move into positions around the White House.

Nursing a wound and doing his best to ignore it, Maj Gordon Sheriff is conducting rounds of his men to check they are alright. He is accompanied by battalion commander Lt Col Payton-Reid and they bump into someone who says something in German.

Sheriff is quickest to recover from the surprise and, despite his wound, leaps onto the man, grabbing him around the throat. Lt Col Payton-Reid pulls his sidearm from its holster, tries to shoot the German. Sheriff keeps getting in the way and, in the end, manages to strangle the man, who seems likely to have been part of a scouting party.

Comrades of the German try to help him by hurling a stick grenade, which falls short and explodes. Payton-Reid and Sherrif hear 'a frightful wailing' and find it is being generated by 'a goat that had been hit.'[170]

In the evening of September 20, many of the survivors of the 1st, 3rd and 11th Bns of the Parachute Regt are gathered at the Oude Kerk.

They are now led by Maj Dickie Lonsdale, the second-incommand of the 11th Para Bn, who has suffered wounds in a leg and both hands. He even sustained one of his wounds just before he jumped, caused when enemy AA shrapnel penetrated the Dakota he was aboard.

The force holding the line in the southeast corner of the perimeter is under the overall command of Lt Col WFK 'Sherriff' Thompson, CO of the 1st Air Landing Light (Artillery) Regt and he has given Lonsdale permission to pull them back from the open ground where they have been dug in. After valiantly resisting intense enemy attacks, it is imperative they regroup and consolidate their defences.

Despite his wounds, Lonsdale pulls himself up into the pulpit and makes a rousing speech to the troops. He seeks to stir his so-called Lonsdale Force from encroaching torpor settling on them after three days of vicious fighting with little sleep, water or food to sustain them.

He tells them: 'We must fight for our lives and stick together. We fought the Germans in North Africa, Sicily and Italy. They weren't good enough for us then. They're not bloody good enough for us now. They are up against the finest soldiers in the world. When you go back outside to take up positions, remember ammo is scarce so when you shoot, shoot to kill. Good luck to you all.'[171]

Among the weary, filthy, and battered Airborne soldiers sitting in the pews – cleaning their weapons, or just glad to have a rest indoors and something to eat – is Cpl Harry Tucker. After Lonsdale's pep talk, he and the other men leave the church to take up their new positions.

Above all, they must prevent the Germans from pushing across the perimeter's southern end and cutting the division off from the Rhine. It is still hoped XXX Corps will arrive, project itself into the perimeter and expand it into a substantial beachhead. There are even wild rumours about the Second Army already arriving. *The Airborne have finally linked up with XXX Corps!*

This provokes delight among the civilians in the cellars of the battered houses. Bottles of schnapps are brought out to toast the excellent news with resident British troops. After all this excitement there follows a quiet night – the cellar dwellers praying the end of their ordeal is near.

–

At the Arnhem road bridge, the last British holdouts are just about hanging on.

During the fight for Caen in Normandy, air and artillery bombardment reduced that stone-built mediaeval city to rubble during Allied attempts to snuff out German resistance. It merely succeeded in providing the defenders with better cover, killing thousands of civilians, while also making streets impassable for vehicles. This is not entirely the case in Arnhem.

> 'All the buildings one by one caught fire and burnt ... they were largely built of wood and went on smouldering for a considerable time, so there was no refuge in the rubble, as there can be when there are buildings largely made of stone. Sometimes they [ruins] are more effective than the actual building itself. But [at Arnhem] once a building caught fire there was no means of extinguishing the flames. They became no man's land.'[172]

For all that, there is still a considerable amount of masonry and other rubble. *Panzergrenadiers* often have to close with the foe, naked of tank support, dismounting from their half-tracks and plunging into savage hand-to-hand, face-to-face combat.

Even Mackay and his diehards cannot fight on forever, especially as the enemy is determined to finally wipe out all resistance in what remains of the school. 'We stayed in our position till the afternoon, when the Germans brought up a Tiger tank and blew the top off our house,' he reports. 'We had only ten men left [standing]... We carried out the wounded on stretchers and they surrendered. The remainder of the blokes broke through to the east... Everybody ran across through burning houses.'[173] Trying to escape from the Germans with five of his men, Mackay has a stand-up gunfight with 50 enemy troops and two panzers. The British desperadoes walk down the middle of a street, using up their last bullets, the astonished enemy troops dropping 'like half-filled sacks of grain' according to Mackay.

With three men left, Mackay says they should split up, hide out in gardens, and aim to meet down by the bridge that night to plan a proper escape. In seeking to avoid an enemy patrol by playing dead under a bush, Mackay is found and stabbed in the backside with a bayonet. It goes so deep he feels it lodge with a jar against my pelvis'.[174]

Enraged and already pretty angry at a painful shrapnel wound in a foot, Mackay extracts himself from the bush. He draws his pistol, shouting at the Germans surrounding him: 'What the bloody hell do you mean stabbing a bayonet into a British officer?'

Realising the ludicrous nature of the situation, Mackay bursts out laughing, lobs his pistol over a garden fence and yields. When interrogated by a German officer who speaks English fluently, Mackay can't resist telling him that his side may as well surrender, that he will be more than happy to accept it, Mackay is delighted to find 'that was the end of the interrogation.'[175]

—

Lt Col Frost has been wounded on the Wednesday morning: blown up by a mortar bomb while holding a discussion with senior company commanders. The explosion sent them all flying and everyone was wounded. Frost is not seriously injured, with shrapnel in his right shinbone and left ankle, but it is very painful. He is given morphia to dull the pain and taken down into a cellar to rest.

—

One of the more remarkable sights during combat at the bridge is a British paratrooper officer strolling around wearing a bowler hat and brandishing an umbrella. This is 27-year-old Maj Digby Tatham-Warter, who, prior to joining the Parachute Regt, served in the Ox and Bucks, and now commands A Coy in Frost's battalion.

For all his eccentricities Maj Tatham-Warter is a brave and inspirational leader during what is actually his baptism of fire. On the advance to the Arnhem road bridge, his company was the spearhead, and he decided it was far better to go through back gardens than expose his men to enemy fire in the streets. In doing so, A Coy also killed or took prisoner 150 enemy soldiers.[176]

Tatham-Warter supposedly carries the umbrella because he can never remember the daily password, so thinks anyone seen carrying one will automatically be recognised as a genuine British soldier. In one episode, Maj Tatham-Warter leads an attack on German Mk IV tanks with the furled umbrella in one hand and a pistol in the other. Looking on with considerable admiration, Freddie Gough notes that Tatham-Warter is now wearing a novel form of headgear instead of his customary red beret.

> 'He had found an old bowler hat somewhere and he was rushing along, twirling that battered umbrella, looking for all the world like Charlie Chaplin.'[177]

During a skirmish, Tatham-Warter allegedly uses the umbrella to incapacitate the driver of a Waffen SS armoured car, by poking it rather hard through the unfortunate enemy's soldier's observation slit.

When the 2nd Para Bn's padre is seeking to carry out pastoral duties with the wounded – but cannot get across a street for fear of being shot down – Tatham-Warter appears at his side. With the open umbrella held aloft, he escorts the padre safely across the street.

Lt Pat Barnet, of the 1st Para Bde defence platoon, is sprinting from one building to another amid a storm of mortar bombs and is astonished to see Tatham-Warter calmly strolling about with only the open umbrella for protection. 'That won't do you much good!' Barnet yells as he runs past.

Looking shocked, Tatham-Warter shouts back that he needs the umbrella in case the rain comes on.[178]

Tatham-Warter will become second-command to Frost after the nominated officer, Maj David Wallis, is killed, but, inevitably, the umbrella-toting Major can only push his luck so far. He ends up wounded in the buttocks by shrapnel, though he tries to limp on for a while.

Command of the British force at the bridge then passes to Maj Gough, who comes down to regularly consult Frost. They realise death or surrender looms. 'We were absolutely sealed in by a ring of enemy infantry and armour,' remarks Frost.[179]

Self-propelled guns are firing at point blank range into buildings and there are very few PIAT bombs left, so they just have to sit there and take it.

There is very little ammunition of any kind left.

The senior military doctor at the bridge, Capt Ronnie Gordon, comes to see Frost about the possibility of a truce, telling him: 'I am afraid unless we can put the flames out … 200 wounded men are going to be burned alive including you, Sir.'

Frost agrees to negotiations and so the doctor exits to discuss evacuating the wounded with the enemy. This is agreed, with both British and SS troops bringing the wounded of both sides out of the cellar.

Teenage soldier James Sims, who suffered shrapnel wounds in his left leg during a fight in a back garden, watches as another injured paratrooper suddenly reveals a Sten gun. This man loathes the enemy so much he intends killing any Germans coming down the cellar steps. 'He was quickly overpowered by the equally badly wounded men on either side of him,' relates Sims. 'He sobbed furiously over this…'

Had the paratrooper opened fire, Sims feels the Germans would have been 'quite justified in slinging grenades down among us.'[180]

Joining Pte Sims and the other wounded outside, Frost removes his badges of rank – and is already entertaining the idea of escaping, asking his soldiers not to give him away. He can hear the Germans asking for him by name as he lies on a stretcher, and, all around, SS men consoling his troops. They are 'very sympathetic',[181] with Frost thinking it all very well for the SS to be 'polite and complimentary … but the bitterness I felt was unassuaged.'[182]

Frost and others are put on half-tracks – the stretchers laid across the top of their passenger compartments – and taken to St Elizabeth Hospital to be looked after by German and British medical personnel working alongside Dutch civilian doctors and nurses. The Lt Col's hopes of escaping will be frustrated, as he is taken to Germany the next day, but, even when in a prison hospital, he is not interrogated, so for a while longer his identity remains a secret.

Hundreds of wounded have been evacuated from various buildings and most British strongholds have been overwhelmed, but 130 unwounded (or just lightly wounded) soldiers of 1st Para Bde HQ, under the command of Maj Tony Hibbert, are still at large.

They lurk in various shell battered buildings, watching as the captured men of the 2nd Para Bn are marched away.

Hibbert asks for an assessment of how much ammunition each soldier has left. The answer is a single magazine for each Sten or Bren but no PIAT bombs. Hibbert thinks they may be able to hold out for four or five hours longer in the morning, but they will not be able to dominate the approach to the bridge and influence the course of the overall battle. They will have no impact at all on that, so he decides his men should split up into sections and infiltrate the German lines to the west, aiming to join rest of the division. However, as Hibbert notes rather ruefully, 'very few people got away.'

> '...by this time the fighting had stopped and of course [we were] moving troops through a town at night when the entire place was covered in rubble and broken glass ... so, whenever you walked through anywhere it was bloody noisy and you were immediately [spotted] ... and the place was absolutely stiff with Germans and there were fire-fights going on all 'round...'[183]

Not far away, Maj Deane-Drummond and the other three hideaways are in their third night imprisoned in the lavatory of the house by the river.

It is robustly locked from the inside, for there have been several tries on the handle by the Germans in the house, though fortunately nobody has tried to bash the door in.

The battle around them has been 'extremely noisy [and] those first two nights, the machine guns were going pretty hard,' according to Deane-Drummond. They could hear 'there were star shells going up all over the place. It wasn't a very comfortable position at all.'

It will be suicide to try and break out of the house at this precise moment, and, even if they can, it is likely impossible to get through either to the bridge or the division's positions in the west. Deane-Drummond suggests to the other three soldiers: 'Look, we've got to get across the river, which means we've all got to swim.' If they can succeed, then it may be possible to sneak along the south bank of the Rhine, to either link up with Second Army troops or get back across the river to the 1st Airborne Div.

Thursday

21 September

'Two world powers at war, fighting at a distance of 25 yards from each other...'

—Frans de Soet, Oosterbeek, September 1944

Within a few hours, things become rather more placid, with the machine guns in the house falling silent. It seems the Germans may have withdrawn altogether as their clomping around can no longer be heard, nor their voices. Around midnight, Deane-Drummond and the other three Airborne soldiers emerge from their hiding place, with battle dress blouses wrapped around their – boots to muffle the noise – just in case some of the enemy are still around.

Successfully making the river bank, Deane-Drummond notes there is 'still an awful lot of banging and machine gun fire and everything else going on, but, fortunately, by this time, it was about 500 yards away further upstream.' He tells the others they should rendezvous with him on the other side, 'at the railway crossing ... about a mile further up.' The four men strip off, putting their clothes inside their water-resistant parachutist smocks, keeping tight hold of the bundles as they strike out across the river. Deane-Drummond advises them to 'swim as slowly as you can' and stay calm.

The river appears to be about 400 yards wide at this point and fairly fast flowing, with the four fugitives landing at different points as Deane-Drummond anticipated they would.

To reach the rendezvous point, Deane-Drummond must navigate through a brickworks, which he manages successfully. Then he heads across an orchard and a field, stopping every now and then to listen out for the enemy. On hearing coughing and talking – which has to be German troops – he uses his night vision to try and pick out where they are, pistol at the ready.

> 'I arrived at the embankment to the railway about an hour before dawn… I knew perfectly well [that] in most armies, if there is a company in action [they] start standing to about an hour before dawn to repel any attack that might happen…'

Disaster strikes as he closes with the railway embankment. Eyes straining to try and pick out his fellow Airborne soldiers waiting for him to arrive, he fails to notice a slit trench, which he falls into.

> '…and down at the bottom of this slit trench there was two rather dozy Germans who were just waking up. Because at exactly at that moment a whistle blew and the whole of this [enemy] company stood to…'

Amid all the noisy activity of German NCOs shouting to rouse their men, Deane-Drummond presses the muzzle of his pistol against the head of the enemy soldier he has fallen on top of. He pulls the trigger, killing him with a single shot, the other German jumping on top of Deane-Drummond.

> 'It seemed certain that I was to be shot, but I suppose the second man did not know his comrade was dead and did not fire for fear of hurting him. Instead of being killed I was made a prisoner.'[184]

By dawn on the Thursday, having dodged prowling tanks under cover of the night, Pat Withnall is making good progress towards the Rhine. Then he comes face-to-face with three enemy soldiers.

> 'I can only assume they heard me coming down the trail. This German suddenly stepped out in front of me with his gun pointing at me and gesturing for me to lay down my rifle and put my hands up. The other two emerged and so I didn't have much choice... They started marching me around and around, talking to each other in a very animated fashion. I seriously believed they were contemplating shooting me but they thought better of it and instead marched me off to their field HQ. They fed me before taking me to a town nearby called Apeldoorn where all captured British troops were being kept.'

As for the British at the road bridge, it is all over, the last fighting elements surrendering or trying to escape. Maj Tony Hibbert goes out with the last party of would-be escapees from his position, making a break for it at first light.

> 'It was a pretty bloody miserable end. We got fired at wherever we went. I took them to a burned out building and I thought I was being very clever [as it had] burned out some time ago ... we dug holes in the ashes and then pulled the ashes over the top and [unfortunately] you were then [like] a baked potato in an old bonfire...'[185]

Moving on with the war correspondent Tony Cotterill, Maj Hibbert finds 'what looked to be a super hiding place – a coal shed – and we made an enormous hole in the coal and pulled it back over the top intending to get out the following night.' But the Germans were mounting a determined search for British soldiers on the run. 'They went through it [the coal shed] really thoroughly and fished us out and that was the end of that.'

A few Airborne troops are killed in the act of surrender, others hauled alive from the ruins while some caught trying to escape are either gunned down, wounded, or put their hands up. The British fight to the end with a ferocity that earns the respect of their Waffen SS opponents who have faced plenty of tough opponents in the past.

At least one incident does, however, test the willingness of the SS troops to give their foe mercy. The loss of a much-loved officer named Vogel really enrages some SS troops for, as one of the *panzergrenadiers* relates, he is 'shot in the heart during close-quarter fighting'. An attempt by a medic to give the dying officer aid, sees the medic shot and killed by the British.

According to Rottenführer Rudolf Trapp 'this made the boys very angry' and they were determined 'to do the "Tommies" in!'[186]

Later, on at least one occasion, a Waffen SS officer has to stop his men from executing surrendered British paratroopers. Trapp and his comrades do not take their vengeance and instead give prisoners biscuits and chocolate. One Waffen SS officer does decide a captive is so badly wounded he is not going to live, so puts him out of his misery with a pistol shot to the head.[187]

Outside the St Elizabeth hospital, where many of the British wounded from the bridge fight are being treated alongside the Germans, there will be a notorious incident.

A drunken Waffen SS combat reporter named Karl Gustav Lerche summarily executes a British Airborne doctor, Capt Brian Brownscombe, shooting him in the back of the head. Lerche does not entirely escape justice, for, after the war, he will be put on trial, found guilty of committing a war crime, and sentenced to ten years in jail, though only serves five.[188]

On the whole, the Waffen SS show a level of mercy to the British they would not have accorded the Russians on the Eastern Front. They do in this case abide by civilised rules of war and ensure wounded Airborne troops receive medical aid rather than a bullet.

In one episode, a Waffen SS NCO even offers surrendered British soldiers his cigars. He tells them: 'That was a lovely battle. Have a cigar. We are human too.' The German NCO invites his foes to sit down with him and have a smoke. Lt Tom Ainslie later relates that they 'had a matey chat about the events of the past few days.'[189]

After the war, Lt Col Frost will maintain the enemy did not beat his troops and blames the conditions they were forced to fight in, 'they could not have much chance with no ammunition, no rest and with no positions from which to fight. No body of men could have fought more courageously and tenaciously than the officers and men of the 1st Para Bde at Arnhem bridge.'[190]

Maj Gough makes his own bid to escape, intending to hide out in some waterworks, but, before he can disappear, a German foot patrol comes into sight. He tries to conceal himself under a pile of wood. Unfortunately, a boot heel still shows, and he is unceremoniously hauled out of there.

It is a ludicrous end to his Arnhem adventure. The 43-year-old Airborne warrior, who served as a junior officer in Royal Navy battleships during the First World War – joining the army in the 1920s – is being taken prisoner by enemy soldiers who were not even born during that previous conflict (and indeed not for some years later).

Once Gough is firmly in custody, a Waffen SS officer, who has heard about him commanding the British force at the bridge, comes to see him.

He extends his congratulations for a masterful fight. Explaining that he is a veteran of urban combat at Stalingrad, the Waffen SS officer says he can tell that Gough and his men must also have fought in many such battles too. Gough begs to differ and tells him: 'This was our first effort. We'll be much better next time.'[191]

—

The captured Maj Deane-Drummond, meanwhile, gets his own close-up look at devastation around the northern end of the Arnhem bridge. After being questioned at the battalion HQ of the unit he stumbled into, he is put in an open-topped *Kubelwagen*, which then drives east and across the Rhine.

> '…the battle for that bridge had just finished and it was covered in broken down and burning trucks and half-tracks actually on the bridge itself…'

He is taken to a church where there are quite a number of able-bodied British prisoners being held, plenty of whom he recognises. As he can speak a little German, he buttonholes a guard and tells him the Geneva Convention demands food is provided for all these hungry people. The guard tells him they will be fed soon enough.

—

At Nijmegen, unaware as yet that the road bridge in Arnhem is entirely in enemy hands, the Guards Armoured resume their advance at 11.00am but soon hit trouble.

A German self-propelled gun destroys six Shermans in quick succession, causing a tailback of 48 other British tanks unable to get by to attack the enemy. The curse of radio faults strikes again, frustrating attempts to call down Typhoon fighters to blast the enemy out the way.

Any thoughts of further advance are abandoned while the Guards wait to be supported by the battle-weary troops of the 43rd (Wessex) Div.

They are struggling to make their way through the carnage of 'Hell's Highway', as the besieged main route of attack has become known.

Overnight in Oosterbeek, there has been severe shelling, meaning little sleep for Jan and the others in the cellar below De la Reyweg 9. During a lull in the firing, it is suggested decisive action should be taken.

> 'Taking into account that we have no more food and only a very limited amount of water, Walter suggests this may be an opportunity to move somewhere safer, but where? After a discussion, it is decided to head for Heveadorp where Annie's parents live. However, the two old ladies and the older couple do not, under any circumstances, want to come along. So the party will consist of Mum, Gini, myself, Rika, Walter and Annie. We venture out with as many "fleeing bags" as possible attached to a broomstick held by Walter and myself – and some white cloth on a stick, to signal for us not to be shot at. But grenades explode everywhere. There is smoke and fumes. The street is covered by all kinds of debris from houses and trees that are shot to pieces by artillery fire. When we approach the Utrechtseweg from the Steynweg, moving in the direction of Hartenstein, we can hardly make progress, because of all the mess on the road – dead paratroopers, wrecked vehicles, bits of debris and we can see houses on fire. When a volley of grenades explodes close to us, my mother screams for us not to continue. She turns around,

> we drop everything, including the broomstick with the "fleeing bags" and myself, Mum and Gini hurry back to our "safe" cellar. A few minutes later Rika, Walter and Annie come back too, returned by two paratroopers who announce they had been "walking into hell" and so are better off returning.'

The problem of finding sustenance has not gone away, so Jan and Walter go in search of food in the house, finding 'a few pots of preserved food, so we had a little bit to eat, albeit we could not heat it anymore. But water was short again.'

Cpl Tucker is by now in a house overlooking a junction where a Tiger tank has stopped to let some *panzergrenadiers* climb down. Perhaps the sight of this metal monster might cow others into holding fire but not the defiant paratrooper, who only wishes he had a bigger weapon.

> 'If I had been armed with a PIAT, then I could have taken the blighter out dead easy. The Tiger was firing down the road in the direction of the Hartenstein while these two panzergrenadiers carrying a mortar jumped off. As one of them ran off with the tube of the mortar I shot him. Then his mate made a dash for it carrying the base plate and I shot him as well. Wondering what the heck was going on, the tank commander suddenly popped his head up out of the tank to take a look, so I let off a few rounds at him too.'

Fortunate not to have had his brains blown out – and realising the location from where the fire is coming – the Tiger commander instructs his crew to turn the turret and aim at the house in which Tucker is lurking.

The black maw of the 88mm gun belches fire and smoke, the shell demolishing part of the front of the building, sending

Tucker flying. While he lands in an untidy heap, the other three paratroopers have tumbled out the back of the house.

The dust and debris settle, and, after a little while, the tank moves on, so they come back in to try and find Tucker, expecting to discover him mangled and very dead.

> 'Luckily I only had concussion, but my rifle – an M1 carbine I had acquired – had fallen out of the window as I flew backwards. It now lay on the front doorstep.'

With plenty of enemy snipers eager for kills lurking in the neighbourhood, it would be foolish for Tucker to brazenly expose himself to get the carbine back. It is a lightweight weapon, so he may still be able to retrieve it by applying ingenuity to the process.

> 'Going down into the cellar and looking out a window I could see where it was lying. Using a coat hanger I made a wire hook and spent the next half an hour pulling it back through into the house via the cellar window.'

At the Vredehof villa, de Soet comes up from his cellar to ask the soldiers how the battle beyond is going. *Is liberation nearer?* He is told by the paratroopers they still hope to hold on until the Second Army finally gets across the Rhine. He wonders how this will be possible, as even visiting houses just a few yards away means dicing with death.

> 'Our house lies on a corner [of Weverstraat and Fangmanweg]. It is impossible to cross the roads. We can only reach our neighbour through a little gate in the garden wall. All around our house are English soldiers either in dug-outs or lying flat against walls. Every hedge behind which a German is seen, or supposed to be, is fired at.'

Having cleared the British out from the Arnhem road bridge, the Germans increase their attacks on the divisional perimeter. In response, the Airborne artillery is again firing over de Soet's house.

> 'It is such a terrible noise that you cannot distinguish the English from the German discharges. Explosions, detonation, whistling, hits. Continuous falling of debris and the sound of shrapnel on the stones.'

A British soldier explains to him that this kind of urban fighting is perfect for paratroopers. 'In open country,' he tells de Soet, 'we would long since have been annihilated.'

Worried as ever about the plight of the civilians down in the Vredehof villa's cellar, the paratroopers offer the Dutch tins of sardines, packets of tea and canned meat. All they ask for in return is the cigarettes they had given to them earlier. Four British paratroopers come down into the cellar and Ann de Soet washes their faces with Eau-de-Cologne. One of these exhausted soldiers, a veteran of many other battles, tells de Soet this is 'the hardest fight since D-Day.' He reveals the Germans have them surrounded, but if he gets home – and with so many of his friends having their lives cut short – he intends to go AWOL. He doesn't care if he ends up in prison, remarking heavily: 'Oh, I detest war.'

Beyond the cellar, the fighting reaches a new intensity.

'The tumult around and above us is terrific,' notes de Soet.

For all their weariness, the paratroopers get up to go back out into it, according to de Soet, telling themselves: *'Come on, we want to have Christmas in England.'* Then, 'they shake hands with my wife, kiss my little daughter, take their weapons and go upstairs into the hell of fire. Heroes they are.'

Capt Fletcher of the Glider Pilot Regt is sent out to visit positions around the perimeter, distributing what little food and ammunition is left.

He is also the bearer of false hope.

> 'The men asked when XXX Corps was going to arrive and I lied to them to keep their hopes up. I said: "They'll be here soon." But, in my head, I could hear this Greek chorus, which said "we've had it."'

On the afternoon of 21 September, there is much close quarters fighting in and around the White House position occupied by the KOSB. Capt Jim Livingstone, second in command of C Coy, is among those facing a mob of charging, screaming Waffen SS troops – an assault like something out of the First World War – which threatens to overwhelm the KOSB.

Livingstone waits in his slit trench until they are about 20 yards away and then opens fire, later observing of this moment: 'I killed an awful lot of Germans then, with my Sten.'[192]

By a tree in front of Livingstone's trench is a wounded SS soldier, who is on his knees, but still trying to fire his weapon. Capt David Clayhills, who is standing over by the main hotel building screams: 'Kill the bastard!'

Livingstone fires a burst of Sten gun fire, later confessing: I'm a bit ashamed of it now, but I was bloody angry at the time. The rest of his party were already dead. Mind you, there was some of our dead as well.'[193]

With smoke still drifting over the scene – the stench of cordite in his nostrils and grass wet with blood, his ears ringing from all the firing – Livingstone takes in the carnage. His attention is drawn back to Capt Clayhills 'standing near this big tree, and there were an awful lot of dead Germans lying around it – twenty or thirty at least, young men mostly.'[194]

The Waffen SS do maintain a grip on part of the White House grounds, but a bayonet charge is swiftly organised to eject them, which many of the British soldiers find an excellent release after days of being bombarded by German artillery. The 7th KOSB's own account of the action drily describes its men as being motivated by 'a state of extreme exasperation at the continuous shelling and sniping.'[195]

Time for payback and, as one regimental account puts it, the Borderers 'rose in their wrath and slew them – uttering the most blood-curdling howls…'[196] The charge 'cleared the enemy from the vicinity, leaving large numbers of his dead on the field.'[197]

The KOSB killed an estimated 100 SS troops during the battle for the White House and paid a sly tribute to those who made the mass assault: 'The enemy were picked SS troops and put up a most gallant fight to the last, but they had taken on rather more than they had bargained for.'[198]

In the process, the hotel has been set on fire and suffers serious structural damage and, on the veranda of the White House, is an extraordinary sight. The battalion HQ Company boss, Maj Alex Cochran is lying, pistol in hand, right next to a Waffen SS officer, also dead, and with Luger in hand.

'The Battle of the White House will long be remembered by all those who took part,' says the War Diary of the 7th KOSB. The price paid by the battalion, over the course of two days' fighting, is 150 dead and wounded, a high proportion of them officers and NCOs.

In the aftermath, an aid post in the hotel is moved, and Maj Gen Urquhart agrees with Lt Col Payton-Reid that it is better for the KOSB to withdraw to a position more easily defended in line with the perimeter.

Whereas everywhere is holding fast against the enemy, the Border Regt has been forced off the crucial high ground at Westerbouwing that dominates the river where the Driel ferry has been operating even during the fighting. It is by now out of action. The ferry was never utilised by the British, but the crossing point itself will become crucial to their fate and that of the entire mission.[199]

In addition to increasing numbers of self-propelled guns – along with flame-thrower tanks and mobile anti-aircraft guns – the Germans have assembled more than 100 artillery guns around the perimeter, also bringing in *Nebelwerfer* rocket launchers. All this fire is now pouring into what they have christened *Der Hexenkessel* (*The Witches Cauldron*) or, as it will become known by British veterans, The Cauldron. It is 3,600ft long and 2,400ft wide, enclosing around 3,000 defenders.

In the centre of this storm remain thousands of civilians cowering in the cellars. With sheer terror overwhelming some, they try fleeing to find what they hope are deeper, stronger places that will better withstand the bombardment. De Soet characterises the moment as 'despairingly critical'.

> 'It is 4.30pm. Somebody wants to leave the cellar to go upstairs. I have to refuse. I explain the situation. The Germans may enter the house and cellar at any moment. From now on nobody is allowed to leave his place without my consent. The front door bell is rung continuously. Outside there is a man and a woman. Their house has been burned down. We take them in. The woman scolds the Germans violently. She is hysterical. We succeed in calming her down. We now number 20 in the cellar. This is all it can hold. Again it is quiet in the cellar, but a loaded quietness. We wait for the coming events … modern war is 80 per cent noise and 20 per cent danger. Through the roaring of the guns we hear the tanks coming on. Suddenly there is a big crowd at the top of the stairs; the inhabitants of a house nearby. Their house has had a hit. About 30 people want to get in. Most of the women are half crazy with fear. A father has to use all his strength to hold his fourteen-year-old daughter in check who is kicking and yelling with all her might. Shells whistle and explode everywhere. In the cellar the tension becomes unbearable, Above, a troop of distracted people. I block the cellar stairs. I shout at them, that anybody who cannot keep quiet will be knocked

senseless. Everybody must lay flat on the floor in the hall and the kitchen. Shells keep on exploding all around us. They may hit us at any moment. The crowd obeys, only the girl keeps on yelling and kicking. I tell the father to knock her senseless. "I cannot, Sir", he says, "you do it, please". Within my reach I find a wooden hammer. I threaten her with it. Then she is quiet. I fetch a soothing medicine and her father lets her drink it. These people cannot be allowed in the cellar. Their fear would contaminate the others, and then a panic could not be avoided. An old woman, with a money chest under her arm, slips through under my arms. I let her go. She is quiet. I send one of the men back to the damaged house. I presume the cellar there is still habitable. After three long minutes he comes back and shouts: "We can go back, the cellar has not been hit". The people don't move. I threaten them and say: "When I count three, everybody must have gone". I count "one, two, three" and meekly they go, bowing under the terrible shell fire.'

Houses to the south and east are ablaze, as the Germans are using phosphorous shells, just as they did against buildings near the road bridge stubbornly occupied by Airborne troops. The fires around the Vredehof villa also threaten to consume it and then everybody will have to leave its cellar or die. De Soet goes up into the house to assess how hopeless the situation is.

'The fires around us are growing, roofs and fences fall ... crackling and produce clouds of sparks... It is a dramatic sight to see all those well-known houses perish by fire...'

What chances of survival amid this? How will they last for even a short time if the fire consumes everything above ground?

> 'There are just two gas masks against the smoke.
> Everyone else must put wet towels over the mouths
> and if the fire catches the house on fire then they
> will leave and take shelter outside until the fire has
> finished consuming the house and then go back
> down into cellar. It does not happen, yet.'

Amid all this, the Germans attack the house at 5.00pm, but are repulsed – the frightened people in the cellar reassured by the courageous example of the British soldiers who keep de Soet informed of what is happening. He strikes up a good rapport with their commander, RQMS David Morris of the 11th Bn, the Parachute Regt and Pte Jimmy Carr.

For the rest of the night, the Germans content themselves with probing all around the Vredehof, but do not mount a further attack. David and Jimmy come down into the cellar to get some sleep while a wakeful de Soet ponders the strangeness of war.

> 'I review the situation – next to me Englishmen,
> who last week were still in England, the country to
> which our thoughts had gone out so often. Outside,
> Germans patrolling cautiously. Two world powers at
> war, fighting at a distance of 25 yards from each other
> and between them 20 sleeping civilians.'

In the cellar of the house on the Reyweg, Jan and Walter decide they will make another dash to the water pump by the butcher's shop. Jan's mother protests, urging them not to take the risk. They go with her pleas ringing in their ears. On the way back, carrying three buckets full of sloshing water, such is their hurry they don't even bother to take cover.

'It is a miracle that we get back unharmed,' reflects Jan, 'and also still with the water in the buckets. That evening, the cellar door is opened by "our" paratroopers, who ask us if one of their injured companions can be allowed to spend a few hours in our cellar, which, of course, we permit.'

The battle above ground appears to be taking a turn for the worse, with the Airborne troops still not getting the supplies they need by air, while casualties increase and the enemy bombardment is even more intense.

'The whole night there is shooting and shells fall so close that we regularly feel the air pressure of the explosions in the cellar,' notes Jan. 'A few times, earth falls into the vent hole, and it is certainly not reassuring. Nobody can sleep, even for a minute.'

―

At the Hartenstein, an entry is made at 9.44pm in the Divisional Diary of the 1st Airborne, which notes that nothing has been heard from units in Arnhem itself for 24 hours. It observes that the situation in Oosterbeek is grim, within a 'very tight perimeter' subjected to 'heavy mortaring and machine-gun fire... Our casualties heavy. Rations stretched to utmost. Relief within twenty-four hours vital.'[200]

―

Deane-Drammond and other British prisoners have by now been marched to the village of Velp, around four miles to the east of Arnhem, ending up at a large house with two monkey puzzle trees in its garden.

He meets Tony Hibbert and gets the story of the battle at the bridge. Hibbert tells him they 'inflicted fearful casualties on the Germans' but ran out of ammo and water and the wounded were at risk of being burned alive. As an experienced escaper Deane-Drummond advises Hibbert not to waste any time in formulating a plan.[201]

> 'My advice always was to escape in the first few
> minutes, or first few hours or first few days and don't

get [weighed down by] the anti-climax of being made a prisoner. You don't want to think to yourself you have to wait until the prison camp to get out.'

Looking around the large room they are being kept in, Deane-Drummond can't see any feasible means of escape. His eyes fall on a wall cupboard, which he explores. It is about 6ft high and a foot deep. He pulls out shelves, stacks them up. Best of all, the exterior of the cupboard door is covered over with wallpaper, so isn't too, obvious. The key is still in the lock, which Deane-Drummond slips into his pocket, thinking he can 'just about stand it for a couple of days then the 2nd Army would arrive… So, I got into this cupboard with not very much food, because we'd [only] had a bit of sort of German bully [beef], which was all I'd had for the five days since dropping [into Holland]…'

He has enough water to last a little longer: a quart and 'another pint which I could put on the shelf above me and one could reach 'round and get to it. As far as food was concerned I didn't find it very attractive – I had a lump of German brown bread, which rapidly became extremely stale and was very dry and, really, what one wanted was water rather than food. I poked myself in there and that night they took details of all the people who were in that prison cage, which I avoided and I was not then listed.'

Lt Todd of Jedburgh Team Claude is, by Thursday evening, concealed up a tree in the garden of a house not far from the road bridge.

He had been part of a bid to get away in the early hours of that morning, along with assorted British comrades attempting to slip though enemy lines to reach Oosterbeek. They were spotted by the enemy, with a machine gun opening up, hitting Todd in the leg. In response, he hurled a grenade in the direction of his assailants and blew them up.

Getting to his feet, Todd sprinted through some wrecked buildings, with bullets kicking up dust at his heels. Flattening himself, against a wall to catch his breath, Todd wondered how to get himself out of the fix he was in, especially with no weaponry at all left. On hearing a German patrol approaching, he hauled himself up into the foliage of a tree. Feeling for his leg wound, Todd discovered he had been lucky – the enemy bullet hit an empty Sten gun magazine in a trouser pocket. His leg was only bruised.

Judging the battle now well and truly over – the Germans taking a night off rounding up enemy fugitives – Todd now slides down the tree, pulls himself under a bush, and sinks gratefully into sleep.

Friday

22 September

'Wounding and death, burning towns and rotting bodies, the stench, the carnage and horror of war: all these could become as habitual and acceptable as commuting on the eight-fifteen.'

—Zeno, *The Cauldron*[202]

With German tanks rolling through British positions in the glades and woods, spraying death to left and right, there are also fierce struggles along the streets of Oosterbeek – often house-by-house. There is hand-to-hand combat in small rooms where the dagger, grenade and pistol count for more than the rifle. The tenacity of the British in such circumstances is why the Germans adopt tried-and-tested tactics to flush their enemy out into the open.

Dennis Clay thinks fleeing is the better part of valour when a 60-ton Tiger crashes through the house he is in.

> 'The Germans shelled us first, setting it on fire and then moved in to do a demolition job. As the Tiger came in I ended up moving from room to room and house to house, just managing to stay ahead of it. Others were not so lucky.'

Having lost control of the DZs and LZs, the Airborne troops watch in fury and agony as Allied air forces continue to deliver on schedule, but again drop the majority of supplies to the enemy, paying a heavy price in aircraft shot down and aircrew killed.

Scavenging is widespread as military rations run low. Stan Turner is among those venturing forth as part of the hunt for food, and it nearly costs him his life.

> 'During the day I go in search of food and for some reason pause before crossing a gap between two trees. There is a spatter of machine gun fire, which throws up splinters from the tree to my right. I take cover in a nearby slit trench.'

While those who fight in woods might have little left to forage for, the occupants of houses raid pantries and storage cupboards. British soldiers are delighted to find tinned food along with 'bottled tomatoes, French beans, and other vegetables'.[203] Gardens are ransacked and, for some lucky pantry foragers, it is sometimes possible to rustle up chicken, pork, and beefsteak for their comrades[204], all chucked in the pot for mixed stew. Rabbits left in back garden hutches are not likely to survive long.

In one case a dispute between ranks develops, with a soldier stealing and killing a rabbit that an officer has been feeding with odd bits of lettuce and cabbage. Force to yield the dead animal, it is left by the officer's trench, but a German shell obliterates it before it can be prepared for the pot.[205]

Sgt Lewis Haig of the Glider Pilot Regt – real name Louis Hagen, whose father in the 1930s held a senior position with BMW in Berlin – enjoys delving into preserves and pickle jars his British-born comrades in arms recoil from. Haig – who now considers himself more British than German – had in 1934, escaped a likely brutal death in the Torgau concentration camp, from where he was sprung by a well-connected family friend.

With the memory of 'smug and conceited'[206] Nazi thugs strutting the streets of Potsdam where he grew up still fresh in his mind, Haig is waging an energetic war against his former overlords.

After some close shaves under fire while crawling about in woods and hiding in gardens, he is delighted to chase some of the enemy out of houses by hurling grenades and firing his Sten gun.

Together with an officer, the 27-year-old NCO goes up into the attic of one house and fires PIAT rounds through a hole in the roof at a self-propelled gun halted down below. The explosions do not cause any significant damage, but the Germans are worried enough to withdraw.

For all his warlike spirit Haig decides: 'I hate war. I can't stop thinking of the friends and relatives of anyone who has been hit. I know the Germans. I have seen them do the most vile and frightening things… But I do not enjoy killing or wounding anyone.'[207]

However, when forced to fight, Haig devotes all his powers to it. He does not care about the effect on the enemy – the one-time countrymen upon whom he is pleased to visit revenge.

In the early hours of the battle for Oosterbeek, others do pity a slain enemy and feel for the family he leaves behind, but the experience of combat soon eradicates that. SSgt Arthur Shackleton, of the Glider Pilot Regt, kills a young German soldier whose helmet falls off.

> 'He was a true Aryan – blonde – his eyes were open.
> And I looked at him and I thought "his mother
> doesn't even know he is dead yet". How could I hate
> him?'

Not long after, during another firefight, bullets pepper his own position. 'The man next to me had half his face blown off. So, I lost that [softer] inhibition.'[208]

During lulls in the action, or under cover of darkness, the British soldiers not only go out to search houses for food but also to find sources of water, whether it be from radiators, water butts, toilet cisterns or wells.

In various houses baths were filled with water before the Germans cut the mains supply. These mini reservoirs are drawn on for cooking, even after the ceiling comes down in one bathroom – turning it into a 'thin, unpleasant porridge'[209] of dust and plaster. If water is not available, in some houses wine stocks are plundered to slake thirsts, including champagne and claret but also gin.

—

In his cupboard at the big house in Velp, Deane-Drummond tries to figure out what is happening on the other side of the door. He is 'just half standing … listening to what was going on'. He discerns the prisoners being moved out and furniture moved in.

He realises that the Germans have 'turned the room just outside my cupboard into an interrogation centre and the interrogation officer put the back of the chair just next to where my cupboard was. I was then able to hear this chap questioning all these people I knew quite well.' Deane-Drummond listens in over the next few days, fascinated to be 'a fly on the wall.'

Those being quizzed are asked for personal and military details, ostensibly so they can be passed on to the Red Cross. Surely this is a cover for getting much more than name, rank, and serial number as required under the Geneva Convention? Deane-Drummond judges that nothing given away by his comrades is a security breach.

—

By the morning of 22 September, Cpl Tucker and his three-man squad are holed up in the kitchen of a house close to a cluster of trees. They are on edge, against sudden lunges by the foe.

> 'The Germans were making constant forays, lobbing grenades and firing their machine guns. We had just managed to see them off again and I turned away from the kitchen window for a second – was about to say something to Smithy – when he suddenly started

firing his Sten gun in my direction. I threw myself on the floor and then leapt up, saying: "what the hell are you doing Smithy!?" I was very angry, but calmed down when he explained a German had popped up at the window behind me and was about to plug me with his machine gun. Smithy saved my life by killing that German.'

At the Vredehof villa, de Soet finds easy camaraderie with the British and this extends to even joining them to kill Germans. De Soet asks paratrooper NCO David Morris to give him a gun.

'He hands me one immediately, together with 21 cartridges. I hang the gun with a piece of string around my neck. Sitting on the stairs in the house David explains to me the working of it. It is an automatic gun… Then we go upstairs. The outlook from there is indescribable. It is like a panorama in a war film. Houses are burned down around [us] and in ruins. Between them [are] wrecked jeeps, cars and tanks. It is a cheerless and deserted sight. David points to a wall of a deserted house, burnt out, about 175 yards away from us. Nearby a burnt out tank. [He says:] "There are Germans behind the house. Wait, I'll frighten them up." He shoots.'

Startled, a German soldier leaps out from cover behind the house and throws himself down by 'a heap of rubbish.' Morris suggests to de Soet: 'Now you shoot.' He misses with his first shot and is instructed: 'No, higher.'

De Soet pulls the trigger again.

Morris suggests with a laugh: 'Perhaps you killed a German?'

They go back down into the house and find a couple of paratroopers busy making soup, but enemy shells start falling and so they all take cover in the cellar. De Soet hears someone anxiously enquire of a paratrooper: 'Your guns?'

> 'Hesitatingly the soldier says: "Yes," but his eyes [are] roving over his comrades, and I read in them that he means "Theirs". These valiant Englishmen feel what it means to us civilians to be suddenly in the hell of modern warfare. They sympathise with us as we slowly but surely see our village, our houses and possessions go to ruin.'

De Soet marvels at the cool heads, good manners and decency of the British soldiers who are kind and attentive to his family's needs, even amid all the fighting. 'They play with our little daughter and let us have some of their soup.' The paratroopers go out to fight again, but, later, in the midst of a heavy German tank assault, a soldier, who is perhaps not so relaxed as the others, comes down the cellar steps, gun ready to fire.

He demands: 'Germans here?'

They tell him 'no', and he warns them not to come out of the cellar or it is likely 'they will be shot down.'

A tank can be heard, its engine grumbling as it edges around the house. The cellar's occupants sit in frozen silence. The tank's gun barks – the house shudders to a hit, and de Soet and the others hear the response it provokes. 'Furiously answered by the British anti-tank guns... Death lurks around. We are prepared.'

Their hopes of surviving drain away as time slows down into the agony of waiting for the final blow that will end their lives – they no longer fear death, wishing only for it to be painless.

Nine soldiers creep down into the cellar, among them Morris, who whispers that everyone must be 'absolutely quiet'. The tank stops shooting, and now they can hear Germans directly above, walking around the house.

> 'When my little daughter is a little restless, the faces of the soldiers are painfully twisted. The least little noise may betray them and us. A couple of German hand grenades in the cellar and we will all be finished. We are like rats in a trap.'

A German shouts: 'Nein, hierher.'

De Soet whispers a translation in Morris' ear: *'No, this way.'*

He asks what they should do if the Germans come down into the cellar and Morris replies softly: 'We will surrender, or you will also be shot to death.' The British NCO pulls a pencil from a pocket and ties a white handkerchief to it. De Soet prays his child will not give them away, but fortunately she is distracted. 'My little daughter plays with her mother's purse. She has opened it and calmly tears a bank note of one hundred guilders to pieces.'

That doesn't matter, so long as she doesn't start crying out.

> 'The shooting continues. For hours we sit there. Finally we hear English soldiers calling outside. The greatest danger is over. The English leave the cellar.'

The paratroopers stalk the tank and destroy it with a PIAT shot, David inviting de Soet up into the attic to see their handiwork. 'I can see it burning, not quite 125 yards from us. They are heroes. All of them.'

One by one, the cellar inhabitants go above ground for a brief period to get some fresh air. Not far away, there are bursts of gunfire as the paratroopers hunt down enemy infantry who were with the tank.

De Soet sees that his house has received substantial damage from two hits – the kitchen has been demolished and the bath and toilet have come crashing down from upstairs.

—

North of Nijmegen, as cruel chance would have it, the 43rd (Wessex) Infantry Div faces the very same troops of the SS II Panzer Corps it grappled with during bitter fighting around Caen in Normandy in July. Both formations paid an especially heavy blood price during the bitter fight for Hill 112. That time, the 43rd Div won, playing a key role in forcing the Waffen SS into their traumatic retreat across France. On 22 September, with the help of 43rd Div infantry, who make flanking attacks (with anti-tank weapons), the Guards Armoured hope they will be able to resume their push from Nijmegen – but again, they make no progress, and the advance up the main highway is abandoned, a risk averse attitude that will be heavily criticised after the war.

Lt Col George Taylor, CO of the 5th Bn of the DCLI suggests to Lt General Horrocks that he should be allowed to lead a task force to reach the Rhine by another route. Contact can then be established with the 1st Airborne Div across the river, enabling both reinforcements and supplies to be sent across. Armoured cars of the 2nd Household Cavalry had already reached Driel and made contact with the Poles, though the Germans subsequently blocked the route they used.

In the meantime, the artillery of the 43rd Div is weighing into the fight at Oosterbeek. It conducts long-range fire support missions against German forces trying to snuff out the Airborne forces in The Cauldron. Its intervention has broken up at least one major attack and will shatter others.

Taylor's plan – which he admits is 'a shot in the dark'[210] – centres on using DUKW amphibious transport vessels to take the crucial supplies across the river.[211] Horrocks gives approval by noon, though Taylor thinks just two DUKWs packed with ammunition and other supplies, is somewhat inadequate, observing: 'we've got to get more than this across to them.'[212]

At 5.00pm, Taylor's force sets off – half-track troop carriers, lorries, the DUKWs, escorted by tanks of the Dragoon Guards with more infantry riding on them. They go at high speed, using side roads to try and evade any lurking enemy blocking forces.

Then, Taylor spots a couple of Tigers slowly churning their way towards a road his force is just about to head down. He decides to keep that information to himself, so his troops won't hesitate and hopefully stand a better chance of slipping past the panzers. Taylor dismounts his vehicle and stands at the side of the road waving the 5 DCLI column through.

Taylor prays the enemy will remain blind to what is happening. He tells a fellow officer who has just spotted the enemy tanks that he should keep quiet too, remarking: 'We cannot stop now.' Taylor then mounts his own vehicle and speeds off, later remarking of the dash to the Rhine: 'Any time lost would have given the enemy time to move up a blocking force.'[213]

The light begins to fade as Taylor's force – which, as it passes through villages en route, is cheered on by the Dutch – finally reaches the Rhine, at 5.30pm. The relief force suffers its first tank casualty, caused by a mine placed in the road by Polish paratroopers at Driel.[214]

Around 2,000 Poles are now on the south bank of the Rhine, the brigade's 3rd Bn taking up a position directly across the river from the church in Oosterbeek while the 2nd Bn covers the Driel ferry crossing. Having reached Polish-held territory, Lt Col Taylor still entertains the idea that troops and tanks under his command can swing east along the banks of the river, attacking the southern end of the bridge. They may yet make a link with the British Airborne troops holding the northern end. Such hopes are soon dashed.

Visiting Maj Gen Sosabowski's headquarters, located in a commandeered farmhouse, Taylor meets two 1st Airborne officers – a British engineer and the Polish liaison officer attached to Urquhart's staff – who have swum across the river. They tell him Frost's force at the bridge has been wiped out. Taylor's heart sinks further when he is informed the 1st Airborne Div is on the brink of annihilation.

That night, an alternate plan is put into action anyway. Polish paratroopers will go across the Rhine in dinghies with the assistance of combat engineers on both sides of the river. The engineers will also ensure there is a safe launch point on one side and landing spot on the other for the DUKWs, which can then make an attempt to cross at first light on 23 September. Taylor is also determined to send his troops across to help the hard-pressed Airborne, if he can.

As 5 DCLI troops not in the motorised vanguard of the relief task force make their way to the southern banks of the Rhine, they have a fight with an enemy armoured force. Once again, they show their old foes in the Waffen SS they know how to take on and destroy panzers.

Using expertly placed mines and a storm of PIAT fire they destroy the enemy force, knocking out three Tigers; two others are abandoned by their crews after trying to reverse out of the fight in a panic and getting stuck in ditches. A recklessly brave infantryman finishes off a Tiger already crippled by mines. He dashes forward to within a few feet and puts a PIAT shot into the armoured giant. Pte Brown loses an eye in the back-blast but, as he is carried away for medical treatment, remarks with grim pride and typical Cornish grit: 'I don't care, I knocked the bugger out.'[215]

Such heroic stoicism is inspiring, but what the British need above all is a stroke of luck that will enable XXX Corps to exploit the initiative of Taylor's lunge across the polder to Driel. It can then throw its might over the Rhine to relieve the 1st Airborne Div and ensure its sacrifice is not in vain.

That night, at the Vredehof villa in Oosterbeek, attempts are made to clear up some of the debris inside the house before civilians and also some of the soldiers bed down in the cellar. De Soet asks himself, more in hope than realistic expectation: 'Shall we be liberated tomorrow?'

It rains, with de Soet thinking it 'sounds like the crackling of a fire', so he goes up to look outside. British troops are crouching in their slit trenches in his garden, trying to find shelter under their waterproofs, waiting wearily for the next German assault.

Saturday

23 September

'We shall make a fortress of this house...'

—RQMS David Morris, 11th Para Bn[216]

The Germans continue pouring fire and brimstone into The Cauldron from all sides. Despite this terrible pummelling, Maj Gen Urquhart is still hopeful of holding on so that a bridgehead can be established on the north bank of the Rhine by XXX Corps.

Starting at 9.00pm the previous evening, Polish paratroopers made their valiant effort to get across the Rhine in dinghies, also conveying rafts carrying supplies. The Germans soon spotted something was going on and opened fire, killing many of the brave Poles. Only 50 men made it across the river along with a paltry amount of supplies.

Once in Oosterbeek, the Poles continue their quest for vengeance against the Germans, taking every opportunity to kill as many as possible. When British troops make their way through Polish positions they are extra careful not to be shot by trigger-happy defenders. They sometimes take a Polish paratrooper with them to shout requests not to fire on their friends. The Germans know they can expect no quarter from the Poles who, according to one British admirer, fight 'like demons.'[217]

The arrival of the Polish brigade on the south bank of the Rhine causes the Germans to divert forces that might otherwise be sent against the Oosterbeek perimeter. It is feared the 10th SS might find itself cut off as it battles to prevent the enemy from reaching Arnhem along the main highway.

The next attempt to get across the river is mounted in the early hours of 23 September. Dozens of soldiers from the 5 DCLI are on hand each side of the cumbersome, heavily laden DUKWs to try and ensure the vehicles do not slip into ditches. At 2.00am, the DUKWs begin their move towards the Rhine, but bad luck strikes again, for the surface of the narrow road is covered in both thick mud and – nearer the river – a layer of mist. This makes it impossible to distinguish road from ditch.

Despite the efforts of many hands to hold them on the roadway, the two DUKWs slither into ditches just yards from the river. They are stuck fast, and Lt Col Taylor is forced to call the operation off. Other DUKWS will later make it across the Rhine but then get marooned in the mud on the other side and are abandoned.

The rest of the 43rd Div is by now trying desperately to reach the river – also using side roads – but, back down Hell's Highway, German counter-attacks are severing the main route in several places. Troops and tanks are forced to halt their advance and turn to meet these assaults rather than press on for Arnhem.

—

Even now Stan Turner and his comrades within the grounds of the Hartenstein have yet to be subjected to the worst the enemy can do. As the perimeter contracts – with anti-tank guns of the division whittled down while the foe's firepower builds up despite the distraction of the south bank Poles – the storm of fire descending on the centre of the pocket will grow.

> 'We had heard rumours of tanks and self-propelled guns. Today they become a fact. Looking up a hill from our position we see a very large tank. We say to ourselves: "What can we do against it with the rifles and sten guns?" There is a lull in the German

shelling because they don't want to hit their own tank. Luckily it moves off, but then the shelling starts again.'

One bombardment catches Sgt Gordon Walker in the open. He has ventured out of cover to fetch water from a well and, as he and a fellow soldier lower the bucket, they expect 'a bullet in the back at any second.'[218]

Returning to their position, enemy mortar bombs and shells burst in the trees around them, sending hot shrapnel flying. Walker hurls himself into what he thinks is an empty trench only to find it has a tiny inhabitant – a squirrel. Not keen on sharing his space with the frantic animal, Walker scoops it up and throws it into the trees.

The enraged squirrel is having none of that and scampers back, biting Walker, who is pressed right down into the bottom of the trench. Squirming around him, the squirrel burrows into the earth underneath.

Walker – who survived the Dunkirk evacuation and service with the Desert Rats in North Africa without a scratch before joining the Parachute Regt – later describes this bizarre episode as being 'the stupid position of me, a soldier, fighting a little squirrel for possession of a slit trench.'[219]

Actually, it is not that unusual for such a contest to take place between soldiers and squirrels for, as Walker adds, 'they couldn't live in the woods [due to the battle] and very sensibly occupied slit trenches and were not at all keen on a human being there too. Sharp little teeth they've got.'[220]

There are other surreal incidents that demonstrate ordinary everyday concerns persist, including caring for domesticated animals, and that, amid the brutality there is room for common, decent humanity. A young girl emerges from the cellar below the house where Cpl Tucker is waiting grimly for more German attacks.

'She offered me, Smithy, Lownes and Miller apple slices from a china plate,' Tucker recalled. 'We had not much water or food, so her offer was very much appreciated.'

Later, the girl comes back up and says she is worried about a horse she keeps in stables out the back. 'Can I go and look to see if the horse is safe?' the girl asks, in perfect English.

'No you can't because the Germans will shoot you,' Tucker replies.

The girl won't go back down into the cellar and pleads with him to let her take care of the horse. 'I must go... I must go,' she insists. Tucker relents, opening the kitchen door and cautiously taking a look outside.

> 'The firing appeared to have quietened down a little and I persuaded myself, against my better judgement and the advice of the others, that we could have a go at tending to the horse.'

Tucker goes out first, every sense straining, and expecting a fusillade of bullets any moment. At the bottom of the kitchen steps, the girl dips a bucket in a water barrel and follows Tucker across the backyard to the stables. Surprisingly, the horse is still alive, although the stables are peppered with bullet holes and shrapnel tears.

> 'I told the girl to hurry up with feeding and watering the horse. We then went back across the yard and she thanked me for helping her. The thing that still amazes me is that not a single shot was fired at us during the whole episode. Maybe the Germans were showing us some mercy, or maybe they were just temporarily out of ammo.'

For paratroopers in the Vredehof villa, ammunition is running low, the Germans gradually closing the ring around them. There is, however, enough food for three weeks stowed away in various places. De Soet brings it all down into the cellar, but water is getting short, though the baby has some condensed milk.

Pte Carr goes out to a brook to get some water – using an empty condensed milk can – but a bullet holes it. He takes another can out and has better luck, returning to the cellar without it getting punctured. Next Carr takes food across to civilians in another cellar.

Chatting with RQMS Morris, de Soet asks why the German tanks only mount solo forays and is told it is because the enemy do not have that many. Morris promises de Soet the Second Army will soon arrive – and they will have thousands of tanks. This seasoned veteran is dismissive of the enemy infantry whom he describes as being 'like children'. He again hands de Soet a gun, suggests they go up to the attic, to have another go at shooting Germans. 'We look through a hole in the roof over the sea of debris, wrecked cars, and tanks,' reports de Soet.

> 'Suddenly on the left near a rather intact house, about 175 yards away from us, I see three Germans raise up. One has his back turned to us. Two others I see sideways. I touch David. He sees them too. Calmly he takes aim, a shot ... the middle one drops down. The others dive down in cover. The collapsed German raises one hand, like [he is] seeking hold. "Heil Hitler," whispers David softly.'

As enemy shells begin falling around the house, Morris quickly instructs de Soet in how to work his gun.

> 'The Germans seem to be attacking again, for at intervals they jump up from behind the debris, run a

> few paces and drop down again. When they jump up we shoot them down. We fire in turns or simultaneously. The rifle is heavy. I perceive that I am weak through lack of food and sleep. We are shooting through holes in the roof. My rifle is empty. David loads it again.'

The assault is coming in from all sides, and de Soet feels his actions are symbolic of an entire nation's struggle, its hopes of rising to cast off the yoke of the occupiers.

> 'I realise my unique position, defending my country, from my own house. It looks more like something in mediaeval times than of our 20th Century. The thought, that they are human beings that are being killed, human beings with their own remembrances and longings, on whose return others are waiting who have been brought up with love and care, this thought is strangely repulsed. They are simply "Germans" who are trying to annihilate these fine valiant fellows… Germans who want to destroy my home. David instructs me, when I am not shooting, to keep my finger away from the trigger for safety's sake. I shoot once more. David twice.'

De Soet's eye is drawn to a surreal sight: 'I see a couple of escaped rabbits on a little lawn near a dead German.'

Two paratroopers come up to take over in the attic. Morris indicates to them where the Germans are before he and de Soet descend to the cellar. Morris informs its occupants that there is to be an attack against the Germans at 3.00pm. Ann de Soet asks how best to help when the soldiers get wounded. Not wanting to put civilians in harm's way, Morris replies:

> 'Leave us where we are, and don't come near us. We will help ourselves and each other.'

The British soldiers exit the house to make their attack, leaving the cellar dwellers feeling bereft, or, as de Soet puts it, 'isolated and deserted'. They become fatalistic as the Germans mount a counterattack.

> 'The tumult of an oncoming all-destroying tank is terrific. Finally life is not complicated any more. There is only one thing worth considering, that is, to live... We don't care for food any longer. Our earthly belongings are slowly crumbling to pieces above us. There is not even the possibility of a wash. Yes, there is only one thing that is absorbing all our thoughts, that is the soldiers. Those heroes, who outside in the dark carry their anti-tank gun from one side to the other – they are at it again, they won't surrender. It will not be their fault if this battle is lost... One of them comes downstairs, his face blackened with gun-powder. With one hand he wipes the sweat from his forehead with the other he dives into his pocket and says "Here are some sweets for the children," and on [out into the fight] he goes again.'

De Soet sees that each person in the cellar copes differently with the nearness of death – finding courage via their own particular means of distraction.

> 'Some of them have pulled their blankets over their heads, feeling safer perhaps this way. Others are moaning softly. There is also an old gentleman, his raincoat and his hat on, and an umbrella in his hand. He sits there as if he expects the conductor to call out at any moment, "Terminal station, all get out here".'

At the Vredehof villa there is a desperate cry at the kitchen door from Pte Carr, who has found it locked and cannot get back into the house. The key has been 'lost somewhere in the debris' and de Soet leaves the cellar to help. He fetches a hatchet to help the increasingly frantic paratrooper, who fears he will be killed at any moment. Even hacking away at the door fails to budge it, while outside the sound of machine gun fire rises in intensity.

Carr yells: 'Get out of the way! I'll shoot the lock open.'

He fires three times, but it doesn't work, so de Soet tries that hatchet again but despite chopping at the lock, the door still won't open. Carr decides to use his rifle butt, stumbling through the shattered remains of the door, declaring it 'a narrow escape!'

Carr has a dog with him – the animal has been his companion since he first turned up at the Vredehof villa – and which has just been wounded slightly in a leg. Down in the cellar, Carr dresses the dog's leg wound, then attends to that of the teenage girl who was injured earlier.

De Soet counts 20 people and three dogs now sheltering in the cellar, living off British 'sweets, biscuits and chocolates' and tinned sardines, while also grateful for the soup cooked up by the soldiers.

After taking a brief rest down below, some paratroopers with blackened faces fix bayonets to their rifles as a precursor to going back into battle. De Soet asks one of them if he has ever used it.

'So far, only once,' he replies.

An officer calls down from above: 'Come up into this bloody fight!'

De Soet looks on in awe as they return to 'the hell of fire, steel and gunpowder.'

The exact nature of 'this bloody fight' the officer has ordered the paratroopers to join him in the street outside the Vredehof villa – possibly even in its garden – can only be imagined by de Soet.

One paratrooper who fought at Oosterbeek describes such a tussle to the death as 'a confused mass of struggling, leaping figures' grappling with each other in slit trenches and bushes, where pistols and bayonets are the best weapons to use. Sten gun shots have to be very carefully aimed and preferably at

Germans on the periphery of the fight, where they can be picked off without killing one of your own side. Death is delivered at intimate ranges, with no quarter asked and none given. A Waffen SS trooper who has vanquished one paratrooper – leaving him dead in a bloodied, crumpled heap at the bottom of a slit trench – may himself be killed by another British soldier who jams a gun in his face and pulls the trigger.[221]

For the paratroopers at the Vredehof villa it appears the moment of truth is here. Morris comes down into the cellar to explain, talking very fast:

> 'This is the end of the line. From now on we retire no more. We shall make a fortress of this house. We shall barricade the doors and windows, and we shall not leave this house again.'

Going back up with the paratrooper NCO, de Soet indicates furniture suitable for fortifying his home.

> 'We have two pianos, and a baby grand, which can be of good service. Old cherished pieces are heaped alongside. This is not important. We must hold this house until the Second Army arrives. We must, we must.'

De Soet informs the cellar occupants the house has now become a 'British fortress' though this news provokes some objections, from fear of the ferocity of the German attack that it may provoke. At 7.00pm, Morris calls de Soet upstairs and to the front door where he is greeted with 'a unique sight'.

> 'A dozen German SS soldiers stand with their hands up against the wall of our house. They are all staunch fellows... Four Britishers are busy disarming them. The helmets are thrown on the ground. One covers them with his Bren gun. In threes they are led down the street, two Britishers behind them.'

De Soet takes in the scene, finding his garden host to dead soldiers and a wrecked jeep, the ground also 'covered with branches and leaves of the trees, fences, and all kinds of war material.'

An explosion makes him leap back into the cover of the house. 'The group of prisoners fly apart. Some of them lay still.'

Morris comes over and reveals that one of the SS soldiers – who did not want to stay captured – set off a grenade.

By nightfall, there are 20 British soldiers holed up in the house, waiting for the enemy assault. Morris declines an offer of space in the cellar for his men. They need to be upstairs, ready throughout the house to repel the enemy. The Airborne soldiers settle down on the floors of various rooms, with de Soet and Morris handing out blankets to keep them warm.

Sunday

24 September

*'We remember the previous Sunday, the churchgoers and
our happiness to be liberated. Alas...'*

—Frans de Soet, Oosterbeek, September 1944

Just before dawn, de Soet and Morris go back up to the attic. The paratrooper lets off a few rounds to see if any enemy troops amid the rubble of the street below react and expose themselves. De Soet watches as he 'peers into the darkness of the early morning...'

> 'A German jumps up. A little further he falls down behind a wall. More of them follow. We are shooting in turns. Shells are coming over. It is getting lighter; David says he needs field glasses. I go downstairs to fetch them. I also take my camera upstairs. While David is looking out I take a few shots [with the camera]. "Three killed, and one wounded," he says. I see them too. After a little while David proposes to go down and get some breakfast.'

Morris again sends two soldiers up to the attic to take their turn on over-watch duty. He and de Soet manage to get an oil stove going, making some tea and an omelette.

In conversation with L/Cpl Harold Cook, de Soet learns that the soldier once saw Queen Wilhelmina of the Netherlands in

London and that he has fought in North Africa and Italy among other places. He reveals he was captured in Italy, but escaped.

Now Cook fancies helping to beat Germany and then taking part in the defeat of Japan. De Soet remarks how that is certainly one way to see the world. Cook observes drily that his current predicament in Oosterbeek is perhaps not the best means of realising that ambition.

The vibration of shells exploding not far away reaches the cellar, one of the paratroopers remarks to de Soet: 'It is a good thing, you have such a good cellar, else you would already all have been killed.'

At least British fighter planes are in action now, their strafing and rocketing runs described by the British as: 'Music to our ears'. However, the Airborne artillery is declining in effectiveness and the German vice shows no sign of loosening.

That morning, at the house in which Cpl Harry Tucker hides out in, L/Cpl Smith goes missing. Sent out to see if he can get more ammo and food, he doesn't come back. Such is the wielding of the scythe in The Cauldron.

'To this day I do not know what happened to Smithy,' recalls Tucker. 'Maybe he was killed by a sniper, or wounded and later died in captivity. So many disappeared never to be seen again.'

As the temporary truce to bring the wounded out and take them to St Elizabeth Hospital concludes, the fury descends again. In addition to increasing their bombardment, the Germans throw more self-propelled guns and tanks into battle.

These include 60 gigantic King Tigers shipped in by rail from the Reich to better grind the British into the dust. At one point three of these monsters stand off from a house containing Airborne troops and systematically demolish it with their 88mm guns.

Not far away, Cpl Tucker decides the house he and two surviving comrades are in is becoming too exposed. How long before it also becomes nothing more than a pile of bricks, tiles and shattered wood, mixed in with their body parts?

> 'We had also lost contact with anyone else and I wanted to try and link up with other troops near the divisional HQ. All three of us ran out the front door of the house. I took up cover in a large bush in the garden opposite ... the other two were either side of me...'

None of them sees a *panzergrenadier* sneak up to lob a grenade into the bush, the explosion ripping Tucker's legs to shreds. Ignoring his wounds – adrenalin surging through his body – Tucker leaps up and, under a hail of machine gun fire, makes another break for it.

> 'All I can remember is falling through the front door of a house, where these Dutch people dragged me down into the cellar. I then blacked out.'

At the Vredehof villa fighting resumes, with the usual pattern of the paratroopers going out to take on the tanks. There is more punishment for the house itself, with several shell hits and the cellar dwellers hearing a wall crashing down above them. The long anticipated decisive moment in the siege of de Soet's once peaceful home cannot be far off. 'There is a hit near the cellar entrance,' records de Soet.

> 'We gasp for air. Everybody is covered with chalk and dust The candle has gone out. Some cry out aloud. I shout out above the noise that nothing is the matter and that the dust will settle again in a moment. When the candle is lit again, the light can hardly be seen through the dust, but gradually it

becomes clearer. The cellar stairs are full of debris. A tank is firing quite close to our house. The walls are swaying as if made of rubber. We hear the English drag their anti-tank gun from one part of the garden to another. Like timid sheep we sit together. Half crazed by the tumult, our ears and brains can hardly sustain this noise. Suddenly Jimmy tumbles into the cellar. Hurriedly he hands me a large German knife in a sheath. "Here," he says, "a souvenir for you". Then he is gone again. I burrow it under the potatoes in the cellar. The battle lasts hours. We hear the tank drive off. But it is coming back. It may be another one. Again I change my train of thoughts from English into German, so that I shall be able to speak German when the necessity arises.'

Cpl Harry Tucker has regained consciousness and wonders what happened to his companions. The Dutch civilians who dragged him down into their cellar are worried he will die from his wounds, fearing the consequences if the Germans find even his corpse down there. They use the Oosterbeek telephone system – incredibly, still working – to call the Hartenstein Hotel and an Airborne medic is ordered to make his way there.

The intention is to take Tucker to a large house belonging to Kate ter Horst, a Dutch woman who has willingly opened the doors of her home to wounded soldiers and, along with a local teenage boy, is assisting the British medics with nursing more than 200 casualties.

After being helped to take Tucker up the cellar steps to its entrance, the Airborne medic thanks the Dutch civilians. He says he will manage the rest of the trip alone, which, of course, they are relieved to hear.

'This is going to hurt you a lot, but I have no choice,' the medic tells Tucker as he hoists the wounded corporal onto his back.

As the medic runs along the street, bullets hit the woodwork of windows and doors, chipping brickwork, chewing up the road and pavement. Tucker is too overwhelmed by pain to feel afraid and loses consciousness. When he comes around again, he is lying on the floor of the ter Horst house, amid other British wounded.

> 'Kate ter Horst appeared and went from man to man with some soup. She also gave each of us a bit of a wash. She didn't flinch as shells slammed into the house, showering us with debris and shrapnel. I heard a British military padre in the house say the wounded were being killed and he was going to try and negotiate a surrender.'

The wounded are given no break from the bombardment. Many are killed by fresh wounds as they lie there when shells hit and bullets fly in. They are starving and suffering from dreadful thirst too, though water had been obtained from a pump near the house until it turned red with blood.[222]

As she moves among the wounded, through once immaculate rooms now turned into a squalid mess, Kate ter Horst comforts wounded men lying 'on mattresses of straw amid the stench of wounds and death'[223] by reading the 91st Psalm.

> *Thou shalt not be afraid for the terror by night,*
> *nor for the arrow that flieth by day, nor for the*
> *pestilence that walketh in darkness, nor for the*
> *destruction that wasteth at noonday.*

There is no lull in the fighting for possession of the Vredehof villa, with Morris and his men putting up a stiff resistance, even as the enemy dismantles even more of the house. A panzer and enemy infantry close in, some of the paratroopers deciding the only place to find cover is below ground. 'A few English soldiers descend the cellar stairs,' reports de Soet.

> We don't know these. We ask them no more, and they don't say anything, only their eyes glitter, in their gun-powder blackened faces. The tank rumbles and takes the house under fire. Walls crumble down upon us [in the house above]. The cellar walls are swaying. No intervals between explosions – whistling and a hit. All noises melt into one. A hellish symphony. Three times a fierce flame shoots through the cellar. Luckily no one is in the way. I shout at people to remain quiet. My wife sits beside me. She has our little daughter on her lap. The little one looks around with great big eyes … seeking to discover where all this noise comes from. We whisper each other good-bye. "Hand grenades in the house," says Harold [Cook], looking at us in fear. We hear them yelling and shrieking above us and around the house. Then, it is suddenly quiet. A couple of seconds. I hear German spoken close to the cellar window, under which we are sitting. I peep through a split between the planks with which we have covered our cellar skylight. I see grey uniformed legs. Germans at a distance of two metres. We are in deathly peril. It is mouse-still in the cellar. I whisper in my wife's ear "We are lost – Germans!" Then our child gives a little cry. That betrays us. The planks are torn away from the sky light.'

A German soldier shouts down into the cellar: 'People in there, get out!'

De Soet dambers through the cellar window, tumbling to the ground, to be encircled by a dozen nervous Germans, 'rifles at the ready and grenades in their hands.'

De Soet yells in German: 'Only 20 civilians in the cellar!'

A German shouts into the cellar: 'All get out! Come out immediately!'

As the cellar's occupants begin to emerge – deathly pale after more than 100 hours below ground and several weeping – a German soldier looks down the road to where one of his own machine gunners lies, finger on trigger. He bellows: 'Don't shoot!'

> 'A girl scrambles out, then another one, I take my little daughter ... and when my wife appears I give the child to her, and start pulling the lame man by his hand and arms out of the cellar.'

Then, a German grabs de Soet by the arm and demands:

'Where are the other Tommies?'

He is pointing at British soldiers sprawled in death across the garden, de Soet's gaze passing over them to fall on the small barn next to his house. In its entrance he sees 'a dead English soldier, his rifle still in his hands. I answer the German that I don't know.'

De Soet stares at a horse, lying dead on the ground next to a tree, head still tied to it with a piece of rope. It had been outside throughout the battle and somehow survived for most of it, though suffering a few wounds.

Looking around again, de Soet sees L/Cpl Cook climbing out of the cellar to be taken prisoner.

A German asks de Soet: 'How did the Tommies treat you?'

He replies that they handed out food but – wary of further questions about what else went on in the house – de Soet moves away, explaining he has to see everybody is alright after their ordeal of seven days and nights in the cellar. As de Soet does so, he turns to the German soldier and asks:

'Are you SS troops?'

He is told emphatically: 'No!'

More British soldiers emerge from the ruins with their hands up and are immediately disarmed by the nervous Germans, though de Soet does not recognise any of them. As he walks away from his destroyed home de Soet is stunned by the 'indescribable chaos'.

> 'A monster Tiger tank stands close to the fence. It does not shoot any longer. I never saw [such] gigantic steel colossuses, [sic] not even during the flight of the German army out of France and Belgium. Next and behind the tank are Germans, their rifles at the ready, and hand grenades, looking silently on.'

He wonders how it is possible for human beings to make such a mess of things in such a short space of time. De Soet feels he, his family and the others must get away from the house. He senses there are still some British soldiers in there and so fighting may erupt again at any moment.

De Soet calls out for everybody to follow him.

—

Even as the situation looks increasingly hopeless, efforts are still being made to get reinforcements into The Cauldron to try and stave off the inevitable. Polish paratroopers attempt another south-to-north crossing of the Rhine, again under heavy enemy fire. Those who make it to Oosterbeek are absorbed into the units weathering the maelstrom. Stan Turner watches the arrival of some.

> 'We see our first Polish paratroopers who have been ferried across the Rhine. They are not pleased to have been landed in a very poor situation. The latest rumours are that XXX Corps has been held up.'

At divisional HQ, Maj Gen Urquhart calls over Lt Col Murray and Capt Fletcher, telling them to make their way to the 4th Para Bde HQ position, a slit trench on the eastern side of the perimeter. Urquhart claims Brig Hackett is stubbornly refusing to go to an aid station after being wounded. The general tells the two Glider Pilot Regt officers: 'I want you to take over from him if his wounds are serious and make sure he goes back for treatment.'

Fletcher and Murray find Hackett with dead British and German soldiers lying all around him. The brigadier has been constantly on the move despite the enemy fire, exhorting the troops to keep on fighting. He was actually on his way to an aid post but had stopped, despite his own serious stomach wound, to supervise retrieval of an injured soldier.

Capt Fletcher recalls: 'He explained the situation by waving a hand around and saying, "the Germans are teasing us a bit".'

Lt Col Murray tells Fletcher to help the brigadier back to the aid post and then return to the divisional HQ in case Urquhart needs him for any urgent tasks.[224] Back in the cellar at the Hartenstein, Maj Gen Urquhart calls Capt Fletcher over and, on a big map, shows him a position in some nearby woods where a Tiger tank is located. 'I want you to get a hold of some people and attack that tank,' he tells Fletcher, whose blood runs cold, but he hides his terror.

> 'I was absolutely scared stiff but I dutifully went off and assembled a motley crew of eight glider pilots. They grumbled a bit when they heard what our task was, for we only had rifles. In fact, I had given my own Sten gun away to some chap who went out on patrol and had now picked up a German rifle along the way. A lot of us had German weapons because we thought they were better. Strangely, many of the Germans picked ours up because they thought they

> were an improvement over their own. Anyway, I admitted to my little band that it was a tall order but promised we wouldn't do anything silly. We'd have a go and then come back.'

Things have quietened down around the Hartenstein by the time Capt Fletcher and his haggard would-be heroes creep up through the trees towards the Tiger.

> 'The Germans who manned it were just sitting around, basically idling. They were obviously enjoying their break, too. I indicated the boys should fire. Then these machine guns opened up from all over the place and I yelled: "Back! Back!" We retreated and, on the way, I fired the last of my German rifle's ammo.'

Capt Fletcher reports to the HQ staff, saying his group has hopefully hit a few Germans, but that it lost three killed. The aim of such attacks is both to hide the fragility of the 1st Airborne Div's state from the Germans and to give its men something active to do, rather than simply wait for inevitable death or capture. As Capt Fletcher has seen already, some of its men have experienced psychological collapse under the relentless German bombardment. They are hiding in the cellars of a house near the divisional HQ. These are men 'who had had enough and were unwilling or incapable of any more fighting'.[225]

The official history of the British Airborne forces in the Second World War will judge: 'It would be wrong to maintain that this bombardment had no effect on the spirits of Urquhart's men. It had to remain cheerful [and] needed a constant effort of the will. The remedy – one which never failed – was to take some action against the enemy.'[226]

L/Cpl Clay, witnesses one of these efforts from a slit trench in the British perimeter, where he is also doing his bit to try and fend off German attacks.

Clay watches a small group of paratroopers led by a keen young officer charging forward, guns blazing – an amazingly brave act that cannot possibly end well.

> 'A few seconds later the officer came walking back, a bullet having gone through his mouth, which, incredibly, had not killed him. I escorted him to an aid post.'

Some who attack the enemy take what most people would regard as insane risks. There are four Victoria Crosses awarded on the ground during the battle and one for heroism in the air to Flight Lieutenant (Flt Lt) David Lord, the pilot of a Dakota that carried on dropping supplies even while on fire and falling apart.[227]

In positions to the north of the Oude Kerk – occupying houses and dug into their gardens, while also in possession of a laundry – are the men of a company in the South Staffs. They are under the command of the indefatigable Maj Robert Cain, who carries out the most extraordinary feats to win one of the VCs.

The Staffs' positions come under attack numerous times from tanks and self-propelled guns, and they knock out quite a few of them. At one stage the South Staffs are working with an incredibly brave Polish 6pdr anti-tank gun team who deliberately leave their gun totally exposed in the middle of the road so they can get the best shot – straight down it at any approaching tanks.

The Poles suffer a commensurate level of casualties but cause the Germans a lot of pain, as does Maj Cain by adopting equally daring tactics.

At one point, he even takes on a Tiger single-handedly, firing his PIAT from a distance of only 60ft, prompting the tank to halt and fire its 88mm gun and machine guns at where he is lying next to a house.

A whole corner of it is blasted away, and Cain is showered with masonry fragments, sustaining wounds but he carries on firing the PIAT, immobilising the Tiger after several more rounds.

Cain then persuades the Light Battery at the church to lend him one of their 75mm howitzers and its men which, firing on a flat trajectory over open sights, utterly destroys the crippled Tiger. Satisfied with the outcome, Cain finally consents to receiving medical treatment for his wounds and is back in action by the morning.

He is just one of many incredibly brave men who take severe risks to pit flesh and blood against panzer steel, but Cain is surely among the most valiant, and the epitome of the Airborne division's fighting spirit.

During one contest between the South Staffs and German armour, there is a self-propelled gun that remains stubbornly undestroyed. Cain teams up with Lt Ian Meikle of the Light Battery, who performs target spotting duties. Under Meikle's direction, Cain launches PIAT bombs right over an intervening house so they will, hopefully, drop onto the self-propelled gun and destroy it. This provokes return fire, a shell slamming into the house and toppling a chimney, which kills Meikle. Cain survives but is rendered deaf, putting dressings on his bleeding ears and carrying on.

Cain manages to work his way up to a shed and enters it to get a good angle on the foe. His PIAT shot explodes under it. Just as Cain is beating a hasty retreat out the other side, its final shell rips the shed asunder.

Spotting a tank coming down the road, Cain sneaks up on it and fires his PIAT. This provokes a response from the tank whose shot obscures it in a cloud of dust and smoke. With the outline of the tank reappearing as this dissipates, Cain fires again. 'This also raised a lot of dust again, and through it I saw the crew of the tank bailing out,' remarks Cain[228], watching as Bren guns open fire and kill the fleeing panzermen.

To make sure the tank is not recoverable, Cain again fires the PIAT, but its bomb detonates in the launcher. He is thrown back almost comically, with both his hands thrown into air in shock and swearing 'like a hooligan', as Cain himself puts it. British soldiers rush forward to help him. They are horrified by his smoke-blackened face with blood seeping from numerous pinprick wounds and an impressive pair of black eyes.

'I think I'm blind,' Cain remarks as he is taken away.

A soldier watching thinks Cain is surely finished now, observing: 'That poor bloody bastard...'[229]

It does not stop Cain. Half an hour later – with his sight restored, and refusing morphia in case it dulls his mental acuity – he is again attacking tanks and self-propelled guns. When the PIAT bombs run out, he switches to assailing enemy infantry and armour with a 2-inch mortar fired from the hip. Earlier, he had even tried his hand with a 6pdr anti-tank gun to assail advancing panzers. Seeing so many of his friends killed during the abortive attempt to get through to the bridge on 19 September is what enrages the normally calm and reasonable Cain to such heights of heroism.

It is also mixed in with the native pugnacity that imbues many of Britannia's bravest warriors. Some graffiti scrawled on wallpaper in a room at Pieterbergseweg 34 by 21st Indep Para Coy sniper Tony Crane sums up the bloody-minded resistance of many Airborne troops:

'NEVER SURRENDER. FUCK THE GERRY'S [sic]'[230]

Below this is listed a day-by-day tally of enemy claimed by a sniper, with each foe slain or wounded denoted by a swastika symbol.

Between 21 September and 23 September, there is no score, the graffiti recording: 'Nothing'. On 24 September there are six swastikas. On the following day – perhaps reflecting the increasing frequency of repulsed enemy infantry attacks – there will be ten. It also indicates just how much tighter the German noose around the 1st Airborne Div has become.

While the truces have managed to see hundreds of casualties evacuated from within the perimeter, there are many left in the various frequently shelled aid stations.

Allied commanders realise medical supplies are urgently needed, along with hands-on assistance, and they make the dire situation known in communications with XXX Corps.

133 Parachute Field Ambulance (PFA) of the Royal Army Medical Corps (RAMC), is part of the 1st Airborne Div, the majority of whose men have jumped in with the 4th Para Bde. They are already up to their necks in muck and bullets along with the 16 PFA and 181 PFA, fighting to save lives with the other two brigades.

But a proposal to send help is being worked on urgently, led by the German-speaking boss of XXX Corps' 163 Field Ambulance, Lt Col Martin Herford. He has held discussions with senior officers after hearing the 1st Airborne Div is 'surrounded and they were desperately in need of medical supplies.'[231]

An estimated 1,500–2,000 British wounded are reported at Oosterbeek, although it could be more. Herford takes charge of a mercy convoy, consisting of 'thirty fully loaded ambulances with medical supplies' plus 40 other vehicles, but he is 'completely in the dark' about how to get them across the river.

Nonetheless, Herford takes it up Hell's Highway to Driel. He encounters an enraged Maj Gen Ivo Thomas, the commander of the 43rd Div, who shouts: 'What the hell are ambulances doing here? I want guns. Get off the road!'

Herford acknowledges that perhaps the general's ire is understandable. 'He was quite right, we couldn't do anything until they got control of the situation.' To get them off the road, Herford tells the crews of the ambulances and other vehicles to park in a field, so they don't block fighting reinforcements.

He assesses that prospects of getting across the Rhine are 'pretty dim', with 'considerable noise and fury' and confusion all around. Yet something will have to be done.

> 'I thought I'd go and see General Thomas again and get permission to go across with a party to see if contact could be made with the Airborne on the other side.'

He finds Thomas with Lt Gen Horrocks, and they seem to be discussing withdrawing the 1st Airborne Div but pause in their chat to grant Herford permission to try and get across the river. 'I wanted to do a recce to see if I could contact the Airborne and perhaps make arrangements for a night crossing with larger supplies.'

Volunteering for the attempt to get across the river is Capt Percy Louis, a Medical Officer (doctor) of the 133 PFA who flew into Holland with the Airborne Corps HQ, landing near Nijmegen.

A veteran of the French campaign and Dunkirk evacuation of 1940, Capt Louis is eager to do whatever he can to help his comrades in arms at Oosterbeek. Louis and four medics from 163 Field Ambulance, also volunteers, will accompany Lt Col Herford, in trying to enter The Cauldron with medical supplies. Herford will also attempt to arrange a truce with the Germans to evacuate the wounded.

To describe their mission as risky would be an understatement. Most sane people would rather be getting out of The Cauldron than trying to get into it, but Herford is battle hardened. His recent experiences have qualified him well for such a mission, having first encountered the Nazis when working as a volunteer civilian doctor in the Spanish Civil War of the late 1930s. Herford also served as a volunteer medic for the Finns during their war with the Soviet Union in 1940. He subsequently served as a British Army medical officer in most of the Allied land battles in the Mediterranean from 1941 onwards. Capt Louis is taking an extra level of risk, as he is Jewish, and if he ends up going into captivity to care for the Airborne wounded could risk execution.

During daylight on 24 September, the medical group sets out on its mission. Availing themselves of a collapsible boat courtesy of the Royal Engrs, they launch it from the mud on the southern bank of the Rhine at 2.00pm, displaying a Red Cross flag on it as they paddle.

Getting across with no problems and landing 10cwt of medical supplies – blood plasma, drugs, dressings[232] – Lt Col Herford tells

Capt Louis and the medics to wait under the riverbank, where they will be out of sight of the enemy. He heads off, carrying the Red Cross flag to show the Germans he is not there to fight but on a mission of mercy.

> 'I wanted to see if I could get a pass to visit a senior German officer and try and parley for medical supplies to be allowed to go over that night to reinforce the supplies that were obviously dwindling for the Airborne.'

He feels fairly safe, observing: 'I didn't expect them to shoot. The Germans aren't all savages, and, on the whole, they respected the Red Cross flag...' Coming to a stream – actually not much more than a ditch – but with barbed wire strung all down the other side, Herford finds himself 'wondering where Hell to pass as I didn't want to get my boots wet... Suddenly, behind a privet hedge ... very near to the ditch, four or five Germans rose up pointing their rifles and threatening to throw grenades if I didn't hurry up and cross.'

Herford waves, indicating he can't see how to get past the wire, so walks further along while the Germans get more edgy, their guns still aimed firmly at him. He finds a place to jump across, telling the Germans he wants to see one of their senior officers to parley. Herford suggests that if this isn't possible they must at least guarantee they will send the British medics down by the river safely back across the Rhine.

Herford gives them the Red Cross flag and again insists the Germans go back and look after his team, also repeating his request to see a senior officer.

> 'I said I wanted to arrange to make arrangements for the many Airborne who had been wounded. They said they'd send the [British] party [by the river] back.'

Herford is blindfolded – to ensure he cannot glean any intelligence on enemy dispositions – and guided by a German soldier through the lines. After a fair bit of searching for a senior officer who can parley, they finally find one and the blindfold is taken off. Herford is then taken to an even more senior officer, again while blindfolded.

As he is led about, there are numerous bangs and flashes on all sides and on a few occasions the German escorting him pulls Herford down under cover. At one point, Herford finds himself being leaned against what seems to be a tree. Fearing the worst, he calms himself down by reflecting that the Germans will surely not bring him all this way just to shoot him.

At the next meeting with a senior officer, Herford is interrogated about his intent and what he wants, and also who he is exactly. In a rather offbeat twist, Herford has brought a piece of paper with him, on which is scrawled a list of British units the Germans will know are engaged in the fighting.

This is to prove Herford is authentic, but also inserted in the list are references to bogus 'secret weapons' – just for fun and to give the Germans something to chew over. Reading through his list, they realise this is just a prank and are not terribly amused. Typical British humour!

Herford is told that, rather than being allowed to return to British lines, he 'must be regarded as a prisoner…'. His mission to gain a truce and bring casualties out across the river has failed. Herford endures 'a pretty chilly night in a room with a bed with no mattress… In the morning I was put in a car but taken not to Arnhem, but to Apeldoorn.'

He is then escorted to a meeting with Oberstleutnant Zingerlin, the chief medical officer for German forces in the Arnhem area. 'Zingerlin offered me some very nice coffee in cups of royal China. It was all very civilised and he was obviously a very reasonable man… We talked as two doctors about the needs of the wounded.'

Zingerlin tells Herford a truce has been arranged in Oosterbeek to get the wounded out of the firing line and better cared for. It will ultimately be agreed that Herford will care for the British wounded, working alongside captured Airborne medics in a hospital established in a nearby military barracks.[233]

To make their escape from the battle, de Soet and his fellow refugees have been forced to head through gardens, as the roads are impassable – littered with wrecked tanks, debris, dead bodies, bits of trees.

German soldiers point the way the civilians must go, which takes them past more troops and tanks waiting for orders to attack the British. The tanks have their guns pointed in the direction of de Soet's house.

He realises how overwhelming the German force now is and that it is a hopeless fight that has only lasted so long due to the sheer stubborn heroism of the Airborne troops. De Soet leads the group past more dead British and Germans – they lie everywhere – some of them 'an awful sight'. In a few gardens are dead civilians. A Dutch SS[234] soldier shouts as they pass: 'You see, you have shouted victory at half time!'

As they go along a raised road called De Dam, shells start landing nearby, with German machine gunners to their front opening fire.

> 'I kneel over my daughter, my wife next to me. English machine-gun fire responds. Shells are fired in the direction of our house. They are coming so closely over, that it seems as if they are grazing our hair.'

After a few minutes, the firing falls away and they can raise their heads. 'The Germans beckon us to go on,' says de Soet. 'We go forward with bowed heads. Some hundred yards further down [the road] a German hands my wife a suitcase, which later we find contains a large ham, bread and a pair of socks.' Going by a label on it, the suitcase belonged to an Oosterbeek resident. The de Soets have left all their own things behind, including a suitcase packed with 'flight things' they planned to bring with them if forced to flee.

There are large smoke columns rising up and fires blazing in the direction of the Vredehof villa, and de Soet suspects it is getting another pounding. Back down the road, he sees a man from his cellar, who is carrying the lame man on his back, de Soet thinking: 'he is a hero'.

Since 22 September, life for Jan Loos, and others in the cellar of De la Reyweg 9, has become one big fearful blur, and he ends up with 'no clear memories of individual events across three days, except for noise, stench, hunger, thirst, dust...'

> 'Gradually everyone in our cellar becomes apathetic and I suspect that most of us think we will not live through it. My mother is wondering whether or not Pa is still alive and, if so, where could he be? Occasionally the artillery falls silent for a moment and then Walter briefly opens the cellar flap to let in cool air. On one of these occasions we can see that the roof of the house above has been partly shot off and that it is full of debris. There are still a number of Paras in the house, who are firing in different directions. It is clear that the Germans are getting closer. That is again underlined during the night of Saturday/Sunday when, for hours, we hear a wounded German soldier lying nearby calling for his mother. Apparently nobody dares to bring him to safety and eventually he is silent, as he is dead.'

Just down the road, in the cellars of the Hartenstein, Maj Gen Urquhart is composing an encrypted wireless message. It explains the situation in the bleakest of terms – dispensing with efforts to always sound positive that he had previously made in case the enemy intercept and decode messages.

He still makes it clear his force is not going to capitulate, no matter how bad things get. It gets to Airborne Corps HQ, via the Phantom radio net, at 9.15pm.

> 'From URQUHART to BROWNING.
> 'Must WARN you UNLESS PHYSICAL contact in strength is made with us EARLY 25 SEP, consider it unlikely we can hold out (long enough). All RANKS now EXHAUSTED. Lack of rations, water, ammo and weapons with high officer casualty rate of defending [force] had effect. Even slight enemy offensive activity may cause complete disintegration. If this happens all will be ordered to break TOWARD bridgehead if only RATHER THAN surrender. Movement at present in FACE of enemy not possible. Have done our best and will so as long as possible.'[235]

Monday and Tuesday

25 and 26 September

'I had been evacuated from Dunkirk in 1940. I wasn't left behind then and there was no way I was going to be left behind at Arnhem.'

—L/Cpl Dennis Clay[236]

Despite the inevitability of stiff enemy resistance to a crossing, soldiers of the 4th Bn, the Dorsetshire Regt are launched across the Rhine in the early hours of 25 September to reinforce the 1st Airborne.

They take artillery-forward observers with them to help bring down barrages with precision on German forces squeezing the perimeter, an effort to save it from collapse.

Capt Louis goes with them, in a new bid to convey medical supplies and care for the wounded in The Cauldron. He is accompanied by Lt J Tiernan, an officer from the 181st (Air Landing) Field Ambulance, along with 20 medics in boats and DUKWS carrying plasma, sulfa drugs, blankets and bandages. It is an ill-fated venture, with the DUKWS and boats holed after running up on the beach, and it is impossible to offload the medical supplies due to enemy fire and thick, sucking mud.

The majority of Dorsets who make it through heavy enemy fire across the river fight almost until the last bullet and are then ordered by their battalion commander to lay down their arms. 'There was no way back or hope of relief,' reports an astonished Pte NL Francis.

> 'His orders [to us] were to surrender. We were stunned. We had expected the might of the British Army behind us to reinforce the bridgehead we had made…'[237]

Of the 315 soldiers of the 4th Dorsets sent across the Rhine just 75 make it back, the others being killed, wounded or captured, either during the crossing or on the other side. What exactly happened to 29-year-old Airborne doctor Capt Percy Louis will never be known for certain, though it is suspected he either drowned when an assault boat sank or was killed during a firefight ashore. His body is not recovered, although Lt Tiernan will swim back across the river on the night of 25 September.

Such is the valour shown on their hopeless mission, the 4th Dorsets will be given the accolade of displaying the battle honour 'Arnhem' and flying the Airborne pennant – though that is not much consolation for such a vain sacrifice.[238] It is a bitter turn of events for the battalion, which was also mauled in battles against the II SS Panzer Corps in Normandy and has been forced to fight its way through those same enemy units to reach Driel.

—

Overnight on 24/25 September, de Soet and his family find shelter in another cellar, below a house in which German troops are quartered. Chatting with one of them, de Soet asks if captured British soldiers will be shot. The German tells him that won't happen, which is a relief.

At 2.00am, on 25 September the shells of a British artillery barrage begin landing around the house, the shock waves knocking tiles off the roof. The de Soets resolve to get even further away once there is a lull in the bombardment. Carrying their child wrapped in a blanket they make a break for it.

> 'The streets are deserted. Here and there burned houses. The tramway system has been wrecked.'

They are heading along the Schelmseweg and, with rain pouring down, press on past more Tiger tanks before seeking shelter under a railway bridge. They see a German soldier on guard nearby and ask for water. He takes them to a small farm, which has been looted, but where there is a water pump. They find a tin with some sugar in it, which they give to the baby.

> 'On we go. Everywhere the signs of the battle – parachutes, shells, and a single dead soldier. Now we reach the woods. At last no shells, no moaning of the wounded. The scene of the battle is behind us. We breathe the pure forest air.'

–

However, for some civilians – still trapped in cellars – the fighting continues to rage around them, though Jan Loos and other inhabitants of the De la Reyweg 9 find Monday morning brings an end to their oppressive, terrifying subterranean ordeal.

> 'We hear Germans calling each other, though above our heads we still hear the paratroopers shooting. A German is close to the house, because suddenly we hear someone shouting: "Civilians come out!" We call back that we will come out. We open the cellar flap and go out as fast as we dare and can, waving one of the white flags we made earlier. Taking cover against the hedge of the neighbouring house is a German soldier. He makes it clear to us that we must make sure we go away, towards Paul Krugerstraat. The shooting stops very briefly at that moment and we cross unharmed between the British and Germans – and, to this day, I wonder if that happened deliberately. At the top of the road are a few Germans who have been killed, lying behind a

large stone on the corner near a cottage. Another
German soldier points out which direction we are
to go. In Paul Krugerstraat several houses are burned
out and, in the ruins of one of the three bakeries,
there is an SS man with a machine pistol and a
grenade in his hand. I will never know what inspired
him, but he winks at me and, when I get closer, he
asks me twice what age I am, looks me over from top
to toe and then asks if I am hungry. After my affirm-
ative answer he pulls a piece of bread and a bar of
chocolate from a sort of waist bag and gives them to
me. He says: "And now get away quickly. Whoever
comes back will be shot." Everywhere is debris,
broken and burned out houses, burned out vehicles,
parachutes hanging from the trees and from roofs,
but it is remarkably quiet. What is also noticeable
is that no other civilians are to be seen. Apparently
everyone has already gone. Along the Dreijenseweg
we find large German tanks and self-propelled guns,
the so-called STUGs – Sturmgeschütze – and piles of
British supplies that have fallen into German hands
when dropped by parachute. The German soldiers
are clearly enjoying the contents of the baskets and
containers.'

Jan Loos, his mother, sister, and the others head through woods
and across heathland to the north of the Amsterdamseweg while
during their flight from Oosterbeek, the de Soets come across a
house that has barbed wire arranged all around it. In a neighbouring field the Germans are burying their dead, in very precise
rows, with flowers already laid on the graves.

'We manage to get through the barbed wire. There is
no sentry. We enter the house and are suddenly in a
room against the walls of which German soldiers are
sleeping. We sit down on the chairs at the table in the

middle of the room. Some Germans are staring at us with vacant looks. They are exhausted. They don t take any notice of our presence. My wife examines our baby's bottom. It is quite inflamed. It has not been possible to wash the little dear and give her clean towels the last few days. A German gets up. He says something unintelligible. We remain in our chairs, indifferent. We only form a little part of the wretchedness caused by this war. Presently a German approaches us with his canteen. The child drinks from it. He says: "If you wait a moment, I'll have hot coffee for you". He talks about the "furuchtbare Krieg" – "this terrible war" – and "Verlorene Sack" – "the lost issue". He is moved by our misery. "You may as well surrender," my wife says. He would like to give us something to eat, he says, but he has got nothing left. I ask him to give me a bicycle. I noticed quite a number of them inside the barbed wire.'

The soldier says they belong to his comrades and so he can't, then exits the room. After a short while he comes back, giving the de Soets some German bread. He says there is an English bike that they can have. De Soet decides this German soldier is 'not such a bad sort' and hopes: 'May the war soon be over for him, too... Then we depart. The baby sits on the bicycle with good English tyres but without a chain.'

There is a stream of people from Arnhem passing by who reveal they have been told to leave by the Germans and must head for Apeldoorn. Later, the de Soets stop at a house and ask for a piece of board and something to tie it to the handlebars, so the baby can lie down. The occupants seem reluctant to help until de Soet shames them by explaining that others have lost lives and their entire homes in the past few days.

German tanks are heading the other way, and, as the mass of civilians trudge on, trucks pass by, also heading towards Apeldoorn. 'We cry out our good-byes when we see the red English caps,' says de Soet, 'and they give the victory sign with two fingers in the air... Didn't I see David with his dark head among them? How we do hope to see him again.'

Within The Cauldron, the battle continues, though in the higher levels of Allied command, it is obvious the situation is beyond retrieval. Monty finally yields to the conclusion of his field commanders that all that may now be done is to evacuate the remnants of the 1st Airborne Div across the Rhine. This is to be the primary mission of the 43rd Div and Canadian Army engineers on the southern bank, assisted by the Polish paratroopers and other British units.

Shortly after 6.00am on 25 September, a letter from Maj Gen Thomas is delivered into the hands of Urquhart. It reveals his pleas for immediate and decisive action have been heard but formally confirms Second Army no longer intends 'to form a bridgehead over the NEDER RIJN near ARNHEM.'[239] The letter also sets out the plan for withdrawing the 1st Airborne Div across the river 'on whatever date should be agreed'. This prompts Maj Gen Urquhart to get on the radio to inform 43rd Div HQ that 'withdrawal must take place on the night 25/26...' It is to be codenamed Operation Berlin.[240] and the mechanics of how exactly the Airborne division will disengage and get across the Rhine – without the enemy realising what is going on – will be down to Urquhart.

On the Monday afternoon, the order to evacuate is passed around what survives of the 1st Airborne Div, though, as General Urquhart will later admit, the enemy could by then have easily pushed through and snuffed out all resistance. It is a mystery why they don't do this.

At 6.00pm that evening, the artillery of the 43rd Div begins an intensive bombardment of enemy positions close to the Oosterbeek perimeter. It is meant to keep German heads down, so the enemy won't notice the staged withdrawal of the British. Capt Fletcher is brutally honest about how he feels.

> 'I was absolutely delighted to be going. Quite frankly, I was frightened the whole time of the battle and the news that we were going across the Rhine that night was wonderful. Almost from the beginning to the end we had been at the mercy of the Germans with hardly any fighter cover. The three times our fighters did attack the Germans it worked and their guns fell silent, but it wasn't enough.'[241]

The Allied aerial resupply effort had never faltered – several valiant aircrews carrying on with their drops even as flames engulfed their aircraft, but most of it was squandered despite repeated attempts by the Airborne troops to signal alternate DZs. The lives of many brave aircrews in those aircraft have been sacrificed for nothing, thinks Capt Fletcher, who remarks bitterly: 'One of the few supply containers that came our way was full of red berets, not food or ammo.'

As the 1st Airborne Div prepares to make its withdrawal across the Rhine, Jan Loos and his refugee group have reached the ironically named restaurant "Rust wat" – *Rest Awhile* – on the Kemperbergerweg, in Schaarsbergen. The scene that greets them is very far from restful.

> 'It is just like an anthill – people with prams, with bikes, with handcarts, loaded with mattresses, blankets, furniture, bird cages with their animals in… unimaginable. And here we are, alongside the road with only the clothes that we are standing up in, trying to make a decision what to do next. Soon we hear that all these people come from Arnhem

and that they have been sent away by the Germans and are now trying to find out where to go. And then, in the crowd, there is a woman, who apparently recognizes my mother and who tells her: "I just saw your husband ... and he is somewhere around here hoping to find you." A little later we are reunited, crying, laughing and our family is at last together. But soon we come back to reality. Where will we go? Where can we get something to eat and drink? Where can we find a place to rest? Someone from the Red Cross says to us that we can go to a school near the church, where refugees are being taken care of. We should register later with the Red Cross who have set up a post in the restaurant. When we arrive at the school we are told that we can find a spot in one of the classrooms, where mattresses have been laid on the floor. Then, so we are told, we can get some hot porridge or soup at a sort of field kitchen behind the school. It is delicious! Ma and my sister lie down on "our" mattress to rest while Pa and I go to the restaurant to register. We have only just joined the queue when Allied bombers come over and all hell breaks loose. Everywhere there are bombs dropping, glass and debris flying around, and everyone is trying to crawl under cover somewhere. We end up with 20 people under a billiard table. An image that has always stayed with me is of a man lying on the floor under one of the windows with a colander on his head. If I had not been so scared, I would probably have been laughing hard. Once the explosions are over we go back outside and find pandemonium: people wounded, dead or crazy with fear. Dad and I go back to the school in a hurry, to find all the ceilings have come down and all the glass has been blown out of the window frames. Ma and sister are nowhere to be seen, but soon they emerge from an earth-covered, protective trench behind the school. Amid all this misery the weather is also terrible. Many people decide to spend the night in the "shelter" and so do we. I do not remember how many people there were; I do know, however, that there were a number of people who continuously beseeched the higher powers for help, which drove us crazy. So, we crawled out and went back into the school, shook the dirt off a few mattresses and fell into a deep, deep sleep.'

—

After dark, the first wave of Airborne soldiers, including those wounded who are able to walk, cover their boots with rags to muffle them. They also tie down any equipment that might rattle. Each group – which is to number fourteen, in order to correspond with the maximum each boat can carry – will be escorted down to the river by glider pilots. Urquhart has stipulated that 'if fired on' groups are 'to take evasive action and only fight if compelled to, so as to avoid the danger of indiscriminate firing.' Once they reach the river each of the parties is ordered 'to lie down under cover of the bank and await their turn for a boat'.[242]

The 43rd Div artillery keeps up a continuous barrage throughout the night. The crash and roar of explosions mixes in with the noise of torrential rain helping to mask what's going on. The hundreds of British wounded left behind contribute, where possible, by firing their weapons.

Radio operators will maintain normal transmissions to units already withdrawn from the perimeter as if they are still there.

Right up until they depart, troops douse enemy positions with as much fire as possible, to deter enemy patrols, though the Germans incline towards inactivity at night anyway.

Some men are inevitably casualties on the way down the river, from shrapnel or bullets courtesy of both British and German guns. One group is challenged by the enemy trying to pick them out with a searchlight, which garners a hail of grenades. The Germans are fortunately, at that point, failing to land mortar shells among the British troops waiting at the water's edge.

To mark the landing point on the other side of the Rhine that evacuation boats must head for, 43rd Div AA guns fire red tracer shells over the river. Some soldiers grow impatient and decide to try and swim across. Among them is an officer who has proudly worn a kilt throughout the fighting – he drowns because the weight of his kilt when soaked is too much.

L/Cpl Clay is among those chancing a solo crossing.

> 'In the end I couldn't stand the wait and jumped in, swam out a bit and then grabbed the side of a boat and let it pull me across. I had been evacuated from Dunkirk in 1940. I wasn't left behind then and there was no way I was going to be left behind at Arnhem.'[243]

Capt Fletcher's group finds a small boat abandoned on the riverbank, and, rather than hang around, they climb in. He tells them: 'Use your helmets to paddle with.'

With some men muttering prayers, they push the boat off the mud and start paddling. Fletcher's craft reaches the other side of the Rhine to be greeted by 43rd Div soldiers and Canadians busy putting white tape on the riverbank for Airborne troops to follow up to safety.

One of those coming across the river from The Cauldron is Canadian war correspondent Stanley Maxted, a BBC broadcaster who landed at Arnhem with a group of newspaper reporters, along with Airborne photographers and cameramen, most of whom make it out alive.

Maxted is later full of admiration for the heroic stand of the 1st Airborne Div. 'They stood against the enemy's armour and none had weakened. These knights of Arnhem had no armour. Their strength was in their own courage and in each other.'[244]

The Airborne soldiers have indeed conquered their deepest, most primal fears in battle, but, tonight, it is all about getting out alive, of returning home to see loved ones. It would be terrible to make it through the hellfire only to succumb now.

German born glider pilot Sgt Lewis Haig jumps into the water fully equipped – still wearing a helmet, with Sten gun slung across his back.

It is hard to let go of protection even though swimming for your life, especially when the enemy is still trying to kill you. He also has his boots hung around his neck. At first, Haig is buoyed by the air trapped in his combat smock and enjoys his immersion after several days without bathing. By the time he is halfway across the 250 yards-wide Rhine, that buoyancy has dissipated, and he starts to struggle. The warm waters of the river are not so wonderful now. He begins to thrash uselessly, breathing accelerating, his mind racing with fear – but then Haig realises it is the sheer panic that will kill him. 'Like a flash it came to me that was the one fatal thing to do and the best possible way to get drowned.' It would be stupid to die 'by drowning in the calm warm waters of the Rhine after evading every kind of violent death in the last seven days'[245], especially as he has been a keen swimmer since the age of four.

Haig turns onto his back, giving himself time to rest and gather his thoughts, letting the current take him. There are flares drifting overhead, making the surface of the Rhine twinkle, while German tracer bullets skim low over the surface, criss-crossing with the red tracer of the British AA guns firing from the south bank. British artillery shells cut through the air overhead to explode on the northern bank.

Submerging and keeping himself upright, Haig slips the Sten gun off, bubbles streaming from it as the weapon falls away into the blackness below. Next to go are the helmet and boots, then grenades, Sten gun magazines, even the notes kept during the battle and the pen he used to write them. All are discarded, even the identity papers bearing his false British name. Having divested himself of all this – in some ways to be born again – Haig strikes out for the southern bank. He finds eager 43rd Div hands to help him across the mud and up into a lorry for transportation to an aid post.

The reception Pte Roberts of the 21st Indep Para Coy gets upon swimming the Rhine is not so friendly. Having been wounded earlier during combat on the other side of the river, he suffers the further misfortune of being hit again by enemy fire. Roberts dies three days later in a field hospital at Nijmegen.

One group in the 1st Airborne Div's midst that may, for its own interests, give away the escape of the Airborne soldiers is formed of the 200 German prisoners held in the Hartenstein's tennis courts.

As their own side poured fire into The Cauldron, they had been forced to dig themselves slit trenches to get under cover. During the evening of 24 September, according to the 1st Airborne Div's own report of the battle, some of them had complained about 'beginning to feel the effects of short rations and of their own shelling and mortaring, and were beginning to quote Geneva Conventions.[246] Even so, one of their own officers told them off for moaning about lack of food when their captors had little enough to eat themselves. The job of keeping the prisoners quiet during the division's exit falls to volunteers, who agree to guard them until 1.30am when they will, according to orders, 'withdraw as unostentatiously as possible',[247] to minimise the chances of the prisoners realising what is going on.

By dawn on 26 September, 1,700 1st Airborne Div troops and 420 soldiers of the Glider Pilot Regt have been ferried across the Rhine. A further 234 soldiers are also evacuated by boat (composed of 160 Polish paratroopers and soldiers of the Dorsetshire Regt).[248]

Others have to get away by swimming across the Rhine. RSM John Siely of the Light Battery is one of the last to escape – having tried to keep the troops calm while they wait their turn – taking his own plunge in the light of morning.

'I stripped completely, because I had just seen three men drown, weighed down by their clothes,' he will explain.[249]

Making it to the other side, Siely and an officer – who had also thrown off his clothes for the swim – head for a house where they hunt for something dry to put on. The officer picks a blouse while RSM Siely pulls on, 'a lady's very nice dark cloth coat'.[250]

Divisional Intelligence officer Capt CP Scott-Malden also gets rid of his uniform and equipment before swimming across the Rhine, ending up wrapped in 'several yards of flannel',[251] secured around his waist by a belt. Safely with British troops on the other side, he enjoys a breakfast of Irish stew washed down by two glasses of Cointreau, after which he sleeps for 12 hours – so still that it appears he may be dead. He is, of course, one of the lucky ones who avoided capture and got out alive.

—

During the battle, the British suffered 1,200 dead, with 6,378 unaccounted for, the Polish brigade losing 342 men to all causes. Within the 1st Airborne Div, the battalion that had suffered the most dead was the Borders, with 126 out of its 793 men killed and with 235[252] evacuated across the river.

Then there are those who are sometimes overlooked – the aircrews who died either flying the 1st Airborne Div into action or during the resupply missions – and the Dutch civilians.

The air effort saw 474 men killed, belonging to the RAF and the USAAF. It has been calculated 453 civilians were killed during the battle, including 188 losing their lives in Arnhem itself during the battle and 83 in Oosterbeek[253] – 40 of them executed by firing squad for in some way assisting the Allies.[254] It is reckoned from all causes, including Allied bombardments and air attack, 2,000 more were killed.[255]

The Germans had 3,300 casualties, including 1,300 dead.[256] Nazi propagandists crowed about their side's triumph, while an officer in one of the SS divisions tells a group of Dutch civilians: 'We'll be back in Paris by Christmas'.[257] Those Airborne troops who did not return across the Rhine on 25/26 September were either dead, prisoners of the enemy — 1,700 wounded among them — or on the run and in hiding. Some stayed missing forever, swallowed up without a trace in the chaos of battle.

Aftermath

> *'It was a bridge too far and perhaps the whole plan was doomed to failure from the start, but we had to try, didn't we?'*
>
> —Capt Peter Fletcher, Glider Pilot Regt[258]

Pte Stan Turner is among those actually forgotten and left behind, due to some cock-up that sees evacuation orders not being passed on. He discovers this cruel twist on the morning of 26 September.

'I wake up and it is daylight. I immediately know things are not as they should be as British troops always stand to before dawn,' he later writes in his diary about this terrible moment of realisation.

> 'The grounds of the [Hartenstein] hotel look deserted compared to how they have been over the past few days. I go over to the German POWs in the tennis courts hoping one of them can speak English. A German prisoner makes a remark, which goes something like this: "Tommy, they are all gone." Scarcely able to believe what has happened, myself and the other soldier who shared my trench go over to the hotel building. We are astounded to see a huge pile of British dead, all of them very young. It is a sight never to be forgotten. We meet a medical officer who tells us the 1st Airborne Division was evacuated in the night and he has been left behind to look after the wounded. He tells us we will be taken prisoner.'[259]

Lt Peter Baillie, who led his Border Regt platoon through intense fighting in the Battle of the Woods – until wounded in a mortar bomb explosion on 23 September, suffering a mental breakdown that saw him confined to a cellar – is struck by silence 'so quiet you could have heard a pin drop...'[260]

On hearing German voices, he and another officer emerge from the cellar with their hands up, explaining to enemy soldiers that there are 'many wounded chaps below...' Taking in the terrible vista around him, Baillie sees and smells things that he will never be able to forget, giving him nightmares for a long time.

> 'There were dead bodies by the dozens, lying about and stinking – not just lifeless corpses ... but bits of bodies. Bodies without heads, arms or legs. Bodies burnt, riddled with bullets.'

Nearby houses have been demolished and wrecked military vehicles lie all around, with 'everything smashed to smithereens ... I'm not ashamed to confess that I just knelt down and cried. All these poor swine killed – for what! For what! For what!' Baillie feels 'as weak as a kitten, and terribly tired.'

As he and the other officer watch, the wounded are brought up from the cellars by German soldiers. Other enemy troops pull up in a captured Airborne forces jeep and start handing out British cigarettes and food mistakenly delivered into their hands by Allied air forces.

As Turner, Lt Baillie, and others disconsolately await their fate, survivors of the 1st Airborne Div who escaped are assembling at Nijmegen, which is now firmly in Allied hands.

Those soldiers of the 1st Airborne Div and the Glider Pilot Regt who had been taken across by boat are marched to a rendezvous point to the south of Driel where rum, tea, hot food and a blanket were provided by 43 Div[261] and then on to Nijmegen aboard lorries, DUKWs and whatever vehicles are available.

There are bitter words exchanged in some places between the Airborne troops and the Guards Armoured Division, along the lines of the former wanting to know where the latter has been.

Angry Guards soldiers point out they have been fighting for months since landing in Normandy, or as it is put by one of them: 'Some people have all the fucking luck – one battle and home to England.'[262] Meanwhile, 1st Airborne Div soldiers explain that many of them – including plenty of those killed or captured on the north bank of the Rhine – have been fighting the Germans for years.

In their blankets, thrown over filthy torn and bloodied combat jackets, they were a sorry sight – but within a few hours are in smart, clean uniforms brought across by the seaborne tail of the division.[263]

They are accommodated temporarily in three buildings located in the same part of town – one set aside for the survivors of the two parachute brigades, one for the air landing brigade and the third for the divisional support troops and glider pilots. Already in Nijmegen with three of his men is the indefatigable Capt Eric Mackay, who had swiftly managed to escape from enemy custody.

His first attempt – leaping from a truck while being taken away from Arnhem – ended with Mackay being caught and beaten by guards until he passed out. This rough treatment was probably prompted by Mackay trying to strangle a guard during the escape bid.

Delivered to a holding camp near Emmerich, Germany, and after his first night's sleep in four days, Mackay organised an officer and two NCOs from the 1st Parachute Squadron Royal Engineers RE to try and get away again.

Using a hacksaw blade and hand tools secreted earlier, they cut through bars on a cookhouse window and made their exit.

'As soon as it was dark we created a diversion,' according to Mackay. 'There was no food so we raised hell. While the noise was going on we left.' Other men later followed through the same hole but were caught.

Using a map acquired earlier, Mackay and the other three manage to find their way into Holland and to the River Waal. The next day they lie low in a shed. 'As soon as it was dark we nipped out and jumped [stole] a boat,' reports Mackay. '[We] Bargain with [passing] bargees for food because we hadn't had any for four days. Drifted down the Rhine until we got to Nijmegen,' which they reached in the early hours of 23 September.

Mackay is delighted to wave 1st Airborne Div survivors in but outraged to find only one man from his unit among them.[264]

Under the shroud of defeat, the men of the 1st Airborne Div try to extract something positive from failure, though it is not easy.

'We gave our best but it was a bloody fiasco,' thinks Dennis Clay. Others are a little more forgiving, perhaps not of Market Garden itself but with sympathy for those ordered to make it work. In the end, so Capt Fletcher is forced to conclude: 'We had experienced a dreadful ordeal and I was lucky to escape with my life.'

> 'It was a bridge too far and perhaps the whole plan was doomed to failure from the start, but we had to try, didn't we? That's how we felt then under the shock of it all, and that's how we feel even decades later. When it came to the people who had failed to reach us there was a feeling of "where the bloody hell were you?" However, they had paid their price too, especially those 43rd Division units that tried so hard only to fail within sight of us.'

Following a roll call parade at Nijmegen, Capt Fletcher is sent back to England ahead of the rest of the Glider Pilot Regt survivors to report on its casualties and exploits to senior officers. On reaching the regiment's home base at Harwell in Oxfordshire, Fletcher heads for an officers' bar as soon as he can. He downs a few gin and tonics to toast the memory of fallen comrades, then phones his family. 'Having seen the news, they thought I was dead. I was very glad to inform them that I wasn't.'

Back in Nijmegen, Lt Gen Browning comes to see the Airborne troops late on the afternoon of 27 September to try and put what had happened in a broader perspective. It is a job he has been dreading.[265]

After reviewing what remains of the division during a parade, Browning goes from building to building, speaking to each group separately and complimenting them on their 'achievements.'[266] In one of the buildings he climbs up onto a table, surrounded on all four sides by the men and in spare detail explains the rationale behind the plan.

Lt Col Michael Packe, who had served in the divisional HQ during the battle, conveys the feelings of the men: 'Their mood was dumb weariness, and a tremendous dignity. He realised that they were beyond authority, having no more to give; truth would be clear to them, insincerity would be scabrous.'[267]

Browning says they should not feel they have failed. They have enabled 'a springboard into Germany to be established at Nijmegen.'[268]

That was not the objective at all for their own particular part in the operation, but at least Browning doesn't claim they actually won at Arnhem. While they try to put a brave face on it, among some there is bound to be much bitterness below the surface about one of the finest divisions in the British Army destroyed without securing a single Rhine crossing.

Within days, the 1st Airborne Div survivors are sent back down the corridor, where fighting still rages, to Eindhoven and then on to Louvain before going to Brussels to wait for a flight home.

The glider pilots fly back on 29 September, as does Maj Gen Urquhart who is met at Cranwell airfield by Allied Airborne Army boss Lt Gen Brereton among others. During the flight Urquhart reads a sheet of paper thrust into his hands by FM Montgomery during a brief stop at Eindhoven on the way out of Holland. The 1st Airborne Div commander briefed the Field Marshal on the fight for the Rhine bridges, but Monty said little other than to reassure Urquhart that he knew that his troops had done all they could. On the sheet of paper, trembling from the vibration of the aircraft, has been typed an official letter to Urquhart, which, so he was informed shortly before take-off, is also to be released to the press.

The words convey Monty's appreciation of everything Urquhart did and 'the magnificent fighting spirit' of the 1st Airborne Div. The Field Marshal writes that he feels sure all Britain will be proud.

The letter concludes: 'In years to come it will be a great thing for a man to be able to say: "I fought at Arnhem".'[269]

At that very moment – as he stares out the aircraft window at the clouds passing by and, through gaps, sees the twinkling surface of the sea revealed below – Urquhart is conflicted. There is pride in how his men fought, but he feels drained and appalled at the sheer waste. He will not feel right for some time, and the battle still rages in his head.[270]

Once back in the UK, within a very short time, Urquhart reports on the battle to King George VI and receives an award. When he later visits Queen Wilhelmina of the Netherlands, Urquhart expresses regret over the destruction of Arnhem and Oosterbeek and the civilian casualties. In return, the Queen praises the courage of his men and expresses her nation's gratitude, saying she wishes to present decorations immediately.

By 30 September, all the 1st Airborne Div survivors who made it over the river to Driel on 25/26 September are once again at their respective bases in the UK. The 1st Airborne Div after-action report notes: 'This ended operation MARKET, the sixteenth operation planned by the division since 6 June 44.'

—

For those who did not fly back home that September, the story is far from over. Pte Turner, Cpl Tucker, SSgt Withnall and thousands of other Airborne troops are loaded into railway cattle trucks and taken to prison camps in the Reich.

Even before that, Tucker tastes how the victors of the battle intend to rule their captives, though he has no time for such nonsense and remains as defiant as ever.

> 'The Germans had walked into Kate ter Horst's house on the morning after the evacuation. This SS swine said: "Hand over all weapons, binoculars and compasses or you will be shot!"'

Cpl Tucker stuck a pair of binoculars and a compass up the chimney.

> 'I thought they might be of use to me if I could escape later and make my way back there. I never made it back to that house and always wonder if someone found them up the chimney years later and puzzled over how they got there.'

Among those heading by rail into the Reich is one of Tucker's officers in the 1st Bn, Lt Bingley, who reflects on the fate of his own platoon, which suffered a dozen men killed and 18 wounded out of 30: a 100 percent casualty rate. It had been 'a rather one-sided battle with the Germans holding all the trump cards.'[271]

After suffering his serious head wound during the Battle of the Woods, Pte Newhouse has, along with another five Airborne soldiers, been well cared for by the nurses and doctors in the Wolfheze asylum.

> 'My memories of Arnhem are not the bloody mess that things were, but of being in this hospital on my 20th birthday. One of the nurses had found out somehow and brought me a bunch of marigolds and those are my living memories of that battle...'

The Germans visit the asylum and want to take the six soldiers away. In a ruse to keep them out of their hands, a Dutch doctor claims they are too ill to move and will die soon anyway. *So what is the point of disturbing them?*

On 25 September, the asylum is quickly evacuated when word reaches the staff, probably via the Dutch Resistance, that the RAF is going to attack German artillery guns located in the surrounding woods and the hospital grounds. As he is taken to safety, Pte Newhouse spots a Typhoon fighter bomber, which he thinks 'a dangerous looking plane...'

> '...that thing was coming straight towards me and it let a rocket off [which was] coming straight towards me as well, but it hit a church about 20 metres away from where we were.'

It is decided to evacuate everyone from the asylum on a more permanent basis, but there remains the problem of how to smuggle the wounded British soldiers through the Germans, who occupy the area in strength. To get them past checkpoints, Newhouse and the others are wrapped in blankets and told to act as if they have some kind of mental disability or are suffering psychological trauma.

The British soldiers spend the night in a barn, sleeping on beds of straw, although, by dawn, three of them have decided to take their chances and have disappeared.

A woman arrives with a horse and cart full of straw, telling the soldiers to hide under it, so she can convey them to the nearby town of Ede. Newhouse and the others are lodged in a house and keep a low profile. They are told they will soon be taken to somewhere where they can be better looked after. To that end they receive a visitor:

> 'This chap was in a nice uniform and we thought he was a [official] Red Cross. In fact he was a Dutch Nazi. He took us to a German field hospital [which was] a right horrible place.'

For many Dutch people, if not the Nazis in their midst, the aftermath is terrible. Not only are up to 200,000 people forced out of Arnhem, Oosterbeek, and elsewhere on the northern bank of the Rhine. There is widespread, systematic plundering of ruined neighbourhoods by the Germans – everything from kitchen utensils to jewellery and antique furniture is seized. Gardens are dug up in the hunt for treasure their occupants may have tried to hide. Walls are broken down too, in case people have hidden things behind them.

The Dutch territory still under occupation will also suffer a famine in the winter of 1944/45, partly due to the Nazis taking retaliation for a railway strike that aims to hasten the Allied liberation. Frozen canals, flooded zones, bombed infrastructure, destroyed ports, and unusually harsh weather contribute to food supply difficulties. Around 20,000 people die as a result, though the Germans and the Allies agree that food aid can be delivered by air.

But all that further hardship is yet to come, as early on the morning of 26 September – even as the Airborne troops complete their evacuation – Jan Loos and his family are told they and many others will have to move on from the *Rest Awhile* restaurant. 'More refugees are expected,' reports Jan, on 'a rainy day, not the weather you would like to be outdoors. After a bit to eat and a hot drink we continue our journey without a destination in the general direction of North.'

> 'After three-hours walking via de Koningsweg en de Apeldoornseweg we come to Woeste Hoeve, a wayside restaurant. Again the Red Cross is present, providing us with hot drinks and suggesting people that have no place to go should find a spot on one of the farm wagons waiting there, which will take them to the place where the owner of the respective wagon lives. We find out that most of the wagons come

from small farming villages north of Apeldoorn and so we decide to hop on. Every wagon can hold 12 to 14 persons, and as soon one is fully loaded it starts moving in the direction of Apeldoorn. From time to time German vehicles pass us going in the direction of Arnhem. Occasionally, German trucks carrying English prisoners of war go past us, towards Apeldoorn. As we enter Beekbergen our column of farm wagons is shot up by English fighter planes. People jump from the wagons to find protection in foxholes along the road. Horses bolt and some are hit and drop onto the road. People are hit – it is big pandemonium. We flee into the garden of a house nearby and scramble through the back door into the kitchen of the house. There is food on the table but all chairs are tipped back and lying on the floor – whoever was about to have a meal has made a hasty exit. We stay in there until we cannot hear planes anymore and then go back outside to find "our" wagon. Horse, farmer and wagon are there. No damage except for two holes in the wagon. The farmer asks us to get back aboard as soon as possible, because he wants to leave immediately. My sister cannot be convinced to get back on the wagon and chooses to walk behind it. Pa decides to walk with her. My sister does that for at least two hours but becomes so tired she has to be lifted onto the cart. Towards the end of the afternoon we arrive at Epe, approximately 25 kilometres beyond Apeldoorn. There is a large Red Cross tent where we are registered, given something to eat and drink. Then we go to our evacuation address with a helper from the Red Cross. The greeting of the hostess is not exactly warm. I think that, at the sight of the unkempt family standing in front of her on the sidewalk, the lady of the house is shocked. What annoys my mother most of all is the question:

"Do you mean you have not brought any sheets or blankets?" I remember that we spent two or three nights there. Then Pa – who regularly goes to the local market to see if there are any familiar faces around and to hear the latest news – comes back and proposes that we should move to a different address. He had met a colleague who lived in Epe. That man said that he had enough space to give our family a roof over our heads. After consulting with the Red Cross, we move in and camp there until we are allowed to return to Oosterbeek at the end of May 1945.'

Despite all this, the people of the Netherlands who tasted freedom so fleetingly do not entirely give up hope. 'The liberation of our country was [merely] postponed,' thinks Frans de Soet. 'The country has entered the most difficult phase of its existence as an independent country.'

> 'The battle of Arnhem was lost. The Fatherland has to drink the bitter cup to the bottom. Untold misery suffered by thousands of fugitives. Famine threatening the densely populated centres. The loss of all possessions, the loss of every means of livelihood, the ever increasing war debts, unrolls itself as a gloomy panorama.'

In one of those cruel ironies that war often delivers, the road bridge at Arnhem – which the 1st Airborne sacrificed itself to try and capture – is, on 7 October 1944[272], destroyed by Allied bombers, to stop the Germans from using it to reinforce attacks across the Rhine. Civilians going over it during the raid try to save themselves by jumping into the Rhine.[273]

Two days before the Arnhem road bridge is knocked down, Frans de Soet cycles back to Oosterbeek from where he is living at Apeldoorn, hoping he can make it through to the Vredehof villa and salvage a few things. The north bank of the Lower Rhine is now the front line in the war with the protagonists spending the miserable autumn and winter of 1944/5 staring at each other across the cold, slow flowing river, carrying out the occasional fighting patrol and artillery bombardment.

Venturing back to his home is a very risky proposition for de Soet, not least due to Allied artillery firing across the Rhine, trying to destroy German batteries hidden in woods.

As he cycles towards his house, de Soet notices 'here and there... English coats in the trees. Everywhere a chaotic mess of war material and conserves.' Lying all around are abandoned machine guns, motorcycles and gas masks. He hopes his home 'has not been destroyed altogether, or at least that the cellar has remained intact.' Close to Wolfheze, the fields are still 'littered with burned gliders ... A single glider on the field is still intact...' There are abandoned British positions by the former Landing Zones and Drop Zones, indicated by sandbags and slit trenches with parachutes stuffed into them for bedding.

> 'Nowhere do I see soldiers or civilians. Nearing Wolfheze the bomb craters increase and the houses are totally wrecked. The road is already passable again. In front of the burnt out Institute for the Blind stands a piano and an organ. Parachutes of all colours lay everywhere, or hang in trees or houses.'

He stops to cut some silk and ribbon from a parachute, as his wife might find it useful. Cycling on, there are now shell cases, broken rifles and machine gun bullets scattered everywhere – de Soet thinks this deeply ironic, as between 1942 and 1944, metal was so short in Holland 'not even a nail could be bought'. Going down the Utrechtseweg, he comes across a dead British soldier, lying on his back next to a Bren Gun Carrier. 'Everywhere else the dead have been removed. Is this last one a means of propaganda for the passing German troops?'

The Germans de Soet rides by ignore him, and he reaches Oosterbeek unimpeded and then Weverstraat itself. As he cycles down it, on either side are civilians searching the remains of their homes.

Whole sections of the street have been wiped off the face of the earth, and he finds he can't ride any further. Forced to clamber over debris while pushing his bike, he then dodges through the wreckage of military equipment. Finally, he reaches his own house, or what is left of it.

> 'There it, is. A Tiger tank stands in front of it. Of the white "Vredehof" there are only a couple of singed walls [still standing], pierced by shell fire, left … The stove in the back room peeps over the top of the debris. I walk over to the places where our rooms used to be. All is gone.'

The cellar has not collapsed in on itself, but everything within it is burned. 'Helmets, rifles, and hand grenades of our British friends lay in the corner … Of our "flight suitcase" I only find the small locks and a leather strap. Emerging, I have to look out not to step on the numerous German hand grenades that lie everywhere. The dead have, of course, been removed. Only the dead horse has been left.'

A German working on the Tiger tank calls de Soet over, asking to see his papers, explaining there have been 'English agents' sneaking around.

Reassured he is just a Dutch civilian, the German helps de Soet load stuff on the bike, which he has left leaning against a tree.

His would-be cargo includes baby clothes retrieved from the wreckage. As they pick these up, some tins of British explosive tumble out, causing the German some alarm. He warns de Soet not to even touch them. De Soet notices the garden 'is covered with parts of German and English uniforms. The German says that on this spot the fighting has been very severe...'

A machine gun starts firing, apparently at the British dug in on a dyke across the other side of the river. Heavy British shells start falling and exploding in the distance.

> 'When a British plane comes over the Germans take cover against the walls of the house. I tell them that 20 civilians passed six days and nights in that cellar. They cannot understand that they got out alive. They praise the courage of the English soldiers. Very many of their comrades have fallen on this spot.'

De Soet leaves, pushing the bicycle carrying baby clothes salvaged from the ruins of his home. 'On top of Weverstraat I take some apples out of the shop window of the greengrocer...'

Then he heads back towards Apeldoorn, passing 'rows of burned down houses'. Near a bend in the road, on a spot of land beside a burned-out inn, he comes across 'a few simple wooden crosses.' On one there is the inscription, which reads 'English soldier'. A bunch of orange flowers lies on this grave. As de Soet cycles on he ponders what must have happened at his house after he and the other cellar dwellers left the scene.

> 'Judging by the many German uniforms and outfits in the garden, and by the narratives of the Germans themselves I conclude that after our flight the resistance had not been given up, indeed the Germans had several times been repulsed. Probably, after we left, the English counter-attacked from out of the house with hand grenades, whereupon the Germans attacked the house with flame throwers and finished it. But life goes on. Since the heroic Oosterbeek episode, other and greater battles have raged.'

De Soet feels that, just as Holland will never forget 10 May 1940 – the day the Germans invaded – it will not forget 17 September 1944, when liberators came from the skies. De Soet feels Holland might sink into 'depths of misery'.

It may even come on the verge of dying, but he knows it will survive, its people better for it. De Soet believes they will have 'grown inwardly in character and solidarity. They will be exhausted, poor and beggarly, but with an enrichment of inner life of which later generations will be envious.'

Of all this de Soet is sure as he pedals away from the smoking battleground and back towards his wife and child.

Airborne Diaspora

'We suffered together and we saw each other's suffering.'

—Jan Loos

The odyssey of Maj Tony Deane-Drummond has to be one of the most incredible stories of the battle's aftermath.

After four days in the book cupboard in the house at Velp, he is being very careful to conserve his water, restricting himself to a sip in the morning, one at midday, and another in the evening. The weather 'fortunately wasn't too hot', and, to maintain his circulation, at various times Deane-Drummond kneels down and also leans against the side, as gently as he can, to avoid giving himself away with a bump.

> 'I could move a little bit. Sometimes when I was standing at the back, I went to sleep. One's knees then collapsed, as it were, and I hit the side of the cupboard but this fortunately did not arouse attention.'

After 'four or five days, they had questioned most of the people they wanted to', and, with the Airborne prisoners shipped out to Germany the house becomes a barracks for occupying troops. This is terrible news for the man in the cupboard, as the room is converted into a guardroom, with several metal beds in there for enemy soldiers.

Using his basic German and eavesdropping on their conversations, Deane-Drummond realises they are still looking for

Airborne troops on the run – ironically with one hidden just a few feet away.

Eight days later Deane-Drummond is getting 'rather short of water. There was still a certain amount left ... and I realised the time was coming when I'd have to do something about it.'

That night, the guards leave the room, going outside out to hang over a wall, looking at tanks going past on the main road. Deane-Drummond pulls the cupboard key from his pocket, very stealthily unlocks the door and opens it a crack. He peeps through it but freezes on spotting a soldier lying on one of the beds. The next night the guards leave the room again to watch another military column roar by. 'The tanks made a tremendous noise and the lorries following also made quite a lot of noise.' The soldiers from the guardroom 'didn't look back at the house...'

> They were just looking at the German troops going by on the road. I got out of the cupboard shut the door behind me as gently as I could, opened a window, dropped down into bushes ... and decided I would wait until it got really dark.'

He is in thick shrubs about four feet high, which nobody can see into, so provided he stays still, he will not be discovered. The guards go back into the house, and Deane-Drummond emerges from his hiding place and goes around the back of the house.

Rooting around in a vegetable patch he digs up a beetroot and finds a couple of apples, though eating them after nothing but water and mouldy bread for almost a fortnight doesn't do his stomach any good.

Next on his to do list is finding shelter. So Deane-Drummond makes his way into the village and starts knocking on doors, trying to find someone who will take him in. To those who open their doors, he puts a simple question: 'I am a British soldier, can you help me?' The reply at four houses is a firm 'no', for 'they didn't want the trouble...' Going around the back of a house, he finds and eats a large plate of scraps, presumably left out for the cat, and next door finds another one, which he also consumes.

Giving up on trying to get someone to take him in, Deane-Drummond spends the night in a large hut behind a house, dossing down on some straw. Knocking on the back door in the morning he finds the man of the house receptive and friendly but, when she sees him, the man's wife is horrified by the spectre in front of her – a dirty, unshaven soldier. His mere presence raises the terrible possibility of summary execution by the Germans for harbouring a fugitive.

She screams: *'Krijgen hem weg!'*

'Get him away!'

Deane-Drummond apologises and promises he will only stay in the shed for the rest of the day and in the evening will disappear. To go now, in daylight, will not be a good idea. He asks for food and is brought stew 'which was the best thing I'd had for a very long time.'

One of the other houses he called at has obviously informed the Germans about a British soldier on the loose and there is a commotion in the neighbourhood. A party of soldiers is searching houses and sheds.

The obvious place to hide in Deane-Drummond's shed is where the bales of straw are kept, which is on a raised platform about ten feet up. That being the case Deane-Drummond decides to hide under piles of seed trays.

An hour later, German soldiers go into the house, turning everything upside down and then search the shed. They poke about in the straw, find nothing, but do not look under the seed trays.

Having survived that, in the evening Deane-Drummond heads out into the streets and decides to try a church, hoping someone there will give him assistance. A priest who answers the door tells him: 'You are lucky you came to this one as the other side of the house is being used by a German anti-aircraft gun unit.'

Deane-Drummond is sent to see the warden of the church whom he finds to be 'a great chap' who uses his Dutch Resistance contacts to sort out some secure lodgings in the countryside. Deane-Drummond is able to sleep in a bed for the first time in weeks and, after two days recuperating, has a shave. He cycles one night to a house two or three miles away where a couple and their two children, are already looking after some escapees.

Hundreds of Airborne troops actually evade immediate capture and will be at large for months, among them Brig Hackett. His wounds were so serious that he was evacuated to the St Elizabeth Hospital where he was fortunate to be operated on by one of the Airborne division's medical officers, Capt Alex Lipman Kessel. The Germans had suggested such a wound warranted immediate euthanasia.[274]

> 'My life was saved by a parachuting surgeon of ours … who sewed up 12 perforations and two sections of the lower intestine – one "good" perforation is lethal… I was spirited out of that hospital by the Dutch Underground and taken to a house in the village of Ede where I spent the next four and half months being nursed and cherished by an angelic Christian family of four middle aged ladies and the son and daughter of one of them, in a house which was 50 yards away from a German military police billet; evidence of the courage and fortitude of the Dutch. That was a very interesting four months to spend.'

Hackett regained his fitness and, eventually, in early 1945, would escape back to Allied lines by circuitous route and via bicycle and canoe.

Maj Deane-Drummond also bides his time waiting to escape and tries to keep up with news from the outside world. He visits homes along a street in the village to listen to secret radios. The street is allowed electricity for it is also host to a German HQ. During one listening session Deane-Drummond meets Baroness van Heemstra – whose family come from Arnhem and who has a 15-year-old daughter named Edda (who will after the war be known to the world as the Hollywood actress Audrey Hepburn). One night Baroness van Heemstra says to Deane-Drummond: 'You look as though you need a bottle of champagne.'

He enquires: 'Where do you get champagne from?'

'I've got a cellar – this is where I live,' the Baroness tells him.

True to her word, a bottle of Krug champagne arrives at the house where Deane-Drummond is staying 'with her love…'

Eventually Deane-Drummond embarks on what he hopes is his journey home, in a Dutch Red Cross lorry, along with other 1st Airborne troops hiding under bags of potatoes. It heads across to Renkum, just to the north of the Rhine, and from there with the rest of a 130-strong, fully armed group of British escapees he is guided down to the Rhine.

A German patrol encounters them but, fearing they are about to be overwhelmed, just fire a few shots and run away. A Bofors gun is firing a stream of tracer over the river where they are to cross in British assault boats manned by REs of XXX Corps. A covering force of paratroopers from the 101st Airborne Div will provide protection.[275]

As far as Deane-Drummond's family is concerned, he is back from the dead. His wife, Evie, was pregnant when he left for Operation Market Garden. Deane-Drummond was listed missing believed killed. To get to the bottom of things, Evie met his CO in London, who told her that, regretfully, Tony could not be alive. Her husband was last seen in a house that burned down and nobody escaped.

Subsequently, while staying with her parents, Evie wakes up in the middle of the night, with a premonition that he is, in fact, alive. In the morning she reveals this to her parents who say: 'We all hope he's going to be alright but you have to be prepared for the worst.'

'I know he's alright,' she insists.

Two days later, Tony Deane-Drummond rings home, revealing to his astonished wife that he has just escaped from Holland.

–

The belated return of Airborne troops from the battlefield was a minor piece of good cheer in a dismal story that no number of medals handed out to those who took part could hide.

Market Garden faltered within sight of victory – possession of the bridge at Arnhem that would supposedly have been the gateway into the black heart of Nazi Germany, to deliver a killer blow to the Third Reich. It lay just beyond the fingertips of the soldiers dashing to link up with the 1st Airborne Div.

Had the Allies, by mid-September 1944, been facing an enemy still on the run – the disorganised, fragmented formations they had relentlessly pushed before them since the Normandy breakout – things might have been very different. The pause by Second Army on the Belgian-Dutch frontier enabled the Germans to gather strength – to display once again their formidable ability to create workable combat formations out of the remnants of destroyed units or those drawn from training schools and other sources.

Not only that, but the failure to destroy the 65,000-strong 15th Army, allowing it to escape across the Scheldt into Holland, ensured that additional forces were available to bolster the line, while reinforcements soon arrived from Germany. The Germans decided to make a stand because, after all, if the Allies could see the opportunities offered by a war-ending thrust into the Ruhr, so could they. Defeat it, and they may gain time for the Führer's supposedly war-winning V weapons to force the Western allies into a negotiated settlement, so Germany could then focus on fending off the Soviets. How different Europe might have been but for those brave and desperate hours on the Rhine when the chance of final victory by Christmas slipped away. The tragic irony for the German victors at Arnhem – the last time Hitler's armies triumphed over the Allies in the West – was they ensured the hated Russians got to Berlin first, to devastate the city, pillage what was left of it, and rape 110,000 of its women.[276] The Iron Curtain came crashing down, dividing Germany for more than 40 years.

The Germans might have been better off allowing Monty's plan to work, but, in the end, Eisenhower's broad front policy was not designed to capture Berlin – despite his protestations after the war that it was worth giving Monty's narrow thrust a go.[277] That, in fact, was never the aim, for he knew that such a battle would be hugely costly, and it was far better to let the Russians take it on.

Also, any territories in the east the Western allies took, and which fell within the spheres of influence agreed by Stalin, Roosevelt, and Churchill at the Yalta conference, would have to be yielded. Therefore, what was the point in shedding blood to take them? Berlin lay firmly within the agreed Soviet zone. Monty's single thrust deep into the Ruhr would have been hard to sustain logistically and that most likely would have enabled the Germans – always tenacious when cornered – to concentrate force against a component of the Allied armies and gain enough local superiority to defeat it.[278]

In October and November 1944, the British and Canadians finally did what Monty should have ordered them to do as their over-riding priority – securing the approaches to (and opening the port of) Antwerp.

The offensive, while a difficult and bloody slog on the landward side, included a successful assault in early November by the 52nd Div (not used at Arnhem), a Royal Marine commando brigade (from the sea), plus army green berets and Canadian troops, to take German occupied Walcheren Island – which dominates the Schelde Estuary – and its causeway.

A last gasp German offensive for Antwerp in December 1944 – driving through the Ardennes to try and cut the Allies off from their supplies – was mounted by massive armoured forces, resulting in the so-called Battle of the Bulge. It showed once again the amazing resilience of the Germans, though it wasted valuable divisions better used in defending the Reich against the Russians. The units involved included the II SS Panzer Corps, fighting the 101st and 82nd US Airborne who had been rushed into the front line. After the poor weather that prevented Allied air power from bringing its weight to bear cleared up, the German advance was halted, its troops and armour destroyed, many of them sitting ducks due to running out of fuel. Reinforcements sent into the Battle of the Bulge to help rescue beleaguered Americans included the British 6th Airborne Div, fighting as ground infantry. It was a crushing defeat for the Germans.

Generalfeldmarschall Model – the victor of Arnhem – was left in such a state of despair that, when ordered by the Führer in spring 1945 to send what troops he had left to defend Berlin he walked into a wood and blew his brains out.

After the winter stasis, a decisive moment is needed to give the Allied push into Germany momentum. The British army group has yet to get across the Rhine, though Patton's troops cross in January.

As the Allied armies prepare to redouble their efforts in the spring, the men who fought at Arnhem, but who are now captives of the enemy, will be caught up in the brutal turmoil of the conflict's end.

Near starvation and an encounter with the Russians features in the odyssey of Frank Newhouse, who, after being handed over by a Dutch Nazi to the Germans in September 1944, was, like thousands of his comrades, put in a railway cattle truck.

Following a journey by rail of several hours, he ends up in a small prison camp on the outskirts of Dresden, the so-called

'Florence on the Elbe'.[279] Both sides in the conflict use POWs as labourers, though not officers, who are exempt from such work under the Geneva Convention. In the case of Newhouse and others in their Dresden cage this means being marched into the city to work for the local authority.

Dresden is so far comparatively untouched compared to other German cities, so they only clear up damage caused by the occasional bomb dropped by an Allied aircraft. The prisoners do perform menial tasks, such as unblocking sewers and while doing so are required to wear a long green coat with a red triangle sewn on it. Polish *kapos* – prisoners who have agreed to enforce camp discipline for their Nazi overlords – are put in charge of work groups. They can be brutal, beating POWs with a wooden club if they don't appear to be working hard enough.

Despite all the horrific casualties caused by Allied saturation bombing elsewhere and Germany's sons killed in battles with the Allies, Newhouse and his fellow prisoners do not experience any significant animosity from the people of Dresden. Although, during the Battle of the Bulge Newhouse found 'they suddenly became aggressive, because they were winning again.'[280] That feeling of Germany being in the ascendency once more does not last long and as the Russians close from the east and the Americans from the west, Dresden is bombed. High level fears about another enemy resurgence drive the decision to devastate the city. The Ardennes offensive was a real shocker and there are serious concerns about revolutionary new U-boats severing the transatlantic convoys.

The sooner the Nazi regime collapses the better. There also is intense pressure from the Soviets for the British and Americans to do more. The Dresden raid partly aims to kill thousands of civilians in order to terrorise Germany into surrender, following similar aerial assaults on Hamburg, Berlin and Cologne. A mass exodus of refugees will, it is hoped, impose immense strain on the railway network and divert resources away from the Nazi war effort. Dresden is also home to various important war industries and a major military command and control centre. The Russians push the British and Americans to act by feeding them an intelligence report suggesting two enemy armoured divisions have recently come north from Italy and are in and around Dresden.[281]

Between 13 February and 15 February 1945 – out of clear blue skies and in brilliant sunshine[282] – Dresden is devastated by a RAF raid involving 783 Lancaster bombers, which, in two waves, drops 2,600 tons of bombs[283] including incendiaries. This is followed by 311 Flying Fortresses and Liberators of the USAAF unloading 771 tons of bombs. Dresden's massive railway junctions are largely undamaged, but the historic city centre itself is destroyed by a massive fire-typhoon, along with 25,000 of its citizens.[284]

Some days later, during a dinner at Chequers hosted by Winston Churchill, the boss of RAF bomber command, Air Marshal Sir Arthur Harris, is asked about the scale of destruction inflicted on Dresden.

He responds: 'There is no such place as Dresden.'[285]

When Frank Newhouse is sent into Dresden within hours of the bombings, there is no aggression towards him or fellow prisoners from the survivors. Newhouse is shocked to his core by what he finds, feeling the raids are 'an atrocious thing to do. I still can't understand it.'

> 'The casualty figures that you've seen published for the deaths in Dresden are very, very conservative ... we saw flames and smoke and bodies and all sorts of things, the place was still on fire. It was horrendous.'

Aside from clearing up the debris, the POWs are required to recover the bodies of the slain, or what remains of them, with Newhouse seeing 'piles and piles of bodies in a square [and they are] covered in quick lime and then burned.' He marvels at the magnificent 200-year-old Frauenkirche, which has been badly damaged but is somehow still standing. A few days later it falls in on itself, killing people sheltering inside.

Amid the smoking ruins of Dresden, the prisoners are in 'a survival situation', looking for food scraps or oddments they can sell, or barter, for food. Newhouse spots a couple of things but soon wishes he hadn't. 'I picked this thing up and I thought it was the end of a cigar to flog for bread… and it was a little child's finger. I picked up a shoe and there was a little child's foot in it. It was shocking…'

Airborne soldiers who fought to gain a crossing over the Rhine in autumn 1944 fly into combat again on 24 March 1945 when the 21st Army Group finally makes it over the river in force at Wesel, during Operation Varsity.

Varsity features a massive combined amphibious and airborne assault, involving the British 6th Airborne and the US 17th Airborne Div, a total of 17,300 air landing infantry, paratroopers and other air-portable units all sent into action in one massive lift. The 1st Airborne Div is not capable of taking part and will not see combat again as a unified formation.[286] Among those flying into action, is Capt Peter Fletcher once again at the controls of a Horsa glider, facing a tricky moment as clouds of smoke and dust, created by Allied bombing of Wesel, obscure the LZ.

Aside from his glider losing a wing on clipping a telegraph pole, Capt Fletcher has a good landing. After the troops his Horsa is carrying depart, he heads for a farmhouse designated as the Glider Pilot Regt HQ for the operation. Sten gun at the ready – just in case – Capt Fletcher makes his way across the field only to be greeted by 'this motley crew of Ukrainians and other foreigners the Germans had pressed into service emerging from the farmhouse cellars saying "*kamerad*" as they surrendered.'[287]

This is a good sign that, unlike Market Garden, the Varsity operation will, hopefully, end in a victory for the British and their allies.

While other Airborne warriors are leading the way into the Reich, Frank Newhouse witnesses the Nazis' draconian measures to keep order as Germany collapses.

While out on a working party, a French-Canadian POW, nicknamed 'Canada', manages to acquire a small piece of bacon and hide it in his clothes. He is searched on returning to the camp and the contraband discovered. Put on trial for looting, he is sentenced to death.

One morning, Newhouse and another prisoner are told they are not doing their usual work and instead will take shovels and follow a guard through Dresden to some woods above the city.

The rather elderly guard orders them to dig a hole two metres long, two metres deep and half a metre wide. During a break from his labours, Newhouse notices a large piece of card on the ground with some writing on it. Using the rudimentary German he has acquired he translates what it says: 'A Prisoner of War shot for Looting'.

This message is as much for German civilians as anyone else, for, at the time, the SS are shooting them for looting without even a trial.

Going back to his fellow prisoner, Newhouse tells him about his discovery – a sign for 'Canada's' grave – which they must be digging.

The prisoners confront the guard, telling him: 'No more digging!'

The guard shakes his head and orders: 'Work!'

He cocks his old French rifle with the bayonet on it and points it at them. The prisoners know the old man doesn't have the heart to shoot, so they again refuse to carry on digging. Then, a group of men emerge from the woods, led by an SS officer.

His charges are apparently new recruits under training and, stopping to find out what is going on, the SS man talks to the guard who tells him the prisoners are refusing to work. The SS officer is an entirely different sort of person, and the prisoners can tell he won't hesitate to kill them. They resume digging 'Canada's' grave in which his bullet-riddled corpse is soon interred.

With Russians getting closer, the prison camp is abandoned with a group of prisoners including Newhouse ordered to march[288] to Czechoslovakia. They are accompanied by a few guards who are less than enthusiastic about the task. One by one, the guards disappear, leaving the four POWs to wander the mountains of northern Czechoslovakia.

At this time, the most treasured possession Newhouse possesses is a rusty tin that he can drink from after dipping it into fast flowing mountain streams. When it comes to food, the prisoners beg for scraps in villages and forage in the fields, also stealing from back garden vegetable plots.

One night, they steal potatoes from a woman's garden, then, after consuming them, the next day go and knock on her door asking if she can feed them. She welcomes them into her home and gives them chicken and potato soup, telling them about her son. He is a soldier just like them, a POW in a camp in Canada. Newhouse feels very guilty about his activities the previous evening.

With the war ending on 7 May, but unknown to the British POWs, they continue wandering, Newhouse and the others reaching the spa town of Karlovy Vary, in the German speaking Sudetenland.

They go from door to door begging for food and shelter. A woman in one house tells them the Russians are taking over the town, explaining she and her husband are scared about what might happen.

She offers Newhouse and his fellow travellers refuge in return for their protection. After something to eat and a hot bath, Newhouse sleeps for the first time ever under a duvet.

In a cruel irony, American troops, with whom the British could well have hitched a ride west, had occupied the town on 6 May. However, under the terms of an agreement between the Western allies and the Russians, they were pulled back on 11 May. In fact, fighting is still going on nearby, as fleeing German units, including Estonian Waffen SS, who fear they will be massacred, stage a last stand. Though some get away to surrender to American forces, most of those who capitulate to Czech partisans and Soviet troops are executed.

When predatory Russians come hammering on the door, the lodgers answer it and explain they are British soldiers, and so the unwelcome callers go away.

Newhouse and the others decide they really ought to head west to make contact with their own side. They spend the next month walking to Regensburg, introducing themselves to some well provisioned US troops, who feed them to bursting and then provide some transport.

> 'They took us to an airfield, gave us a couple of jerry cans of petrol and a car and told us to go to Brussels. The four of us got in this car and drove to Brussels and got deloused and then [sent] home.'

Newhouse turns 21 in September 1945, reflecting that since he parachuted into Holland 'a multitude of things have happened… I'd lived a lifetime.' Being wounded in battle, his captivity, witnessing the horror of Dresden, and his wanderings – all have changed him. He now won't take any nonsense from anyone. Had he never gone to war or been captured would he have been more likely to suffer fools gladly? Years later he will revisit the Wolheze asylum and also Arnhem itself, attending a European Youth Conference held to further the cause of peace. To illustrate the horrors of war he tells the youngsters about his wartime experiences.

Yet, despite the pain and the suffering he has endured, the horrors he witnessed, and his odyssey through a starving, war-wrecked Europe, Frank Newhouse will only ever think of himself as 'just a paratrooper'.

—

Some of the British troops captured at Arnhem will owe their own liberation to the Russians whom Monty sought to beat in the quest to take Berlin. In his Silesian POW camp Pat Withnall and other Airborne soldiers know their time in captivity truly is over thanks to a typically Soviet show of brute force.

> They drove a tank through the gates. They then drove a herd of cows in and told us to feed ourselves. We killed the cows and then burned down our huts to cook them.'

Several weeks later, the Russians ship the POWs from that camp to the American zone for repatriation to Britain.

Since being captured, Pte Sims of the 2nd Para Bn has endured starvation and beatings. More than once, when away from his prison camp in western Germany, as part of a POW working party, he has evaded death at the hands of Allied aircraft. Sims has seen terrible sights amid the carnage of war. The worst has been 'a shrapnel-riddled pram with a dead baby inside it.'[289]

After one raid, the angry citizens of a newly devastated town where the British have been working gather to berate them, screaming the names of cities destroyed by RAF bombing.

'Hanover... Cologne... Hamburg... Berlin!'

Sims and his mates unwisely hurl back the names of cities blitzed by the Germans: 'Rotterdam... Belgrade... Coventry... London!'

This totally enrages the mob. 'Things began to look nasty,' notes Sims, 'as the women converged on us carrying bricks, cooking pots, sticks and carving knives. They were much more terrifying than the SS.'[290]

Fortunately, a Luftwaffe officer restores order and puts the POWs to work clearing up rubble until the crowd has dispersed. He then orders their guards to get them back to camp as quickly as possible.

Later, Sims encounters a Flak train with a mixed-sex crew, commanded by a thoroughly cynical, English-speaking warrant officer. He offers Sims a cigar, explaining how he always makes sure his train gets 'the hell out of it down the line' to avoid destruction. He observes of his troops, who make no secret of sleeping with each other: 'It's good for them.'[291]

Later, when USAAF Thunderbolt fighters strafe the Flak train, Pte Sims looks on admiringly from the cover of a ditch as a female soldier – the sole crew member to stay aboard firing cannons – manages to shoot one down. 'She was a magnificent sight,' thinks Sims, of the 'strapping blonde ... Amazon' who is the hero of all her comrades.

As the front lines become fluid, the British Army annihilates remaining pockets of enemy troops in north-western Germany, and Sims is among 300 POWs marched east towards Berlin, allegedly to be held as hostages.

They end up pressing themselves into the mud of a field during a battle between a British self-propelled gun and a Tiger. Their SS guards have already run off, after giving the prisoners their rifles, and now the Tiger retreats and scuttles away, hotly pursued by its foe.

Using bits of cloth, the prisoners spell out 'POW' on the ground. This is spotted by an Allied aircraft and a message passed on, for the following day a Bren Gun Carrier emerges from some woods. It trundles towards the large group of prisoners, who charge forward cheering their lungs out.

'We practically lifted that carrier off the ground as we engulfed it in a human wave,' relates Sims. 'At last it was all over.'[292]

—

As for Cpl Harry Tucker, the tough little Para eventually liberates himself via a long walk. After his wounds heal, he twice escapes from POW camps while out on working parties. The first time is in Silesia during early 1945 when he does a runner in company with a Glider Pilot Regt NCO.

Their plan is to reach the Russians, who are by then advancing rapidly into eastern Germany. Just as they are nearing Red Army positions, the escapees have the misfortune to stumble across a German regimental headquarters in a wood.

The commander of the unit is going to have them both shot. He is persuaded otherwise by a junior officer, so Tucker and the glider pilot are sent to another POW camp, this time in western Germany.

Cpl Tucker is not going to spend any more time behind the wire. Sharing his new cage with American troops, he conspires with one of them to take his place in a working party.

> 'I swapped clothes and papers with this Yank prisoner. We marched down the road a bit and we were put in a barn for some reason. Suddenly there was a commotion and a Yank got a knife from somewhere and tried to cut his own throat, presumably because he couldn't stand being a prisoner anymore. While the guards were distracted dealing with this I legged it down the road.'

After a few days wandering around, Tucker meets some Frenchmen forced to work in German factories but who have, like him, made a bid for freedom. 'The Frenchies had these suitcases and said they wanted to stick with me. They had food and drink, so that was okay by me.'

This motley crew eventually comes face-to-face with a lone American soldier who is possibly an advance scout for a patrol, the suspicious GI asking for identification papers.

> 'I didn't have any and my POW tag was not good enough for him. The fact that I spoke English like a true native wasn't proof because some Germans had been carrying out missions by posing as Allied soldiers. The Frenchies were no good, as they didn't speak English. So, I rolled up my sleeves and showed him my tattoos. Finally, he was convinced when he saw "Dad" on one arm and "Mum" on the other. The Yank smiled and gave me a bar of chocolate. I burst into tears because I was so glad to have finally escaped and made it to friendly lines.'

Harry Tucker did eventually make it to the Arnhem road bridge (albeit a new one built post-war and named after John Frost). On 17 September 1994 – 50 years to the day that he leapt from a Dakota into battle – Harry was in Holland along with a thousand other Airborne veterans of the fight then still alive. He watched as eight hundred British paratroopers from the modern-day Parachute Regt provided a salute by jumping from Hercules transport aircraft to land on the same LZ as their forebears. The bridge Harry walked onto at the age of 75 may not have been the one he fought in vain to reach in 1944, but it still felt wonderful to finally go across the Rhine.

> 'A lot of mates died in the battle, so it means a great deal for me to be in Arnhem and pay my respects to their memory.'[293]

Whenever the veterans went back, they were always deeply moved by the warm reception they got from the people of Oosterbeek and Arnhem, feeling that they didn't deserve it. Jan Loos recalls that returning veterans frequently asked of their Dutch hosts: 'Why are you all so kind to us – after we were the cause of all the misery and destruction?'

For Jan, who regularly gives talks on the battle and his experiences as a teenager caught up in it, 'those days are still in my memory as if they happened yesterday', and the answer is simple:

> 'It lies in the bond that was created by going through it together – Airborne soldiers and Dutch civilians alike. They fought in our gardens, in our houses – sometimes even from room to room – while we were sheltering in the basement. We suffered together and we saw each other's suffering: No water... no food... no sleep. We saw them wounded, frequently took care of them one way or another and we admired

them for what they were doing; putting their lives at stake for the liberation of the people of a foreign country.'[294]

Appendix 1

Looking Back in Anger?

What was the perspective of combat commanders who found themselves plunged into the seething cauldron of battle? Did they look back in anger? Or were they philosophical about the glorious failure that Montgomery branded one of the great fights, in which a man could be proud to have taken part? Did any of them actually think, as Monty tried to claim, that it was 'ninety per cent successful'?

That's a hard one to accept. If something does not achieve its objective – launching the 21st Army Group into heart of the Nazi war machine, to end the war by Christmas – then it's a failure. And when it comes to some of the big beasts in this enterprise (the top generals), what did they really think, after the passing of time, about how things turned out?

'It Was a Relief When the Party Ended.'

Having reached Nijmegen after his own escape across the Rhine, not surprisingly, Maj Gen Urquhart found he was 'not yet ready to analyse the battle, nor even inclined to look back in anger or regret at the causes of this tragic yet inspiring operation of war through which we had just lived.'[295]

For quite some time, he and other members of the 1st Airborne Div who escaped in body across the Rhine found their minds still back in The Cauldron.

Urquhart was afflicted with 'an incredible lassitude that was to persist for weeks...'[296] On the night after the evacuation he and two other officers from the 1st Airborne Div were invited to, what Urquhart described as, an 'extravagant' dinner with Lt Gen Browning and Lt Gen Horrocks. The latter's smooth patter about his exploits combined with the rich menu caused the Airborne division general to feel nauseous. Urquhart recoiled from Horrocks, and indeed, the whole evening, and wanted to be somewhere else. 'The Battle still raged in my head. It was a relief when the party ended.'[297]

Even so, in January 1945, Urquhart would remark of the recent battle in his official report: 'The losses were heavy but all ranks appreciate that the risks involved were reasonable.' He felt his men would 'willingly undertake another operation in similar conditions' and that they all had 'no regrets.'

More than a dozen years later Urquhart stayed true to that perspective, ending his own account of the battle by observing: 'I have the same view today, when all the survivors are scattered all over the world...'[298]

Horrocks would after the war reveal how terrible he felt at the failure to relieve the Airborne division, describing it as 'the blackest moment of my life.'[299]

He felt the responsibility lay with him, though, in his view, the Guards and US Airborne troops did everything they could. He judged 43rd Div should have been sent across the Rhine further to the west of Oosterbeek and then hooked around behind the Germans, but that, in the final analysis, time ran out and the opposition was too strong. Finally, there was the geography, which was a serious impediment to a successful outcome. According to one historian, Horrocks was not armed with all the detailed intelligence on the terrain that he should have been.[300]

Prior to the war, the Dutch had war-gamed what would happen if an assault tried to use the same axis of advance. Those who went straight up the single, elevated highway across the polders were defeated, whereas a decision to make a crossing to the west of the Rhine road bridge and outflank the enemy delivered a win for the Dutch war-gamers.[301]

Horrocks may not have been aware of that at the time, but senior Dutch military officers did warn their British counterparts on Montgomery's staff. They pointed out that a failure to keep the infantry up with the tanks at all times – in order to swiftly outflank enemy blocking positions in terrain that tanks could not advance across – would see the drive up the highway falter.[302]

'...They Were Like Chefs in Haute Cuisine...'

In 1945 the official history of the British Airborne forces in the Second World War explained that the sacrifice of lives – and the destruction of the 1st Airborne Div – was not in vain. It suggested the battle for Oosterbeek and Arnhem showed that 'as a corporate whole this [1st Airborne] Division triumphantly vindicated the soundness of their training and proved beyond doubt or dispute that an airborne army is not a luxury but a necessity.'[303]

John Hackett, according to the same account, reportedly wrote in a letter to Roy Urquhart: 'Thank you for the party. It didn't go quite as we hoped and got a bit rougher than we expected. But speaking for myself, I'd take it on again any time and so, I'm sure, would everybody else.'[304]

That was just a few months after the battle, when Hackett was fresh back from his escapades in Holland – no doubt unwilling to rock the boat in light of the battle's depiction as one of the greatest fights in British military history (which it was, though also a terrible defeat).

Some decades later, by then retired from the Army and installed as a leading academic of some renown, Hackett was less kind. He was pretty stinging in his assessment of the Airborne forces' planners, observing: 'I used to think they were like chefs in haute cuisine that would prepare a delicious dish and then add pepper and salt to taste – pepper and salt being the German troops in this case.' He added: 'The Airborne business ... tended to be manned, and very considerably be [commanded] by brave, highly motivated courageous boy scouts.'[305]

In early September 1944, Hackett felt, there had been 'tremendous optimism not to worry about [the opposition], except a "stomach battalion" – people with gallstones, not fit [and] an officers training school.' When asked post-war when he began to feel the plan was flawed, Hackett replied: 'Before it began.'

During the final pre-operation briefing for his brigade on its part in Market Garden, using 'beautiful maps', as he put it, Hackett outlined the allotted task of setting up an outer perimeter on the northernmost approaches to Arnhem. When that was done, he asked his battalion commanders and other senior brigade staff to stay behind, to give them an idea of the slim prospects of success. He told them their worst casualties would be suffered trying to reach the positions where they could set up the outer perimeter, which duly happened.

In Hackett's view, the British Airborne forces were highly skilled in deploying their troops and equipment onto the field of battle but did not have the required level of expertise when it came to commanding and controlling units after landing. But, to be fair to them, Hackett acknowledged that, whereas the 6th Airborne Div had months to work on its plans, the 1st Airborne had to adapt elements of the cancelled Operation Comet for a much more ambitious venture.

Yet it wasn't really possible to compare the D-Day and Market Garden missions. It was like comparing apples and oranges. For example, in June 1944, the heavyweight back-up was rather closer to hand. There were hundreds of Allied fighter-bombers on call over Normandy – along with considerable naval firepower loitering offshore. Troop reinforcements and armour only had six or seven miles to cover to reach Airborne troops at the bridges over the Caen Canal and Orne River (not the 64 miles to be covered in 48 hours under the Market Garden plan).

Had the 6th Airborne Div faced hardcore Waffen SS panzer troops on D-Day itself, then it could well have found itself in deep trouble, not least because its own brigades were widely scattered across Normandy.

Much of the 6th Airborne's equipment went astray too, with the chaotic, if successful, Merville Battery attack being a case in point. The Merville Battery assault force – the 9th Para Bn – lost its 3-inch mortars and 6pdr guns and ended up with only one heavy machine gun and 150 men out of the 600 thought necessary for the job. The Royal Engineer sappers, meant to blow holes in formidable enemy defences – including barbed wire fences and minefields – and then to destroy the enemy guns, were among those who went astray. Serious opposition may have seen the whole thing fail, for the depleted assault force was only armed with light weapons and whatever explosive charges were to hand. Making the best of what he had had at his disposal, Lt Col Terence Otway ordered his men to attack, and, despite the odds, they managed to achieve the objective.

Chaos is inherent in Airborne operations as the commander of the 3rd Para Bde, Brig James Hill admitted to his troops before D-Day when he said, 'in spite of your excellent training and orders, do not be daunted if chaos reigns. It undoubtedly will.'[306]

The 6th Airborne also had plentiful, accurate, and up-to-date intelligence on the targets and who was defending them, courtesy of the French Resistance. It was far more trusted than the Dutch equivalent, which had been penetrated by enemy agents and severely compromised. The planners for D-Day also did not willingly ignore important intelligence, as Browning did with the information received on the presence of the Waffen SS, including armour, near Arnhem.

The bigger question was whether or not it was entirely feasible for such large-scale Airborne operations to ever succeed in the face of more than the lightest opposition, especially without overwhelming firepower back-up on call from the air and/or from the sea.

They also needed guaranteed resupply and reinforcement from the same directions and on to secure DZs and LZs. Even success could come at huge cost and always needed a lot of luck.

Hence the Germans – pioneers of *coup de main* operations from the air during 1940, when they conquered Holland and Belgium – gave up on major air assaults by their own paratroopers after taking the eastern Mediterranean island of Crete in May 1941. It was a success strategically but, in all other terms, hugely costly and the last such airborne assault by the *Fallschirmjägers*.

To seize Crete from 26,000 British, New Zealand, and Australian troops,[307] the Germans unleashed Operation Mercury, involving 13,000 paratroopers along with 9,000 mountain division troops, using a mix of 500 parachute and transport aircraft along with gliders.

The main targets on Crete were three airfields to be taken by the German paratroopers and glider-borne units, so that more troops could be landed. Though succeeding, there were 4,000 Germans troops killed and a further 2,000 wounded.[308] Plans for further parachute assaults on, for example, Malta, Cyprus, or the Suez Canal, were cancelled. Hitler told Generaloberst Kurt Student, the boss of Germany's airborne troops that he believed 'the days of the paratroopers are over.'

Student would, after the war, admit Crete was 'the graveyard of the paratroops.'[309] He would list among the reasons for such catastrophic losses the fact that intelligence had not picked up the full strength of enemy forces on Crete and also the intervention of enemy tanks at critical moments.[310] That would all sound very familiar to the commanders of the 1st Airborne Div.

'…It Was Not for Want of Trying That We Failed…'

A cardinal sin of the mission to take the bridges over the Rhine at Arnhem was the split lift. John Frost suggested post-war that a second lift on the first day – during perfect weather for Airborne operations – could have been staged. Frost claimed experienced airmen told him, after the war, they could have done more lifts on 17 September.

He suggested Air Vice Marshal LN Hollingshurst, the boss of the RAF's transportation and resupply aircraft was keen to do it, although Lt Gen Brereton, the 1st Allied Airborne Army supremo, said it was not possible. In the final analysis, Frost judged the failure to stage two lifts on 17 September 'the worst thing that ever happened'.

Hackett felt that it would have helped if Browning's Airborne Corps HQ had not come to Holland, as its contribution to the actual fight was negligible. Those gliders could have taken more troops and equipment to Arnhem.

The British split lift meant only one brigade was available for the main attack on the first day, with the other brigade held back to guard DZs and LZs until the second lift could come in on 18 September. A single lift on the first day would have enabled all three brigades to advance on Arnhem bridge within hours of each other, avoiding the fatal delay that saw the Germans block routes.

Tony Hibbert felt those British troops that did advance on the bridge showed lack of flexibility and paused at the wrong moments — the nights of 17 and 18 September — plus didn't press hard or fast enough on any weak points they found in the enemy's defences.

Instead, they waited until the following morning by which time it was too late, and the southern route was closed. He conceded that sort of agility required excellent communications between units to co-ordinate a change of plan — a sort which the British did not possess.

It was a shock because, he said, such a comprehensive communications failure had never happened during previous Airborne operations. Even so, Hibbert felt that, on realising Frost had got through on the southern route, the other battalions should have pressed on come what may. Hibbert felt it was a serious error for Urquhart to have left his HQ to go haring about in a jeep trying to hurry the troops into Arnhem: '…and, of course, as history shows he disappeared … which left the operation without a leader for a very important period.'[311]

Also, while Browning and others may have known about the stronger opposition than expected, Hibbert felt neither Frost, Horrocks, nor Urquhart were made properly aware of the true scale of what they were likely to face. Hibbert conceded it was known there were SS recruit training units in the area and Luftwaffe personnel.

Frost felt the Guards Armoured Division did the best it could but was badly handicapped by having only that one, narrow avenue of attack and that infantry should have pushed harder on the flanks. XII Corps and VIII Corps, which were supposedly doing so should, so Frost felt, have shown more vigour. Despite all that, he believed the higher command genuinely felt the operation could succeed and the Guards Armoured Division had 'a very good chance' of success especially if 'the Nijmegen [road] bridge been available earlier...' Frost felt not enough priority was given to taking the Nijmegen road bridge, preferably securing it on the first day. He also thought the Americans should have dropped some of their men north of Nijmegen road bridge to conduct a simultaneous seizure of both ends.

The enemy did fear the tide of Allied armour, but, the way Market Garden unfolded, they could concentrate their initially meagre – but soon heavily reinforced – forces to hold it back.

The British were also unlucky to land right where the overall boss of enemy forces, Generalfeldmarschall Model, was based, which meant he was instantly able to galvanise his units and put pressure on for reinforcements to be sent from the Reich as soon as possible.

When Frost met Heinz Harmel after the war, the Waffen SS commander revealed Model was 'like a caged tiger and put the fear of God into them – so that was the kind of leadership which was being used by the opposition...' Frost felt that it was 'not quite the same ... on our side.'[312]

When it came to XXX Corps lacking drive and aggression Urquhart agreed, judging, after the war, that 'Horrocks's enthusiasm was not transmitted adequately to those who served under him.'[313] Horrocks denied this and pointed out there was indeed a 'sense of desperate urgency ... and it was not for want of trying that we failed to arrive on time.'[314]

In comparison, the higher command on the Allies side at times seemed to lack focus and drive. Lt Gen Matthew B Ridgway, commander of the US XVIII Airborne Corps, suggested the 'ground armies' in Market Garden were 'sluggish' and short of the 'more vigorous ... supervision from the top' that was necessary.[315] Montgomery was seemingly distracted by the politics of working on Eisenhower for advantage in the next stage – the drive into Germany – while Lt Gen Miles Dempsey, boss of the Second Army, also failed to drive people on at the front line hard enough.

There was a lack of realisation in some quarters that the weak enemy resistance encountered since the breakout from Normandy was a thing of the past now that the contest was on the borders of the Reich – something that Maj Gen Sosabowski had warned would be the case.

Though he treated the Cassandra-like Polish general with disdain for his constant criticism of the plan, Lt Gen Browning privately admitted as much in October 1944.

Touching on the obvious reasons for failure – breakdown in communications between the 1st Airborne and higher commands, the enemy squeezing the 'corridor', the time it took to seize the Nijmegen bridge, bad weather interfering with the lifts schedule, stronger enemy presence at Arnhem – Browning confessed the Germans 'had more people ... than we had expected, and he [the enemy] fought with much greater determination than was ever thought possible.'[316]

With controversy raging to this day over what went wrong and who was most to blame, it is the Americans who are among the most vociferous critics of the so-called tea-drinking Brits.

The British are slammed for allegedly brewing up a nice cuppa on the road to Arnhem after storming across the Nijmegen road bridge instead of charging ahead on those last few miles to the Rhine.

Rather than fulminating about tea breaks, the American critics ought to consider the culpability of the supreme commander of the Allied Expeditionary Force. It was General Eisenhower, after all, who took the overall decision to go with Market Garden. A superb high-level manager of men and armies, Eisenhower faced criticism from both his own and British commanders in the field whenever he seemed to favour one side or the other. Eisenhower could either put the weight of the Allied advance into Germany behind General Omar Bradley's US 12th Army Group (with Patton leading another blitzkrieg) or go with the daring plan of Montgomery.

It was not until 12 September that Eisenhower finally came down on Monty's side – which gave virtually no time to finalise plans. According to the British historian Arthur Bryant, in *Triumph in the West*, this delay meant 'the German strength in Montgomery's path [had] doubled.'[317] When it comes to the matter of it being better to go for opening up Antwerp than Arnhem, it was not actually until October that Eisenhower insisted its approaches be taken.[318] Yet even the Chief of the Imperial General Staff, FM Alan Brooke, felt that it would have been better to deal with opening Antwerp than stage Market Garden, which he felt was premature.[319]

Despite his disputes with Monty, according to the American historian Stephen Ambrose, until the day he died, Eisenhower 'insisted that Market Garden was a risk that had to be run.'[320] Ambrose interviewed Eisenhower several times between 1964 and 1969, and the former supreme commander maintained the Allied armies had to maintain pressure on – to keep pushing.

Eisenhower felt Market Garden offered the quickest and shortest means of attacking into the Reich – via the North German plain. According to Ambrose, Eisenhower believed 'it would have been criminal for him not to have tried.'[321] However, as fellow American military historian Carlo D'Este noted in his biography of Eisenhower[322] ultimately the general would regard Market Garden as a miserable failure.

Ambrose felt that at a tactical level – and this is where it faltered at Nijmegen north of the road bridge – US paratroopers did not co-operate well with British tanks, with whom who they had never trained. Perhaps not even they could have got the Guards Armoured through to Arnhem. In the end, thought Ambrose, the Market Garden thrust was too narrow and took too many risks.[323]

Yet, there were British troops available to go with the tanks. Brian Wilson, who was a junior infantry officer in the 3rd Bn Irish Guards, poured hot criticism on British commanders for not pushing on between Nijmegen and Arnhem. He felt the crucial period on the night of 20 September was 7.00pm to midnight, before the enemy put in place adequate blocking forces.

> '...we sat there all night... We had been informed that the 1st Airborne were in dire straits at Arnhem. It was a moment when you would have expected the commanders to order the Grenadiers to continue hell for leather for Arnhem, with the 3rd Battalion Irish Guards riding on the tanks...'

This, felt Wilson, was 'shameful', and he concluded Market Garden was 'excellent in intention, unrealistic in planning, and poor in execution. The troops on the ground deserved better'.[324]

'It Is Better to Have a Hundred Men Break Their Legs Falling Off Roofs'

In his post-war memoir, Montgomery does not hide the friction between himself and the American generals Bradley and Patton. Monty suggested Bradley wanted to see the Allied armies attack simultaneously into the Ruhr and also Saar, claiming, as soon as Bradley heard about the audacious Market Garden 'he tried to get it cancelled.'[325]

Montgomery pointed out in his memoirs that Eisenhower 'believed in Market Garden'[326], though the supreme commander also favoured an Allied advance on a broad front and leaving the bloody battle for Berlin to the Russians.

Montgomery did concede that 'we did not get our final bridgehead' but proposed that territory the Allies secured in

Holland acted as a springboard for the jump over the Rhine in March 1945. Monty admitted that Market Garden 'did not gain complete success at Arnhem'.[327]

This was, he felt, due to the failure to concentrate all resources on the northern thrust, enabling a diversionary offensive by the US First Army at Aachen and enough fuel and other resources for the British to more quickly launch an attack on a broader front in Holland. He also cited the presence of the Waffen SS and bad weather interrupting the subsequent lifts but accepted blame for not insisting a parachute brigade was 'dropped quite close to the bridge'.[328]

On that note, let's leave the last words in this brief and imperfect autopsy to Airborne warriors who fought in the battle and who have their own strong views on where exactly they should have jumped into action.

The tragic irony of dropping the 1st Airborne's paratroopers several miles from the bridges – throwing away their best advantage of surprise – was summed up with brutal honesty by Val Allerton, the 21st Indep Para Coy NCO who fought at Oosterbeek. In his searing novel *The Cauldron* – based on his experiences with the Pathfinders – a paratrooper he calls 'O'Neill' observes bluntly: 'It is better to have a hundred men break their legs falling off roofs in the town than to have a thousand killed trying to get there.'

Likewise, risking aircraft shot down by enemy AA fire over the town to drop paratroopers by the bridges would, according to 'O'Neil', have been preferable to having planes shot down dropping supplies to DZs and LZs occupied by Germans. He suggests sacrifice to achieve a successful *coup de main* would not have been in vain. Finally, so 'Zeno's' fictional paratrooper suggests, the 'ambitious and daring operation' should have taken account of the likelihood that the enemy would 'react quickly and angrily to an attempt to cross the great plain to Berlin.'[329]

With a full-blooded *coup de main* attempt at Arnhem, the road bridge could have been seized from both ends immediately, though Waffen SS troops would have done their utmost to take it back.

Regardless of the risks, John Frost believed a *coup de main* should have been tried, a view shared by Urquhart who wrote in his own account of the battle that it would likely have cost fewer lives. While Dakotas coming nearer to town to drop paratroopers may have suffered very heavy casualties, Frost felt it was feasible for people to be dropped onto DZs south of the river.

Frost suggested: 'They could [then] have taken the south end of the bridge.' Overall, so he judged: 'The air forces' planning was abysmal.'[330] In his view the 'air force planners' should 'never have denied the use of the relatively small number of aircraft needed for such a coup'.[331]

The successful seizure of the Caen Canal and Orne River bridge in Normandy on D-Day, in Frost's view, set a successful precedent that should have been followed at Arnhem to give the best chance of success within what was, overall, a flawed plan.[332]

Appendix 2

A Truce, But Not Surrender

By the morning of 24 September, the situation for the British and German wounded being cared for under fire in The Cauldron was beyond desperate.

They were being treated amid conditions of absolute squalor, with no water supply, and scarce food and medicines. Many had been wounded again, or killed, when shells and mortar bombs hit British hospitals and aid stations despite them displaying Red Cross flags.

The 1st Airborne Div medical chief, Col Graeme Warrack, decided that a truce must be arranged to remove the wounded from the line of fire. This would not be across the Rhine as Lt Col Martin Herford had hoped but into hospitals controlled by the Germans, though run in some places by British medical staff. Advising Warrack that no impression must be given that the 1st Airborne Div was about to surrender, Urquhart granted permission for him and Lieutenant Commander (Lt Cdr) Wolters, the Dutch liaison officer – with help from the civilian medic Dr Gerritt van Maanen – to hold discussions with the enemy.

Urquhart would later explain in his account of the battle that 'it would be inhuman to deny the wounded their only chance of recovery.'[333]

Wolters was told to assume the identity of 'Johnson',[334] who was supposedly a Canadian officer, to ensure he would not be shot as a renegade. He and Warrack were driven to an enemy HQ in a captured jeep by Sturmbannführer Egon Skalka, an

SS medical officer. They held talks with Obersturmbannführer Walter Harzer, commander of the 9th SS Panzer Div, and were joined by II SS Panzer Corps commander Obergruppenführer Wilhelm Bittrich.

The latter expressed regrets at the conflict between the British and German nations, handing Warrack a bottle of brandy for Urquhart[335] and agreed to the truce so hundreds of wounded could be evacuated.

Warrack and British medical staff stayed behind when the remnants of the 1st Airborne Div later escaped across the Rhine. They cared for seriously wounded who had not been evacuated during the truce or who had suffered injuries since then that precluded them being moved.

Based in German controlled hospitals at Apeldoorn, Col Warrack, Lt Col Herford, and British medics worked alongside German military medical staff, civilian nurses, and doctors. Warrack made sure the Airborne casualties were cared for correctly at all times and, for example, not operated on by inexperienced SS surgeons.

He and other British military doctors did their best to make sure conditions in which wounded were transported to prison camps in Germany were decent and that they were well enough to travel in first place. Warrack was not afraid to engage in heated arguments with SS medical officers to ensure this was the case.

Herford, Warrack and other British medical personnel escaped from Apeldoorn in mid-October. After being caught up in the unsuccessful Pegasus 2 operation[336], Warrack was forced into hiding, finally making it home in early 1945 after linking up with John Hackett and others.

Herford eventually escaped from the Germans the same way he had voluntarily put himself in their hands. He got himself across the Rhine, this time swimming the great river to British lines. Continuing his war service, Herford was involved in the relief of Bergen-Belsen and Neugamme concentration camps where he helped care for liberated survivors.

Appendix 3

Pegasus 1 – the Great Airborne Escape

Thanks to the HBO mini-series *Band of Brothers* and the book upon which it is based, the escape of 1st Airborne Div soldiers from German occupied Holland on the north bank of the Rhine has become a tale of Yanks rescuing Limeys.

The truth of the matter is somewhat different and the star players in the story include none other than Lt Col David Dobie, the CO of the 1st Para Bn, Maj Digby Tatham-Warter of the 2nd Para Bn and Maj Tony Hibbert of the 1st Para Bde HQ. They were ably (and bravely) assisted by a large cast of others, not least Dutch civilians and the Resistance, along with American brothers-in-arms from Easy Company of the 506th Regt, 101st Airborne.

Lt Col Dobie's part in the drama was initiated by his escape from the German controlled St Elizabeth Hospital in Arnhem on 19 September. Hiding out in a ruined house, he was discovered by a local doctor and received further treatment for his wounds. Dobie had been wounded in the eye and an arm during fighting in the town and taken prisoner.

Once the battle was over, and with Arnhem and Oosterbeek being forcibly evacuated, Dobie was lodged at Ede, courtesy of the Dutch Resistance. He was soon in touch with Maj Tatham-Warter, also in Ede, having evaded capture and arrived there with Brig Lathbury, the latter also on the run from St Elizabeth Hospital. Lathbury had been taken there in a semi-paralysed state after being wounded while dodging around Arnhem's streets with Maj Gen Urquhart. Lathbury received treatment from British

Army military doctors and also Dutch nurses and, after a few days, was able to slip out of the hospital.

Maj Hibbert had escaped by leaping from a lorry that was taking him and other British prisoners to Germany. Unfortunately, a jumpy guard opened fire with a submachine gun and killed several of the other POWs. Hibbert got away, though he felt guilty for the rest of his life about those who lost their lives as he did so. Hiding out at Reemst, in company with 39 other Airborne troops, together with other senior officers, he worked on a plan to escape across the Rhine to Allied lines. To make final arrangements, they used a private telephone line (controlled by the Resistance) between power stations at Ede and Nijmegen, which the Germans did not know about.

On the other end of the telephone line in Nijmegen was Maj Airey Neave of MI9 – the military intelligence outfit tasked with assisting Allied personnel escape from enemy-occupied Europe.

Neave had last seen the Waal when he was transported down it aboard a coal barge after being captured at Calais in 1940. Having broken out of the notorious Colditz prison camp he made a successful home run in 1942.

It was decided Lt Col Dobie should, with the help of the Resistance, head for Nijmegen conveying details of the proposed plan. The idea was to gather a substantial number of 1st Airborne Div (and other) evaders together as a military unit and make a crossing at an agreed location, in co-operation with Allied forces. On 15 October, Dobie made it over the Rhine and then crossed the Waal to meet Neave three days later. Dobie was taken to see Lt Gen Horrocks and it was decided that on the night of 22 October, E Coy of the 506th Regt – by then holding part of the line on the south bank of the Rhine – should be the covering force, while boats would be provided and manned by Canadian assault engineers from XXX Corps.

The overall logistical organisation of Operation Pegasus 1 fell to the Resistance – with help from Special Air Service (SAS) operatives. In total there would be 130 British soldiers, five American aircrew (from aircraft shot down over Holland), a paratrooper from the US 82nd Airborne, three Russians, and also fifteen Resistance members ready to escape German occupied territory on the night of 22 October. Around 90 of the British were hiding in Ede while the escape of those at Reemst was being organised by Hibbert. Maj Tony Deane-Drummond was, by then, with that group.

Two Red Cross lorries were used to transport the Airborne troops from Reemst to a rendezvous point with the Ede group after nightfall. Wearing their military uniforms, with many carrying weapons – but some still not fully recovered from their wounds – they pressed themselves to the floors of the lorries. As they climbed down from the vehicles to head off and join up with the Ede group, a German patrol on bicycles came along. The unsuspecting riders rang their bells to clear a path through the throng of people on the road.

The 1st Airborne Div escapees of Pegasus 1 were quickly organised into platoons and sections, all ready to fight.[337] There was a short exchange of fire as the escapees crawled across a meadow to reach the river bank, opposite to where a Bofors AA gun was firing tracer shells over the water to indicate the crossing point. The enemy patrol fled.

Maj Tatham-Warter used a red signal light to send a message, which was spotted across the river where Lt Col Dobie was in overall command of the operation, with assistance from Maj Neave.

At this signal, the rescue boats pushed off into the river, successfully reaching the north bank. Some of the American paratroopers, under the command of Lt Fred Heyliger, headed up over the river bank to contact the escape group while Dobie remained in command of the bridgehead. He was keenly aware of German troop positions 150 yards away, and a strict rule of silence was enforced throughout the operation to avoid alerting them.

At 12.30am a pair of red signal flares was fired by a nervy German patrol in some nearby woods, but still there was no attempt to interdict the escapees. By 1.00am, Heyliger was back, with the first group sent across the river.

Maj Neave waited tensely for their arrival and was hugely relieved as 'the boats appeared out of the darkness ... and, one by one, they touched down against the muddy bank. My duty was to count the men as they arrived.'

Brig Lathbury was first 'in civilian clothes, and then came officers and men, some badly wounded, following the white tapes laid by the Americans across the field to the first-aid post'.[338]

While there was some artillery fire, it was at a distance and, throughout, not a shot was fired at the escapees.

Over next half an hour, the rest reached the river bank, and by 2.00am, with all successfully sent across in the boats, Dobie ordered the withdrawal of the beachhead force. Dobie's verdict on what was known as Pegasus 1 was: 'The operation was completed without casualty, and 100 per cent success.'[339]

Once back across the Rhine, and in friendly territory, the British could properly thank the US paratroopers, with at least one presenting a red beret that he had worn throughout the Arnhem battle as a sign of gratitude. 'Never been so glad to see a bloody Yank,' is how one Red Devil put it.[340]

Unfortunately, a second attempt at pulling off the mass escape feat ended in disaster. Operation Pegasus 2 failed because of a newspaper report on the success of Pegasus 1. Suitably alerted, the Germans boosted their forces patrolling approaches to the Rhine, managing to intercept a group heading for a crossing point on 18 November. The night exploded in gunfire, with the two British soldiers and a Dutch guide leading the group killed, while everybody else dispersed.

Only seven made it across the Rhine that night, though other means of escape from occupied territory were used in subsequent weeks.[341]

Among the would-be escapees was paratrooper RQMS David Morris, who had surrendered at the Vredehof villa on 24 September. During his initial time in German hands, Morris gave a blood transfusion to the badly wounded Brig Hackett at the St Elizabeth Hospital. On 26 September, Morris was put on a train bound for a prison camp in Germany but managed to jump from it and get away. After being on the run for some weeks, he joined the Pegasus 2 escape bid. Captured by the enemy again, Morris would eventually make it home after his POW camp was liberated by American troops in early April 1945.[342]

Appendix 4

The Arnhem VCs

How Robert Cain won his Victoria Cross is related in the main text, but there were four other VCs awarded to men who fought in the battle of Arnhem. They were as follows (with a brief account of their actions).

Capt Lionel Queripel, of the 10th Bn, the Parachute Regt, was in command of a composite company of paratroopers, which, on the afternoon of 19 September, he led forward as part of the attempt to reach the bridge. With his force becoming fragmented and suffering heavy casualties under heavy fire, Queripel several times went back and forth across the road. He also carried a wounded NCO to an aid post, suffering a face wound himself.

Leading an attack against a reinforced enemy position, where the Germans had pressed a captured 6pdr into service, Queripel killed several enemy machine gunners and seized back the anti-tank gun.

The advance down the road was renewed, but, with enemy opposition growing fiercer, Queripel and some of his men took cover in a ditch. He was wounded again, in both arms. With enemy mortar bombs raining down and machine gun fire ripping through the air, he exhorted his group to fight on, hurling grenades, firing pistols, and using a rifle to try and see off the enemy troops. Ordering his men to retreat, Queripel refused entreaties to join then and instead carried on fighting so they could get away.

He was last seen firing a pistol and hurling grenades at the enemy. 'His courage, leadership and devotion to duty were magnificent,' explained his award citation.

—

Lt John Grayburn, of the 2nd Bn, the Parachute Regt, according to his award citation, showed 'great courage and inspiring leadership.' It added: 'He constantly exposed himself to the enemy's fire while moving among, and encouraging, his platoon, and seemed completely oblivious to danger.'

Having already been wounded during a valiant, but futile, attack across the Arnhem road bridge, to try and take its southern end, Grayburn led a ferocious fight to retain possession of a house in a key position dominating approaches to its northern end. Even after being burned out of the house, Grayburn organised his men to carry on, leading out fighting patrols.

When the enemy tried to blow up the bridge, he led the effort to drive them away and defuse demolition charges, though Grayburn was wounded again. Under attack from panzers on the night of 20 September, Grayburn led a fighting withdrawal of his men but was killed.

—

L/Sgt John Baskeyfield, of the 2nd Bn, The South Staffordshire Regt, was in command of a 6pdr gun at Oosterbeek.

On 20 September, during a determined attack by enemy tanks, self-propelled guns (SP), and infantry, his gun destroyed two Tigers and a SP. Baskeyfield waited until each target was less than 300ft away before he opened fire – in the process receiving a serious leg wound. The rest of his gun crew were killed or badly wounded. Refusing to leave the gun for medical treatment, Baskeyfield stayed at his post, yelling encouragement to his comrades. Under a storm of enemy mortar and artillery fire, Baskeyfield operated the gun solo, holding back the panzer assault and inspiring the soldiers in surrounding positions to greater resistance.

When his gun was destroyed, Baskeyfield crawled to another 6pdr whose crew had been killed and fired two rounds at an oncoming SP. An Airborne soldier who tried to crawl across and assist him was killed.

One of the 6pdr shells slammed into the SP and disabled it. As Baskeyfield was about to finish it off with a third shot – and with a panzer firing at him – he was killed by a direct hit on the 6pdr gun. Referring to his 'superb gallantry', the award citation said Baskeyfield 'spurned danger, ignored pain and, by his supreme fighting spirit, infected all who witnessed his conduct with the same aggressiveness and dogged devotion to duty…'

Flt Lt David Lord was the pilot of a RAF Dakota, which he brought in over an Arnhem DZ to make a resupply drop on 19 September. The aircraft was hit repeatedly by anti-aircraft fire, and, with the starboard engine ablaze, Lord could have broken away from the resupply mission or, along with his crew, parachuted to safety.

Instead Flt Lt Lord and his crew stayed with the aircraft to complete the supply drop. He brought the Dakota in over the DZ at 900ft, and, despite the aircraft being the single focus of numerous enemy anti-aircraft guns, kept it level and steady. Supplies were sent on their way, with the exception of two containers.

Lord decided to bring the aircraft around again, despite knowing that, in the words of the citation, 'the collapse of the starboard wing could not be long delayed.' The Dakota endured a further eight minutes of intense AA fire but delivered the two containers, which is when Lord ordered his crew to abandon the aircraft.

It was now at 500ft and well ablaze. He held the Dakota steady to give his crew the best chance of escape, but the starboard wing finally folded, and the aircraft plunged to the ground a mass of flames. 'There was only one survivor,' reported the citation, 'who was flung out while assisting other members of the crew to put on their parachutes.' Flt Lt Lord had stayed at the Dakota's controls 'to give his crew a chance to escape' [and] 'displayed supreme valour and self-sacrifice.'

As was the custom, the VC citations were published in *The London Gazette*, editions dated 23 November 1944 (Baskeyfield), 25 January 1945 (Grayburn), 1 February 1945 (Queripel), 13 November 1945 (Lord). Cain's citation was published in the edition of 2 November 1944.

Acknowledgements

*'As the stars that are starry in the time of our darkness,
To the end, to the end, they remain.'*

—Laurence Binyon, 'For the Fallen'

Top of the list of people to whom I must express my deep appreciation are the veterans of the battle that I interviewed, either face-to-face in their homes or over the telephone. They kept me spellbound for hours as I gently took them through their time in The Cauldron, where they somehow survived those desperate hours on the Rhine.

Their stories struck a deep chord of admiration as I scribbled my notes. Peter Fletcher, Harry Tucker, Pat Withnall, and Dennis Clay, whom I had the pleasure to interview in depth, therefore take pride of place here, along with other veterans of the battle whose stories I found in museum archives and elsewhere.

It seems to me they thought of themselves as just ordinary people caught up in extraordinary events. Though they are no longer with us, their conduct across ten chaotic, bloody days in 1944 will live forever as an example of amazing fortitude against the odds in the face of disaster.

I did not get to visit their battlefield in company with them, but, at the age of 17, I made my own pilgrimage to Arnhem and Oosterbeek.

I think it's worth outlining some of that to help explain to some readers – more accustomed to regarding me as a naval historian – what exactly motivated me to digress into telling the story of this particular land battle.

In 1981, myself and fellow CCF air cadet Andy Sell entered a competition to win the inaugural Portsmouth Grammar School travel scholarship. We proposed a journey down the Rhine from the Basle to Amsterdam – our reason ostensibly being to carry out a study of the trade artery at the heart of the European Economic Community (as it was then known). One of our cunning ploys was to act as emissaries of the Lord Mayor of Portsmouth, carrying a letter of greeting from him to his counterpart in its twin city of Duisburg in the Ruhr. We did not expect to win but, somehow, pulled it off.

At the time, both of us were heading down the path of a career in the British Army. In my case, the plan was to gain a commission in The Royal Highland Fusiliers and then, if I could hack it, try and get a volunteer secondment to the Parachute Regt. At school I was interviewed at regular intervals by an Army lieutenant colonel, to make sure I was on track. He was delighted with the Rhine expedition.

It would involve us walking a couple of hundred miles of the Rhine's more than 700 mile-length. In our heavy backpacks, we carried a two-man tent (broken down between us), along with a field stove apparatus, mess tins, cutlery, clothes, spare footwear, etc. There were many adventures along the way across our five-week summer expedition (and plenty of blisters until our feet properly hardened).

In Oosterbeek, we deliberately picked accommodation that would enable us to retrace at least part of the march by British Airborne troops from their DZs and LZs to the Arnhem road bridge. We were both inspired by reading Cornelius Ryan's *A Bridge Too Far* (and watching the movie version of that epic history). I was also spurred on by reading Zeno's searing novel *The Cauldron*, based on that author's experiences in the battle.

Not having an enemy determined to kill us on the way, our own march along the several miles to the bridge was somewhat less stressful than it would have been in September 1944. Andy went off to visit the centre of the road bridge to pay homage to the sacrifice of the Airborne troops, while I sat on a bench by the river and watched his progress. I also took in the vista of a river I had come to know all too well: damp, misty wooded stretches of the Upper Rhine; the sun-drenched, stunning steep-sided Rhine gorge; now wending its way across the flat, low-lying Netherlands. When Andy returned, I remarked that it wasn't actually the bridge that was fought over. *Didn't he know Allies had blown it up within days of the battle being lost?* I had seen no point in simply marching to the middle of a substitute. Such is the cussedness of youth. I should have accompanied Andy onto the bridge.

I did buy my mother a delft tile (depicting a windmill) at a shop close to it – in streets that didn't exist after the battle either – and we then walked back to Oosterbeek. All in all, not quite the experience endured by Airborne soldiers 37 years earlier whose souvenirs were often mental trauma and physical injury.

In the end, for various reasons, though the Army astonished me by being keen to have me, I changed my mind and went into journalism, which is what eventually led me here. I'm not sure I would ever have made the grade to become a paratrooper anyway. It was, however, wonderful in the late summer of 1994 to embark on writing up the experiences of a small group of Airborne soldiers as my tribute to the heroes of my youth. I was the Defence Reporter and Chief Reporter of the *Evening Herald* newspaper in Plymouth, the historic naval city on the south coast of England. Having been to Normandy three times in 1994 to write about D-Day landings, and subsequent fighting inland, I expressed a wish to do something a little bit special for the 50th anniversary of the next milestone British battle of the war.

That resulted in the 12-page supplement that followed the aforementioned group of veterans – Fletcher, Tucker, Withnall, and Clay – through the battle of Arnhem day-by-day. Sadly, it made only a fleeting appearance on the newsstands of Plymouth. I always felt it was a shame their incredible stories vanished, to merely be used as wrapping paper for fish and chips. Fortunately, I kept a copy of that supplement and the testimony those men gave to me remains an important element of this much more expansive narrative.

I would like to thank Edd Moore, the current Editor of *Plymouth Live* (a latter-day successor to the *Herald*), for granting permission to utilise material from that supplement. It also included extracts from Stan Turner's 'Arnhem Diary'. Stan died in 1992, but his sister, the late Joan Stopperton, a former Lord Mayor of Plymouth, gave me direct permission to use quotes from it in the original *Evening Herald* supplement. I have, therefore, included a few quotes from Stan in this book, to ensure his part in the battle is not forgotten.

One little twist that came late in the day while writing this book was discovering, via my good friend David Pates, that his wife Briony's uncle was involved in the battle. Investigating the fate of 1st Airborne Div medical officer Percy Louis led to the fascinating tale of a vain attempt to get medical help across the Rhine to soldiers trapped in The Cauldron. I hope the details contained in this book go a little way towards solving elements of the mystery surrounding how the brave Capt Louis came to lose his life on the Lower Rhine.

I have always found the people of Holland to be very cheerful and generous. Jan Loos, who allowed me to use (with some extra input) his account of experiences as a teenager caught up in the battle, and Tim Streefkerk, Conservator/Curator at the award-winning Airborne Museum 'Hartenstein' in Oosterbeek, both exhibited those qualities. I am in their debt. Tim forwarded the amazing account of Frans de Soet, which, along with Jan's, enabled me to raise the story to another level. Jan's account and de Soet's ensure the story of the civilians caught up in the fighting is an utterly compelling part of the narrative. Also, in Holland, Geert Maassen helped clarify a few small details for which I am most grateful.

On 17 September 1944, as a three-year-old boy living in Ede, Driekus Heij heard 'hundreds of airplanes that created a great noise' flying over, signalling the beginning of the battle for nearby Arnhem. After a successful career as a submarine captain

– including serving under the sea during the Cold War – Dreikus became chairman of the board of the Airborne Museum 'Hartenstein', and, although retired from that post by the time I contacted him, he deserves a salute for background help.

I got in touch with Dreikus via Rob Forsyth, a one-time Teacher on the Royal Navy's famous Perisher submarine command course, to which the Royal Netherlands Navy used to send its aspiring submarine commanders (including young Dreikus). Rob, along with my other good friends, Doug Littlejohns – another retired submarine CO with a sharp eye for detail – Peter Fellows, Usman Ansari, and Guy Channing (photojournalist, military historian, Battle of Arnhem re-enactor and guru in all things on the British Army in the Second World War) are deserving of my gratitude. They road-tested elements of the book and passed on notes about errors and also general feedback. I apologise for any errors that remain, which are all down to me.

When it comes to UK museums and archives, I would like to thank Wendy George (Assistant Curator at Airborne Assault, the Airborne forces museum at Duxford), Mark Hickman (of the Pegasus Archive), and the staffs of both the Imperial War Museum and National Army Museum in London.

To be given this opportunity to write about the battle of Arnhem in the 75th anniversary year of the battle is nothing short of amazing, and the team at Agora Books have been superb. Kate Evans, Peyton Stableford, and Samantha Brace have, from beginning to end, applied passion to this project. They totally shared my determination to deliver a cracking yarn that adds something fresh to the knowledge of the epic battle (and its aftermath). The excellent maps by Paul Slidel are the icing on the cake. My thanks must also go to Canelo for creating the reprint editions of both *Arnhem* and *Bismarck*. Thanks are also due to Tim Bates, my literary agent at PFD, who spotted the potential for a new book on Arnhem. As ever, the last word has to go to my darling wife Lindsey and my lovely boys Robert and James for enduring, with good patience and humour, the many days when I was somewhere else, deeply immersed in the tumult of the Second World War.

Sources

Airborne Museum 'Hartenstein'

From its Archive: Diary of F de Soet, entitled 'The Last Days of "Vredenhof" House [sic] Report in Diary Form by a Civilian of the Battle of Arnhem', 17–25 September and 5 October 1944.

Imperial War Museum

All accessed via www.iwm.org.uk

Accounts

'The Story of Operation "Market Garden" in Photos', by Ian Carter (Monday 8 January 2018)

Oral History Interviews

Geoffrey Barkway (*Cat No: 10639*)

Anthony Deane-Drummond (*Cat No: 20888*)

Denis Edwards (*Cat No: 23207*)

John Frost (*Cat No: 10045*)

William Gray (*Cat No: 11478*)

John Hackett (*Cat No: 12022*)

Martin Herford (*Cat No: 13130*)

Anthony Hibbert (*Cat No: 21040*)

Frank Newhouse (*Cat No: 22575*)

Jeffrey Noble (*Cat No: 10641*)

Edward Tappenden (*Cat No: 11515*)

John Vaughan (*Cat No: 11548*), *Originated by Eisenhower Centre, University of New Orleans*

The National Archives

'British Response to V1 and V2: How did Britain respond to the threat of attack by missiles in 1943?', The National Archives, Education Service, downloaded PDF. www.nationalarchives.gov.uk

Airborne Assault – the Museum of the Parachute Regiment and Airborne Forces

Documents and information accessed via the ParaData online research portal: www.paradata.org.uk

Accounts of Combatants

'Account of Arnhem by Captain Richard Bingley'

'Shan Hackett at Arnhem: An Article by John Waddy' (compiled for ParaData by Harvey Grenville)

'Personal Account of Major Tony Hibbert's Experiences of the Battle of Arnhem' (updated by Tony Hibbert in 2009, reproduced on ParaData site with kind permission of Max Arthur – author of 'Men of the Red Beret', Hutchison, 1990)

'Personal Account of Cpl Walter 'Bill' Collings (compiled by Bob Hilton)

'Personal Account by Capt EM Mackay of 1st Para Sqn RE in Arnhem'

Personal Profiles

Carl A Scott (by Rod Gibson)

Martin EM Herford (record under construction with assistance from Niall Cherry)

Kenneth Roberts (created with assistance from Phil Jennett)

Richard TH Lonsdale (compiled with the assistance of Bob Hilton)

Percy Louis (with assistance from Niall Cherry)

Richard Bingley

Frederick Gough

Michael St John Packe

Articles

'The Dutch at Arnhem'

'Sicily (Operation Husky) 10/07/1943–17/08/1943'

'1st Parachute Squadron RE'

Official Documents

'German War Reporter's Account of the Battle of Arnhem'

'Arnhem War Diary by Brig Hackett, CO 4th Parachute Brigade'

'Short Diary of Activities of 7th Battalion, KOSB at Arnhem'

'Account of the Battle of Arnhem by Captain EM Macka.'

The Pegasus Archive: The British Airborne Forces 1940–45

Mark Hickham has conducted extensive research in the UK's National Archives, making transcripts of War Diaries available, writing summaries of actions and also the exploits of various soldiers, and much else (including unit histories) available via the impressive and extensive www.pegasusarchive.org

War Diaries

1st Airborne Division

3rd Parachute Battalion

7th (Galloway) Battalion

The King's Own Scottish Borderers

Headquarters, Royal Army Medical Corps

Unit Histories

21st Independent Parachute Company

4th Battalion, The Dorsetshire Regiment (via Pegasus Archive, courtesy of The Airborne Soldier')

Jedburgh Team Claude

7th (Galloway) Battalion, The King's Own Scottish Borderers

2nd Battalion, The Oxfordshire and Buckinghamshire Light Infantry

Biographies

Hilaro Barlow

Cecil Bolton

Bernard Walter Briggs

Denis Edwards

'Pat' Glover

The Gondree Family

Frederick Gough

Jacobus Groenewoud

John Hackett

Martin Herford

Peter Lewis

James Livingstone

Eric Mackay

David Morris

Robert Payton-Reid

Digby Tatham-Warter

'Sheriff' Thompson

Harvey Todd

Jim Wallwork

Order of Battle

II SS Panzer Korps

Reports

'Evasion Report: 21st September–23rd October 1944, by Major AD Tatham Waiter, 2nd Parachute Bn'

'Report on Operation to Liberate Personnel from Northern Holland, by Lt Col DT Dobie'

'The Dutch Resistance During Operation Market Garden' by Stewart W Bentley

National Army Museum

Accessed via www.nam.ac.uk

Account of Battle

'Operation Market Garden'

Object

Signal from Maj Gen Roy Urquhart to Lt General Frederick Browning, 24 September 1944
NAM Accession Number: NAM. 1994-06-201-2

World War II Unit Histories and Officers

Internet database of officers serving in various branches of the British and US armed forces during the conflict and also those in particular units for certain battles. Run by Hans Houterman and Jeroen Koppes.
www.unithistories.com

1st Airborne Division Arnhem, September 1944, Officers

Britnev, Vladimir Alexandrovitch

Noble, Jeffrey Fraser

Official Reports

'1st Airborne Division Report on Operation "Market" Arnhem 17–26 Sep 1944'. *Accessed via US Defense Technical Information Center*

Other

'This is How I experienced the Battle of Arnhem 17–25 September 1944'

A memoir of the battle by Jan Loos, previously unpublished in English. Translated by Iain Ballantyne and Jan Loos specially for this book, with additional text and edits.

'Operation Market Garden Netherlands 17–25 September 1944'

UK MoD booklet published as part of a series to commemorate the 60th anniversary of key battles in the Second World War. Designed and produced by COI Communications, September 2004

Miscellaneous Articles Published on Websites

'The Forgotten American Airborne of Operation Market Garden' by Maj Gen Michael Reynolds (ret.), Warfare History Network (web journal), 1 January 2019.
www.warfarehistorynetwork.com

'The PIAT (Projector Infantry Anti-Tank)', by Paul Rundle, Cornwall's Regimental Museum website (blog), 19 April 2017.
www.cornwallsregimentalmuseum.org

'The Grenade with Instant Fame' [about the Gammon bomb], The South African Military History Society, Military History Journal, Vol 5 No 5, June 1982.
www.samilitaryhistory.org

'Stories of the Lads: Lieutenant Joseph Winston (Pat) Glover – One Man's 8 Days of Hell' and 'Myrtle the Parachick', both published on Friends of the Tenth (website).
www.friendsofthetenth.co.uk

'Major James Anthony Hibbert MBE MC', obituary, Trebah Garden (website), October 2014.
www.trebahgarden.co.uk

'Assessing the Reasons for Failure: 1st British Airborne Divisions Signal Communications during Operation "Market Garden"' by Major John Greenacre, Defence Studies Volume 4, 2004, Issue 3 (published online 29 July 2006).
www.tandfonline.com

'Oosterbeek (Lonsdale) Old Church', description of the church and Maj Lonsdale's pulpit address to troops, by Paul Reed, on his website.
battlefieldsww2.50megs.com

'The King's Own Scottish Borderers, World War II', published on regimental website.
www.kosb.co.uk

'Sgt Gordon "Jock" Walker, Army Film & Photographic Unit – 1st Airborne Division', published on WW2 Market Garden website, Contributed by Neil Walker.
www.ww2marketgarden.com

'World War II: Jews at the Battle of Arnhem (September 1944)' by Martin Sugarman, published by the Jewish Virtual Library.
www.jewishvirtuallibrary.org

'Todd, Harvey Allan 1916–1993, Distinguished Service Cross Recipient', published on website of Marion Illinois History Preservation.
www.mihp.org

'No. 82 "Gammon Bomb" Grenade', revised November 2014, weapon profile published by World War II Database website.
ww2db.com

'The Destruction of Dresden's Frauenkirche', article published by Deutsche Welle.
dw.com

'Bombing of Dresden, World War II', Encyclopaedia Britannica article, revised and updated by Adam Augustyn.
www.britannica.com

'The 4th and 5th Battalions The Dorsetshire Regiment in World War Two', article published on web site of The Keep Military Museum, Dorchester, Dorset.
keepmilitarymuseum.org

'Black British Soldiers – The Forgotten Fighters', by Phil Gregory, article published 14 December 2011, on The Black Presence in Britain website – details of black soldiers

at Arnhem in a web page comment posted by Ronald Smith, 11 October 2018.
blackpresence.co.uk

'Hotel Hartenstein, Airborne Headquarters during Operation Oosterbeek near Arnhem – The Netherlands', pictorial guide to the Airborne Museum Hartenstein.
landmarkscout.com
Includes an image of the British sniper's graffiti on the wallpaper.

'The Universal Carrier of the British 1st Airborne Division at Operation "Market Garden" – 1944', posted 12 October 2012, and 'Forgotten at Market Garden – RAF Fighter Control Officers and Radar Operators – Arnhem 1944', posted 17 February 2017, both on the blog site Arnhem Jim.
arnhemjim.blogspot.com

'The Myth of Dresden and "Revenge Firebombing"', blog post by Richard M Langworth, on his website.
www.richardlangworth.com

'Arnhem 1944 – were the maps good enough?', by Rob Wheeler, article in *Sheetlines*, The journal of The Charles Close Society for the Study of Ordnance Survey Maps, April 2010. PDF document, download.
www.charlesclosesociety.org

Bibliography

Aldrich, Richard J, *Witness to War: Diaries of the Second World War in Europe and the Middle East*, Corgi, 2005.

Ambrose, Stephen E, *Band of Brothers*, Pocket, 2001.
—*D-Day June 6, 1944: The Climactic Battle of World War II*, Pocket, 2002.

By Air to Battle: The Official Account of the British Airborne Divisions, His Majesty's Stationary Office, 1945.

Bailey, Roderick, *Forgotten Voices of D-Day: A New History of the Normandy Landings*, Ebury, 2010.

Beevor, Anthony, *Arnhem: The Battle for the Bridges, 1944*, Viking, 2018.
—*D-Day: The Battle for Normandy*, Viking, 2009.

Bryant, Arthur, *Triumph in the West 1943–1946: Based on the Diaries and Autobiographical Notes of Field Marshal The Viscount Alanbrooke*, Collins, 1959.

Buckingham, William F, *The Complete Story of Operation Market Garden 17–25 September 1944*, Amberley Publishing, 2019.

Cole, Lieutenant Colonel Howard N, *On Wings of Healing: The Story of the Airborne Medical Services 1940–1960*, The Naval and Military Press Ltd, print-on-demand, 2019.

Colville, John, *The Fringes of Power: Downing Street Diaries 1939–1955*, Phoenix, 2005.

David, Saul, *Military Blunders*, Constable, 2012.

Delaforce, Patrick, *The Fighting Wessex Wyverns: From Normandy to Bremerhaven with the 43rd Wessex Division*, Alan Sutton, 1994.

D'Este, Carlo, *Eisenhower: Allied Supreme Commander*, Weidenfeld & Nicolson, 2003.

Ford, Ken, *Operation Market-Garden 1944 (2): The British Airborne Missions*, Osprey, 2016.

Fraser, David, *And We Shall Shock Them: The British Army in the Second World War*, Sceptre, 1988.

Frost, Maj Gen John, *A Drop Too Many*, Pen & Sword, Kindle edition, 2009.

Gregory, Barry, *British Airborne Troops 1940–45*, Macdonald and Jane's, 1974.

Hagen, Louis, *Arnhem Lift*, BCA, 1993.

Harclerode, Peter, *Arnhem: A Tragedy of Errors*, Arms and Armour Press, 1994.

Harris, Marshal of the RAF, Sir Arthur, *Bomber Offensive*, Pen & Sword, 2005.

Hastings, Max, *Armageddon: The Battle for Germany 1944–45*, Pan, 2004.
—*All Hell Let Loose: The World at War 1939–1945*, HarperPress, 2011.
—*Overlord: D-Day & the Battle for Normandy*, Touchstone, 1984.

Horrocks, Lt Gen Sir Brian, *A Full Life*, Collins, 1960.

Howard, John & Bates, Penny, *The Pegasus Diaries: The Private Papers of Major John Howard DSO*, Pen & Sword, 2008.

Keegan, John, ed, *Churchill's Generals*, Warner, 1995.

Kent, Ron, *First In: The Airborne Pathfinders – A History of the 21st Independent Parachute Company, 1942–1946*, Frontline Books, 2015.

Kershaw, Robert, *A Street in Arnhem: The Agony of Occupation and Liberation*, Ian Allan, 2015.
—*It Never Snows in September: The German View of Market-Garden and The Battle of Arnhem, September 1944*, Hippocrene, 1994.

Lamb, Richard, *Montgomery in Europe 1943–45: Success or Failure?*, Buchan & Enright, 1987.

Lewis, Jon E, ed, *The Mammoth Book of How it Happened World War II*, Constable & Robinson, 2002.

Liddell Hart, BH, *A History of the Second World War*, Pan, 2014.

Lowe, Keith, *Savage Continent: Europe in the Aftermath of World War II*, Viking, 2012.

Margry, Karel, ed, *Operation Market Garden Then and Now, Vol 1 & 2*, After the Battle/Battle of Britain International Limited, 2013.

Mead, Richard, *General 'Boy': The Life of Lieutenant General Sir Frederick Browning*, Pen & Sword, Kindle edition, 2011.

Middlebrook, Martin, *Arnhem 1944: The Airborne Battle*, Viking, 1994.

Montgomery, Viscount Bernard Law, *The Memoirs of Field Marshal Montgomery*, Da Capo, 1982.

Norton, GG, *The Red Devils: From Bruneval to the Falklands*, Hipocrene, 1986.

Neave, Airey, *Saturday at M.I.9.*, Pen and Sword, Kindle Edition, 2010.

Packe, Michael, *First Airborne*, Seeker & Warburg, 1948.

Powell, Geoffrey, *The Devil's Birthday: The Bridges to Arnhem 1944*, Papermac, 1985.

Ridgway, Matthew, *Soldier: The Memoirs of Matthew B Ridgway – as told to Harold H Martin*, Harper & Brothers, 1956.

Rogers, Duncan and Williams, Sarah, ed, *On the Bloody Road to Berlin: Frontline Accounts from North-West Europe and the Eastern Front, 1944–45*, Helion/The Military & Aviation Book Club, 2005.

Ryan, Cornelius, *A Bridge Too Far*, Book Club Associates, 1975.
—*The Longest Day*, Corgi, 1974.

Sims, James, *Arnhem Spearhead: A Private Soldier's Story*, Imperial War Museum, 1978.

Skinner, Rebecca, *British Paratrooper 1940–45*, Osprey, 2015.

Urquhart, Maj Gen RE, *Arnhem*, Pan, 1977.

Waddy, John, *A Tour of the Arnhem Battlefields*, Leo Cooper, 1999.

Warner, Phillip, *Horrocks: The General Who Led from The Front*, Class War, Kindle edition, 2014.

Wheal, Elizabeth-Anne and Pope, Stephen, *The Macmillan Dictionary of The Second World War*, Second Edition, Macmillan, 1995.

Whiting, Charles, *Hunters from the Sky: The Extraordinary Story of the German Parachute Regiment*, Corgi, 1975.

Wilmot, Chester, *The Struggle for Europe*, The Reprint Society London, September 1954.

Wilson, Brian, *The Ever Open Eye*, The Pentland Press, 1998.

Fiction

Zeno, *The Cauldron*, Pan, 1977.

DVDs, Blu-Ray Discs and Televisual Downloads

A Bridge Too Far. Directed by Richard Attenborough, MGM Home Entertainment, 1977.

'Arnhem'. *Battlefields*, series produced by Mark Fielder and Nicola Moody, BBC Worldwide/2 entertain, 2001.

Last Words: The Battle for Arnhem Bridge. Directed by Roger Chapman, Simply Media, 2015.

The Longest Day. Directed by Ken Annakin and Andrew Marton, Twentieth Century Fox, 1962.

'Roy Urquhart's Escape from Arnhem'. Episode 8 in the series *'Narrow Escapes of World War II'*, IMG Media, 2012.

Theirs is the Glory: Men of Arnhem. Directed by Brian Desmond Hurst, Strawberry Media, 2014.

Newspapers and Journals

Including reports, features and supplements. Accessed via the publication's web sites, except for Evening Herald.
★ All researched and written by Iain Ballantyne, based on interviews with veterans.

Arthur, Max. 'Obituary: General Sir John Hackett'. *Independent*. 11 September 1997.

Ballantyne, Iain. 'Soldiers who came from the skies'. *Evening Herald, Plymouth*. 30 May 1994.★
—'ARNHEM 1944–1994: An Evening Herald Special Supplement Marking the 50th Anniversary of the Battle of Arnhem'. *Evening Herald, Plymouth*. 14 September 1994.★
—'Parachutist revisits Arnhem battlefields half a century on/Bridge of memories for city veteran'. *Evening Herald, Plymouth*. 17 September 1994.★
—'Across the Rhine and on to victory…'. *Evening Herald, Plymouth*. 28 March 1995★

Braw, Elizabeth. 'Unravelling a World War Two Murder Mystery'. *Newsweek*. 11 December 2014.

Connolly, Kate. 'I saw the British and hid in a bush'. *The Daily Telegraph*. 5 June 2004.

Cox, Alex. 'Audrey Hepburn: an iconic problem'. *The Guardian*. 20 January 2011.

'Maj Gen Tony Deane-Drummond Obituary. *The Daily Telegraph*. 4 December 2012.

'Sir Brian Horrocks is Dead at 89; British General in World War II Obituary. *New York Times*. 9 January 1985.

Wilsher, Kim. 'D-Day's first heroes return to salute the daring Pegasus bridge raid'. *The Guardian*. 1 June 2014.

Notes

1. From *Arnhem*, Urquhart's own account of the battle. In this book 'The Cauldron' encompasses the turbulent situation the Airborne troops were plunged into from the moment their boots hit Dutch soil.

2. Tappenden, IWM Sound Archive.

3. Denis Edwards, quote from his own account in *On the Bloody Road to Berlin*, edited by Duncan Rogers and Sarah Williams, p45.

4. According to Gray, IWM Sound Archive.

5. Ryan, *The Longest Day*, p102.

6. Howard and Bates, *The Pegasus Diaries*, p117.

7. Ibid.

8. Howard, as quoted by Bailey, *Forgotten Voices of D-Day*, p120.

9. *By Air to Battle*, p76.

10. Details of the fly-through film, Howard and Bates, *The Pegasus Diaries*, p112.

11. Barkway, IWM Sound Archive.

12. Ibid.

13. Wallwork, Pegasus Archive bio.

14. Edwards, Pegasus Archive bio.

15. Edwards, IWM Sound Archive.

16. Ambrose, *D-Day June 6, 1944*, p19.

17. *The Daily Telegraph*, 5 June 2004.

18. Ibid.

19. Gray, IWM Sound Archive.

20. According to Vaughan, IWM Sound Archive.

21. Pegasus Archive bio of Gondree family.

22. Tappenden, IWM Sound Archive.

23. Vaughan, IWM Sound Archive.

24. According to John Howard in *The Pegasus Diaries*, p127, Schmidt's companion was probably 'unceremoniously dumped' out of the car as the German raced off to see what was happening.

25. Howard and Bates, p127.

26. As quoted, Bailey, *Forgotten Voices of D-Day*, p134.

27. As recounted Gray, IWM Sound Archive.

28. Mastermind of the Normandy invasion plan – and victor of the subsequent struggle as boss of the combined British and American armies until the breakout.

29. Between 6 June and 15 August 1944 the British 21st Army Group suffered 83,000 casualties with some 16,000 killed.

30. Within weeks of D-Day the balance of forces was weighted towards the Americans – 812,000 US troops in the beachhead compared to 640,000 British, Canadian (and others) by 25 July. The Americans grew still further, but the manpower available to their partners could not keep pace. The Allies in general were vexed by the meatgrinder chewing up infantry but the British were among the worst affected. Montgomery was sometimes accused of being overly cautious to preserve his troops. As Hasting points out in 'Overlord' (p221), even by the beginning of July the shortage of fresh British infantry was leading to some battalions being cannibalised to fill gaps in others.

31. Richard Holmes, in the 'Arnhem' episode of his *Battlefields* documentary series for the BBC.

32. Ryan, *A Bridge Too Far*, p79.

33. Urquhart, *Arnhem*, p42–3.

34. Hackett, IWM Sound Archive.

35. As related by Kent, *First In*, p115.

36. Frost, IWM Sound Archive.

37. This was Sgt Jim Travis of the 21st Independent Parachute Company (Kent, p115).

38. Excellently illustrated with a series of photos on p258 in *The Red Devils* by GG Norton. Containers, in which were machine guns and other equipment, could even be carried under the fuselage of the Dakota and released over the Drop Zone.

39. Ryan, *A Bridge Too Far*, p143.

40. All quotes from Frans de Soet, taken from his diary account lodged with the Airborne Museum Hartenstein. The church mentioned is the Oude Kerk ('Old Church'), one of the most ancient in Holland. It would be damaged during the fighting but restored after the war.

41. Jan Loos in his account 'This is How I experienced the Battle of Arnhem 17–25 September 1944', as are all quotes from him.

42. 'German War Reporter's Account of the Battle of Arnhem', ParaData.

43. Ibid.

44. Ryan, *A Bridge Too Far*, p105.

45. 'British Response to V1 and V2', UK National Archives.

46. The Schutzstaffel (which can be literally translated protection squad, aka the SS) was formed to protect Adolf Hitler in the 1930s. It also had its own army, the Waffen SS (or 'Armed SS'), dedicated to furthering the cause of the Nazis in military campaigns. For the most part, it was a fanatical elite numbering almost a million men, organised in 39 divisions, including panzer forces, infantry and mountain troops. It also recruited from among occupied nations where there were people considered to be Aryans and willing volunteers. The Dutch who served in the Waffen SS saw combat on the Eastern front as part of the SS Division Wiking and other units, but those who fought the Airborne forces at Arnhem and Oosterbeek, were drawn from the Landstorm Nederland. Just weeks earlier they were in combat against free Netherlands troops of the Princess Irene Brigade during battles in Belgium. This so-called Dutch Waffen SS home defence force was more than 3,000 strong, of patchy quality, and in September 1944 found itself under the control of the 9th SS, including being assigned at one stage to Kampfgruppe Spindler. Landstorm Nederland troops subsequently fought the 43rd Div and other Allied units south of the Rhine. As the war ended in defeat for the Nazis, elements of the Dutch SS committed several acts of brutality against their own civilians. For more information on the Dutch Waffen SS, see www.waffen-ss.nl.

47. As detailed by Richard Holmes in *Battlefields*.

48. There were three routes to be used by each of the battalions in the 1st Parachute Brigade, and also by follow-on units. The 2nd Parachute Battalion was to take 'Lion', closest to the river, the 3rd Parachute Battalion the 'Tiger' route through the centre of Oosterbeek and into Arnhem town. The 1st Parachute Battalion was to take the most northernly, via the railway line and the Ede-Arnhem road (aka Amsterdamseweg), known as the 'Leopard' route.

49. Orange is the national colour of The Netherlands and so, to show their patriotic fervour, the Dutch would wave orange scarves and pennants. They would also wear orange clothing.

50. Deane-Drummond, IWM Sound Archive.

51. Greenacre, in 'Assessing the Reasons for Failure' says incorrect radio procedure was a major factor. It has also been pointed out that equipment was suitable, provided the Airborne division stayed within its 'eggs' (parameters) of communication – once they became broken and too far spread out then the net failed, hence the massive failure referred to in the main narrative.

52. Urquhart, *Arnhem*, p49.

53. Sims, *Arnhem Spearhead*, p47–8. Earlier incident recounted by him, p42.

54. Hibbert, as interviewed on camera in 'Roy Urquhart's Escape from Arnhem'.

55. Quoted, Middlebrook, *Arnhem 1944*, p148.

56. Scott was killed either trying to cross the Rhine on 25/26 September, or on an earlier date, according to ParaData, whereas Pegasus Archive says that he was killed in November while on a patrol with troops of the 101st Airborne. When it came to his original mission, greater exploitation of Dutch Resistance was planned by the 1st Airborne Div. Aside from Jedburgh Team Claude, Col Barlow, Second in Command of the 1st Air Ldg Bde, was meant to work with Lt Cdr Arnoldus Wolters of the Royal Netherlands Navy (assigned to the division). Barlow was to become, in effect, the military governor, of liberated Arnhem. As related in the main narrative, he was sent off to command the 1st Air Ldg Bde and killed before he could put into action his plans. Without Barlow to give his efforts authority – and using only his own list of trusted locals – Lt Cdr Wolters found the 1st Airborne Div's staff officers reluctant to trust in assistance from the Dutch Resistance. It was known to have been severely compromised by enemy infiltration. Wolters did manage to recruit some local resistance fighters but their services were not used in any meaningful way. Wolters is still credited by the 1st Airborne Div commander with performing valuable service (see Urquhart's 'Arnhem' p86).

57. Mackay, 'Account of the Battle of Arnhem', ParaData.

58. Kershaw, *It Never Snows in September*, p98.

59. Frost, IWM Sound Archive.

60. Frost, *A Drop Too Many*, Location 3465.

61. Mackay, ParaData.

62. Invented by Captain RS Gammon, of the 1st Parachute Battalion. A Gammon bomb contained a plastic explosive charge of varying power, in a so-called elasticised stockingette bag (or 'cloth skirt' according to the IWM) with the weapon assembled in battle to suit the target. The charge had a fuse in a screw cap attached to it. The Gammon bomb would detonate on impact.

63. Mackay, ParaData.

64. Mackay, quote from his 'Arnhem at the Bridge', as reprinted in Lewis, Jon E, ed, *The Mammoth Book of How it Happened World War II*, p420. This version of Mackay's account was originally published in *Royal Engineers Journal*. Vol LXVIII, No 4.

65. Mackay, ParaData.

66. Frost, IWM Sound Archive.

67. These quotes from Frost, *A Drop Too Many*, Location 3477. In reality Gough was firing a machine gun dismounted from a jeep, by resting it on a window ledge. The vehicles themselves were parked around the back of the building out of the line of fire.

68. Ryan, *A Bridge Too Far*, p257.

69. Frost, *A Drop Too Many*, Location 3516.

70. Ibid.

71. Bingley account, ParaData.

72. Personal medical kits carried by Airborne soldiers included not only bandages but also morphia in a small tin tube onto which could be screwed a hypodermic needle. Not only was this used to dull the pain of the wounded but also, on occasion, to euthanise mortally wounded soldiers. In his novel, 'The Cauldron', about paratroopers in the battle of Arnhem, 'Zeno' presents a scene in which soldiers of the 21st Independent Parachute Company try in vain to rescue a pilot from a burning glider. As flames begin to consume the pilot, morphia is injected straight into the unconscious man's heart. Much of what is depicted in 'The Cauldron' accurately conveys the battle and various actions that occurred during it. For example, Zeno highlights that, to stay awake during the battle

– with sleep, like food and water, a rare commodity – the Airborne troops consumed Benzedrine tablets to keep going. Such amphetamines were used widely during the war on both sides – on land and at sea – in fact wherever and whenever alertness had to be boosted by artificial stimulants to fight the enemy.

73. Deane-Drummond, IWM Sound Archive.

74. Quoted by Ryan, in *A Bridge Too Far*, p300.

75. Deane-Drummond, IWM Sound Archive.

76. The Germans obtained fair warning of the incoming airlifts from observers based on the coast of Holland then passed the information on to the Luftwaffe to task its fighters.

77. Noble, IWM Sound Archive, as are all quotes from this officer in the book.

78. 'Arnhem War Diary by Brig Hackett, CO 4th Parachute Brigade', ParaData. The multi-lingual Hackett was married to Margaret Frena, an Austrian, with whom he fell in love while recovering from wounds incurred fighting the Vichy French in Syria in 1941. They were married in 1942, despite Margaret being classified an 'enemy alien'.

79. Ryan, *A Bridge Too Far*, p134.

80. Waddy, *A Tour of the Arnhem Battlefields*, p99.

81. Ibid.

82. Middlebrook, *Arnhem 1944*, p234.

83. Ibid, p238–9.

84. Ryan, *A Bridge Too Far*, p279.

85. Ibid.

86. Ibid.

87. *By Air to Battle*, p106.

88. Cleminson, to camera interview, *Battlefields* TV doc.

89. Urquhart, *Arnhem*, p75.

90. Bingley account, ParaData.

91. According to Bingley in his IWM Sound Archive interview, the German he grappled with slowly died from stomach wounds inflicted by the Sten gun burst.

This is contradicted by his ParaData written account, from which these quotes are taken. Bingley relates that he ended the fight by firing his Very pistol, in other words killing the enemy soldier by hitting him at point blank range with a flare.

92. Bingley, IWM Sound Archive, including exchange with Britneff.

93. Exchange recorded by Frost in *A Drop Too Many*, Location 3552.

94. 'German War Reporter's Account of the Battle of Arnhem', ParaData.

95. Mackay, ParaData.

96. 'Arnhem War Diary by Brig Hackett, CO 4th Parachute Brigade', ParaData.

97. Urquhart, *Arnhem*, p87.

98. 'Arnhem War Diary by Brig Hackett, CO 4th Parachute Brigade', ParaData.

99. Kershaw, *It Never Snows in September*, p107.

100. Aside from this ParaData account, Bingley explains in his IWM Sound Archive interview that mouseholing entailed making a hole about the size of a dustbin lid through the weaker first floor walls.

101. Bingley, IWM Sound Archive.

102. Urquhart, *Arnhem*, p91.

103. Middlebrook, *Arnhem 1944*, p210–1. As Middlebrook relates in his 1994 book, the only clue for many years, until the account given by Capt McCooke, was provided by Maj John Waddy. In 1954, Waddy visited Arnhem and was given a 'blackened and crumpled silver cigarette case' that turned out to have belonged to Barlow (and, in fact, was presented to the latter by Waddy's father, who had been CO of the 2nd Somerset Light Infantry, in which Barlow served before the war). See Middlebrook's note on p211 of *Arnhem 1944*. The cigarette case had been found less than 500ft from where Barlow was said by McCooke to have been killed. McCooke's quotes also found in a biography of Barlow on the ParaData web site.

104. Ryan, *A Bridge Too Far*, p427.

105. Newhouse, IWM Sound Archive. As are all quotes from him in this book.

106. Middlebrook, *Arnhem 1944*, p216.

107. Derogatory term favoured by many Dutch to describe the German occupiers. It could be traced back to the word 'mof' historically used by the Dutch to describe immigrant labourers.

108. The problems with radio links between the troops on the ground and the rocket-equipped Typhoons of the RAF or Thunderbolts of the USAAF – whether caused by equipment (or lack of it) or using the wrong frequencies – is one thing, but over Arnhem there were rarely, if ever, fighter-bombers to be seen circling in order call them down. This is because Lt Gen Brereton for safety's sake banned Close Air Support (CAS) missions from being flown at all when troops and their equipment were being landed or dropped. However, John Waddy seems to have seen at least one Typhoon intervening during his jump. The 2nd Tactical Air Force (2TAF) was also prevented from flying CAS when supplies were being dropped, to keep the airspace clear. This meant that not only were supplies being dropped to the enemy, but for the duration of those ill-fated sorties it was guaranteed there could be no CAS either. The chopping and changing of when drops were to be carried out extended the periods when CAS was banned too. 2TAF was certainly keen to apply its firepower, but only truly weighed in to assist the beleaguered 1st Airborne on 24 September. It was surely a factor in the failure of the entire enterprise.

109. Frost, IWM Sound Archive. The two sides even taunted each other via the radio. After 'Boy' Wilson's 21st Indep Para Coy snatched three Germans from their positions he received a call from an enemy radio operator who warned the British paratroopers they must return the men, or they would come and kidnap Maj Gen Urquhart. The Germans referred to Urquhart as 'your Sunray', so using the correct call sign for commander of the 1st Airborne Div. According to Urquhart (in *Arnhem*, p148) Wilson laughed at the idea and replied: 'Come and get him if you can.'

110. Ryan, *A Bridge Too Far*, p307.

111. Middlebrook, *Arnhem 1944*, p303.

112. Frost, *A Drop Too Many*, Location 3989.

113. Ryan, *A Bridge Too Far*, p308.

114. Ibid, p309.

115. '1st Airborne Division Report on Operation "Market" Arnhem 17–26 Sep 1944'.

116. 'Short Diary of Activities of 7th Battalion, KOSB at Arnhem', ParaData.

117. Noble, IWM Sound Archive.

118. Ibid.

119. As quoted, Powell, *The Devil's Birthday*, p127. Also, according to 'The King's Own Scottish Borderers, World War II' the 7th KOSB went into Arnhem with

740 men and would come out with just four officers and 72 men. That's almost ninety percent casualties.

120. Ibid, p128.

121. Urquhart, *Arnhem*, p97 as are other quotes from the Maj Gen on this episode.

122. As observed by Glider Pilot Regt NCO Lewis Haig (Louis Hagen). See p84 of his *Arnhem Lift*.

123. 'German War Reporter's Account of the Battle of Arnhem', ParaData.

124. Hagen, *Arnhem Lift*, p42.

125. 'German War Reporter's Account of the Battle of Arnhem', ParaData.

126. Ryan, *A Bridge Too Far*, p306.

127. 'Personal Account by Capt EM Mackay of 1st Para Sqn RE in Arnhem', ParaData.

128. Ibid.

129. Frost, *A Drop Too Many*, Location 3611.

130. Ibid.

131. As recounted in *By Air to Battle*, p117.

132. There is bitter an irony to the battle taking place around and for the Vredehof which, if translated into English literally, means 'peace court', something that Soet notes in his account.

133. As quoted by Middlebrook, *Arnhem 1944*, p332.

134. *By Air to Battle*, p114.

135. Ryan, *A Bridge Too Far*, p342–3.

136. 'Arnhem War Diary by Brig Hackett, CO 4th Parachute Brigade', ParaData.

137. Ibid.

138. '1st Airborne Division Report on Operation "Market" Arnhem 17–26 Sep 1944'.

139. All Forman quotes, Middlebrook, *Arnhem 1944*, p284.

140. *By Air to Battle*, p113.

141. 'Shan Hackett at Arnhem: An Article by John Waddy', ParaData.

142. 'Personal Account by Capt EM Mackay of 1st Para Sqn RE in Arnhem', ParaData and Briggs biography, Pegasus Archive. Mackay overheard this exchange on the radio net. Also recorded in *By Air to Battle*, p117.

143. Cecil Bolton biography, Pegasus Archive.

144. As told by Morgan during on-camera interview in *Last Words: The Battle for Arnhem Bridge*.

145. *By Air to Battle*, p116.

146. Ryan, *A Bridge Too Far*, p356.

147. According to Burriss, during on-camera interview in the 'Arnhem' episode of *Battlefields*, TV documentary series.

148. As quoted by Reynolds in 'The Forgotten American Airborne of Operation Market-Garden'.

149. Wilson, *The Ever Open Eye*, p133.

150. Middlebrook, *Arnhem 1944*, p278.

151. 'Shan Hackett at Arnhem: An Article by John Waddy', ParaData.

152. 'Arnhem War Diary by Brig Hackett, CO 4th Parachute Brigade', ParaData.

153. Waddy's own account of this episode in *A Tour of the Arnhem Battlefields*, p117.

154. Ibid.

155. Hackett, 'Arnhem War Diary', ParaData.

156. Ibid.

157. The commander of light artillery guns supporting the 4th Parachute Bde and second-in-command of the 1st Air Landing Light Regt Royal Artillery (RA).

158. 'Shan Hackett at Arnhem: An Article by John Waddy', ParaData.

159. Hackett, 'Arnhem War Diary', ParaData.

160. Waddy, *A Tour of the Arnhem Battlefields*, p118.

161. Urquhart, *Arnhem*, p119 and Major John Greenacre, 'Assessing the Reasons for Failure: 1st British Airborne Divisions Signal Communications during Operation "Market Garden".'

162. Martin Sugarman, 'World War II: Jews at the Battle of Arnhem (September 1944)'.

163. Phil Gregory, 'Black British Soldiers – The Forgotten Fighters'.

164. Beevor, *Arnhem: The Battle for the Bridges, 1944*, p275.

165. Urquhart, *Arnhem*, p117.

166. 'Personal Account of Cpl Walter "Bill" Collings (compiled by Bob Hilton)', ParaData.

167. Ibid.

168. Collings account, ParaData, as is the quote about Vera Lynn.

169. *By Air to Battle*, p114.

170. As related Robert Payton-Reid biography, Pegasus Archive and *By Air to Battle*, p114.

171. Quoted by Urquhart, *Arnhem*, p106. Lonsdale was wounded on the Thursday, so 'Thompson Force' was handed over to Maj Lonsdale, who became commander overall of that part of the perimeter, under the umbrella name Lonsdale Force.

172. Frost, IWM Sound Archive.

173. 'Personal Account by Capt EM Mackay of 1st Para Sqn RE in Arnhem', ParaData.

174. Quoted by Ryan in, *A Bridge Too Far*, p362–3.

175. Ibid, p363.

176. Biography of Digby Tatham-Waiter, Pegasus Archive. Including umbrella poking incident (recounted below in main text) also.

177. Ryan, *A Bridge Too Far*, p326.

178. Ibid.

179. Frost, IWM Sound Archive.

180. Sims, *Arnhem Spearhead*, p84.

181. Frost, IWM Sound Archive.

182. Frost, *A Drop Too Many*, Location 3658.

183. Hibbert, IWM Sound Archive.

184. *By Air to Battle*, p132. All other quotes, from Deane-Drummond's IWM Sound Archive interview.

185. Hibbert, IWM Sound Archive.

186. Kershaw, *It Never Snows in September*, p185.

187. Middlebrook, *Arnhem 1944*, p314. This was one of Mackay's wounded sappers. Earlier another sapper had been sent to surrender under a flag of truce but was shot at and fatally wounded. According to Middlebrook the same Waffen SS officer shot the SS trooper who had fired at the sapper with the white flag.

188. Elizabeth Braw, 'Unravelling a World War Two Murder Mystery', *Newsweek*, 11 December 2014.

189. Middlebrook, *Arnhem 1944*, p321.

190. Frost, *A Drop Too Many*, Location 3664.

191. Ryan, *A Bridge Too Far*, p366–7. Gough would eventually escape in April 1945, heading for Bavaria where he contacted advancing American forces. He was one of the stars in the documentary-drama *Theirs is the Glory*, a telling of the Arnhem battle (released in cinemas during 1946) and featuring the soldiers who actually fought in it.

192. As quoted by Middlebrook, *Arnhem 1944*, p347.

193. Ibid.

194. Ibid.

195. 'Long war diary of 7th (Galloway) Battalion, The King's Own Scottish Borderers', Pegasus Archive.

196. Ibid.

197. 'Short Diary of Activities of 7th Battalion, KOSB at Arnhem', ParaData.

198. 'Long war diary, 7th KOSB', Pegasus Archive.

199. When an effort was made by the British to secure use of the ferry at Driel, they found it was no longer in its customary place, its cable cut. While they suspected the enemy had done this it is more likely to have been severed by artillery fire. The ferry itself drifted down river and beached close to the railway bridge, according to Ryan, p379.

200. *By Air to Battle*, p128.

201. In early 1941, while serving with the 1st Parachute Battalion, Deane-Drummond was in a 38-strong group dropped into southern Italy to cut off the water supplies of three ports that were supply hubs for Axis forces fighting in North Africa. They were to blow up the Tragino aqueduct. After successfully doing so, and also blowing up a bridge over the River Ginestra, things did not go as planned. The raiding group split into three smaller parties. These were to head for the coast, in order to make a rendezvous with a submarine meant to pick them up. The British were all captured, with Deane-Drummond escaping from a prison camp by year's end. He used the cunning ruse of pretending to scale a perimeter fence to change a bulb on one of its lights. The naïve Italian guards only realised it was a ruse when Deane-Drummond and a fellow escapee dropped over the other side of the fence. Trying to bluff his way out of northern Italy and into Switzerland by pretending to be a Nazi official, Deane-Drummond's crude command of German and Italian gave him away. Determined not to remain caged, he pretended to have gone deaf. Deane-Drummond was transferred to a hospital at Florence for tests and soon broke out. This time he made it into Switzerland, then into Vichy France, and, after making contact with British forces, was picked up from a beach near Marseilles by a Gibraltar-bound Royal Navy vessel.

202. p79–80.

203. Hagen, *Arnhem Lift*, p41.

204. Ibid.

205. Incident recounted in *By Air to Battle*, p126.

206. Hagen, *Arnhem Lift*, p24.

207. Ibid, p41.

208. Quotes taken from on-camera interview in *Last Words: The Battle for Arnhem Bridge*.

209. As related in *By Air to Battle*, p126.

210. Taylor, quoted by Ryan, *A Bridge Too Far*, p395

211. A six-wheel amphibian, the US-origin DUKW, or 'Duck', also had a propeller and was designed to convey both supplies and troops from ship to shore. It made its debut during the Allied invasion of Sicily in the summer of 1943.

212. Taylor, quoted by Ryan, *A Bridge Too Far*, p395.

213. Ibid, p407.

214. Polish paratroopers had entered the village the previous day, after dropping nearby. Marching before them was a captured enemy soldier – with the Sten gun of Lt Stefan Kaczmarek pointed threateningly at him. 'I put the German five metres out in front,' relates Kaczmarek, 'and told him that if he had lied about the other Germans [having left the village] he would get the first bullet from my Sten in his back.' The Poles received an ecstatic reception from local people rather than the gunfire of occupying enemy troops. (As recounted by Middlebrook, *Arnhem 1944*, p404.)

215. Quoted by Delaforce, *The Fighting Wessex Wyverns*, p152.

216. From Frank de Soet's account of the battle.

217. As quoted by Kershaw, *A Street in Arnhem*, p240.

218. Ibid, p267.

219. Ibid, p268.

220. Neil Walker, 'Sgt Gordon "Jock" Walker, Army Film & Photographic Unit – 1st Airborne Division', on 'WW2 Market Garden' website.

221. Zeno, *The Cauldron*, p128. Though a fictional account of the 21st Independent Parachute Company in action at Oosterbeek, this powerful and unflinching novel contains a wealth of detail that conveys the battle as experienced by Sgt Val Allerton (aka Zeno). Allerton had a complex background and even the name he was known by during his wartime service (including being commissioned after Arnhem) was also fake. His real name was Gerald Theodore Lamarque and he wrote *The Cauldron* during the early 1960s, while serving time in prison for murdering a love rival. *The Cauldron* won the Arthur Koestler Award, which was presented to prisoners for creative achievement. After he was released from prison, Zeno wrote *The Four Sergeants*, a novel about pathfinders undertaking a special mission behind enemy lines in Sicily.

222. *By Air to Battle*, p125.

223. Ibid.

224. In 'Arnhem War Diary by Brig Hackett, CO 4th Parachute Brigade' [ParaData] he records his side of the episode as follows: 'Shelling and mortaring now heavy while returning to my HQ. I was hit by splinters from a close burst in the stomach and left thigh about 100 yards from Div HQ.' He records that his runner's leg was also broken and then carries on: 'At first lull walked to Div RAP and sent out party for runner, then had GOC warned of my mishap. Handed over as best as I could to Lt. Col MURRAY (1 Wing GPR) in Div HQ RAP about 1400 hrs. I was put on a jeep and driven with others into

ARNHEM where I am now. Signed J W Hackett, St Elizabeth's Hospital 2 Oct 44'.

225. Fletcher as quoted, Middlebrook, *Arnhem 1944*, p373.

226. *By Air to Battle*, p124.

227. See Appendix on VC winners.

228. *By Air to Battle*, p118.

229. Ryan, *A Bridge Too Far*, p403.

230. The fragment of wallpaper with this sniper's kill tally and imprecation against the enemy is preserved in the Airborne Museum Hartenstein, Oosterbeek.

231. Herford, IWM Sound Archive, as are all quotes from him in this book.

232. War Diary, Headquarters RAMC, Pegasus Archive.

233. See Appendix 2 for how a truce, agreed on 24 September, that saw many wounded evacuated from The Cauldron came about.

234. Likely to have been from the Landstorm Nederland.

235. Signal from Maj Gen Roy Urquhart to Lt Gen Browning, 24 September 1944, National Army Museum and published on its web site. Capped up words as per used in the signal by Urquhart to impart urgency. This signal also quoted in full (but without those words capped up) in *The Memoirs of Field Marshal Montgomery*, p264.

236. From an interview between Iain Ballantyne and L/Cpl Dennis Clay, for *Evening Herald*, Plymouth special supplement on the Battle of Arnhem.

237. Delaforce, *The Fighting Wessex Wyverns*, p161.

238. 'The 4th and 5th Battalions the Dorsetshire Regt in World War Two', blog post on web site of The Keep Military Museum. The 'Arnhem' pennant is proudly on show at what is the museum of the Devonshire and Dorset regiments, in the county town of Dorchester. In fact, The Keep has a display devoted to the battle of Arnhem. For a non-Airborne unit to be allowed to fly the pennant with Pegasus on it from their vehicles, and to display the 'Arnhem' battle honour on regimental colours, was a sign of how highly valued the 4th Dorsets' efforts were. In the same gallery of The Keep (deactivated) weaponry used by both sides at Arnhem can be inspected and even handled.

239. '1st Airborne Division Report on Operation "Market" Arnhem 17–26 Sep 1944'.

240. Ibid. Regardless of the chosen codename for the operation, Urquhart actually took as his inspiration the evacuation of British, Australian and New Zealand forces from their positions ashore in Gallipoli during the First World War. Elaborate masking measures were taken to give the Turks the impression their enemy was still there, with troops gradually exfiltrated from under the very noses of the enemy, using ruses such as rifles being rigged to fire automatically. Some 80,000 troops were evacuated from Gallipoli, with only half a dozen casualties sustained.

241. Interview between Iain Ballantyne and Capt Fletcher.

242. Ibid.

243. From interview between Iain Ballantyne and L/Cpl Clay.

244. From Maxted's voiceover/commentary, *Theirs is the Glory: Men of Arnhem*.

245. Hagen, *Arnhem Lift*, p78.

246. '1st Airborne Division Report on Operation "Market" Arnhem 17–26 Sep 1944'.

247. Ibid.

248. Saul David, *Military Blunders*, p132.

249. *By Air to Battle*, p129.

250. Ibid.

251. Ibid, p130.

252. After the Battle, *Operation Market Garden Then and Now, Vol 1 & 2*, p692, Vol 2.

253. Middlebrook, *Arnhem 1944*, p441.

254. Beevor, *Arnhem*, p344.

255. Ibid.

256. Middlebrook, *Arnhem 1944*, p44.

257. Beevor, *Arnhem*, p337.

258. From interview between Iain Ballantyne and Capt Fletcher.

259. As quoted from diary in Ballantyne, *Evening Herald*, Plymouth, 1994.

260. Aldrich, *Witness to War*, p749. Baillie's diary account is held by the Airborne Forces Museum and these quotes are taken from an extract of it used in this book.

261. '1st Airborne Division Report on Operation "Market" Arnhem 17–26 Sep 1944'. The Poles were treated poorly after the battle, forced to march the 12 miles from Driel to Nijmegen (rather being taken by lorries, which were apparently not available) and then kept in the front line for some time, though the latter was true of US Airborne units too after Market Garden. It was not unusual practice. The 6th Airborne Div fought on for some time after landing/dropping into Normandy, as did those same US divisions. What was left of the British 1st Airborne went straight back to the UK, for it was no longer a fighting formation worth deploying in the field. The Poles were accused by Montgomery of putting in a poor performance while Maj Gen Sosabowski was criticised by Browning for being 'difficult' and failing as a brigade commander. This was grossly unfair to both the Polish paratroopers and Sosabowski who did the best they could in appalling circumstances. Their grit, determination, courage and sacrifice were every bit the equal of their British comrades in arms.

262. Quoted by Beevor, *Arnhem*, p339.

263. The Seaborne Tail of the 1st Airborne Div was composed of around 1,000 vehicles packed with stores and equipment not capable of being delivered by air (or for which there was no need as part of the airlifts). The vehicles and (approx) 2,000 men went by ship across the Channel in August 1944, to be held in Normandy transit camps awaiting further orders before heading across liberated Europe to join the division. Having waited to see which operation eventually went ahead (and where they should go), they went up the corridor to Nijmegen. The original aim was to ensure the division could fight on as a ground force after the Second Army had linked up with it at Arnhem.

264. 'Personal Account by Capt EM Mackay of 1st Para Sqn RE in Arnhem'.

265. Mead, *General 'Boy'*, Location 3510.

266. '1st Airborne Division Report on Operation "Market" Arnhem 17–26 Sep 1944'.

267. As quoted Mead, *General 'Boy'*, Location 3510. This quote was in turn taken from Packe's book on his experiences, *First Airborne*, p1. Packe was commander of Royal Army Service Corps troops in the division.

268. Ibid.

269. In *Arnhem*, p188–95, Maj Gen Urquhart is frank on how he felt at this time and about some of the other senior British commanders. While he first read this

letter from Montgomery during a short flight from Eindhoven to Brussels, I am sure he must have looked at it again aboard the aircraft taking him back to the UK. In his memoir Montgomery claimed that Urquhart asked him to draft the letter so that the latter could be read out 'to the division when it re-assembled in England' (see *The Memoirs of Field-Marshal Montgomery*, p264).

270. For more on how Urquhart felt in the immediate aftermath of the battle, see Appendix 1, 'Looking Back in Anger?'.

271. Bingley, ParaData.

272. The road bridge over the Rhine at Arnhem was a new one, opened in August 1944. The previous one (itself completed in 1935) was destroyed by the Dutch themselves in 1940 to try and impede the German conquest of their country. The pontoon bridge (dismantled by the time the British paratroopers got there in September 1944) was the main road crossing for much of the war. The John Frost bridge that replaced the 1944 road bridge – after its destruction by Allied air attack in October 1944 – was completed in 1948. See Wheeler, 'Arnhem 1944 – were the maps good enough?'.

273. As recounted by Frans de Soet in his diary's passages on the aftermath of the battle.

274. 'Shan Hackett at Arnhem: An Article by John Waddy', ParaData. Hackett's reflections on how his life was saved by an Airborne surgeon and then his time in captivity taken from his IWM Sound Archive interview.

275. See Appendix 2, 'Pegasus 1 – The Great Airborne Escape.'

276. Lowe, *Savage Continent*, p55.

277. See Appendix 1, 'Looking Back in Anger?'.

278. Carlo D'Este, in *Eisenhower* [p618] reveals that in a private letter to Gen George Marshall, the head of the US Army, in March 1944 Eisenhower cautioned against launching Airborne assaults of the kind enacted during Market Garden. D'Este felt that Market Garden was the fault of many people, not least Eisenhower, Montgomery, Browning and Brereton. Even so, D'Este felt it could have succeeded if only the British generals at the sharp end of the so-called pencil thrust into Holland had 'galvanised their tank units' to push on and seize the Arnhem road bridge with the speed and violence Monty himself had urged.

279. Lowe, *Savage Continent*, p8.

280. Newhouse, IWM Sound Archive, as are all his quotes in this book.

281. This was not the case. The intelligence was faulty or fabricated as part of the Soviet pressure on the Allies to bomb Dresden before they mounted an attack on

the city. Stalin demanded of Churchill, when he arrived at Yalta for a conference in early February 1945: 'Why haven't you bombed Dresden?' See Langworth's 'The Myth of Dresden and "Revenge Firebombing".'

282. According to Colville, *The Fringes of Powers*, p530.

283. Hastings, *Armageddon*, p384.

284. Hastings, *All Hell Let Loose*, p610 and Harris, *Bomber Offensive*, p242.

285. Colville, *The Fringes of Power*, p533.

286. Around 6,000 men of the recovered/reconstituted 1st Airborne Div, still under the command of Maj Gen Urquhart, were sent to Norway to take the surrender of 350,000 German troops in May 1945. The division oversaw a smooth liberation by keeping civil order, also making sure the vanquished enemy abided by the surrender terms plus helped with other tasks, such as clearing booby-traps left in various buildings. The division's 1st Parachute Brigade was sent on a similar mission, but on smaller scale, to Denmark. The 1st Airborne Div was disbanded on 15 November 1945, though the 6th Airborne Div continued post-war.

287. Ballantyne, report in *Evening Herald*, Plymouth, 28 March 1995.

288. Prisoners would prepare themselves as best they could on catching wind of such marches, ensuring they got a good pair of boots and warm clothes (if possible) and some form of backpack to carry what little possessions they had.

289. Sims, *Arnhem Spearhead*, p111.

290. Ibid.

291. Ibid, p112.

292. Ibid, p116.

293. Ballantyne, report on Harry Tucker's return to Arnhem, *Evening Herald*, Plymouth, 17 September 1994.

294. Jan Loos to Iain Ballantyne in e-mail communication early 2019. After the war Jan joined the Royal Netherlands Navy and became an aviator. In more recent times, in addition to giving talks, he has become a battlefield guide in his home town.

295. Urquhart, *Arnhem*, p188.

296. Ibid.

297. Ibid, p189–90.

298. Ibid, p208. See same page for the conclusion of Urquhart's official report.

299. *New York Times* obituary, 9 January 1985.

300. Warner, Philip, *Horrocks: The General Who Led from The Front*, Location 2213.

301. Ryan, *A Bridge Too Far*, p381.

302. Ibid, p380.

303. *By Air to Battle*, p133.

304. Quoted in *By Air to Battle*, p134.

305. Hackett, IWM Sound Archive, as are all his comments in this appendix aside from *By Air to Battle* quote as indicated.

306. Beevor, *D-Day*, p55.

307. Liddell Hart, *A History of the Second World War*, p170–1.

308. Wheal, Elizabeth-Anne and Pope, Stephen, *The Macmillan Dictionary of The Second World War*, Second Edition, p115.

309. Whiting, *Hunters from the Sky*, p88.

310. Ibid, p87.

311. Hibbert, to camera interview in the TV drama-doc 'Roy Urquhart's Escape from Arnhem', *Narrow Escapes of World War II*.

312. Frost, IWM Sound Archive, as are all his observations this book. Except where noted to avoid confusion with his own book.

313. Urquhart, *Arnhem*, p203.

314. Horrocks, *A Full Life*, p231.

315. Matthew Ridgway, *Soldier: The Memoirs of Matthew B Ridgway*, p110.

316. Letter from Browning to Hollinghurst, quoted by Mead in *General 'Boy'*, Location 3614.

317. Bryant, *Triumph in the West*, p285.

318. Ibid, p292.

319. *Churchill's Generals*, p100.

320. Ambrose, *Band of Brothers*, p139.

321. Ibid, p39.

322. D'Este, *Eisenhower*, p618.

323. Ambrose, *Band of Brothers*, p139–40.

324. Wilson, *The Ever Open Eye*, p181–2.

325. Montgomery, *The Memoirs of Field Marshal Montgomery*, p259.

326. Ibid.

327. Ibid, p265.

328. Ibid, p266.

329. Zeno, *The Cauldron*, p193–4.

330. Frost, IWM Sound Archive. Urquhart wrote in *Arnhem* (p202) that the flak should have been risked and even 'quite heavy casualties' suffered 'in order to get men south of the Bridge.'

331. Frost, *A Drop Too Many*, Location 4033.

332. As to whether the whole plan was given away by some fool carrying a folder of secret documents into battle, as depicted in the Hollywood movie *A Bridge Too Far*, the blunder is not mentioned in any official accounts. According to Cornelius Ryan in his book *A Bridge Too Far*, a briefcase containing plans was found and taken to Generaloberst Kurt Student. In September 1944, Student commanded the First Parachute Army, which during Market Garden fought desperately to halt the XXX Corps push up the corridor. Student told Ryan the briefcase was found in a Waco glider that had crash-landed near his own HQ. (See *A Bridge Too Far*, p198–9.) Student passed the Allied plan of attack on to Model. The plans had been taken into action against all wisdom and regulations – by someone who may have been American, but could also have been British, as the HQ of the British Airborne Corps landed near Eindhoven. The plans gave away LZs/DZs, all the divisions involved, plus operational objectives, showing the Germans they had to secure or destroy every bridge between Eindhoven and Arnhem. It showed Arnhem bridge was a key objective – which surely Model had worked out for himself – and that the ultimate plan was an attack into the Ruhr. Again, he would have realised that anyway. Whoever did it made a major error by gifting a measure of certainty to the German reaction.

333. Urquhart, *Arnhem*, p161.

334. Ryan, *A Bridge Too Far*, p423.

335. Ibid, p425.

336. See Appendix 3.

337. 'Evasion Report 21st September–23rd October 1944, by Major AD Tatham-Warter, 2nd Parachute Bn', Pegasus Archive.

338. Neave, *Saturday at M.I.9*, Location 4748.

339. 'Report on Operation to Liberate Personnel from Northern Holland, by Lt Col DT Dobie', Pegasus Archive.

340. Ambrose, *Band of Brothers*, p159.

341. Details of Pegasus 2, Middlebrook, *Arnhem 1944*, p438.

342. The post-Arnhem adventures of RQMS Morris recounted in his Pegasus Archive bio.